S. Mary Keely

CHILDREN OF THE RAVEN

ALSO BY THE AUTHOR

Stranger on the Highway
Lie Down in Darkness
The Takers of the City
The Envoys
From Ape to Angel: A History of Social Anthropology
In the Beginnings
The Dangerous Sex
Birds, Beasts and Man: A History of Zoology
Selected Poems 1933–1967
Inside My Own Skin, Poems 1968–1971

EDITED AND TRANSLATED BY H. R. HAYS

Twelve Spanish-American Poets
Selected Writings of Juan Ramón Jiménez
Selected Writings of Jorge Carrera Andrade
Selected Poems of Bertolt Brecht

CHILDREN OF THE RAVEN

The Seven Indian Nations of the Northwest Coast

H. R. Hays

McGraw-Hill Book Company

New York St. Louis San Francisco Toronto

Book design by Paulette Nenner.

1 2 3 4 5 6 7 8 9 K P K P 7 9 8 7 6 5

Library of Congress Cataloging in Publication Data

Hays, Hoffman Reynolds.
Children of the raven.

Bibliography: p.
Includes index.
1. Indians of North America—Northwest coast of North America.
I. Title.
E78.N78H38 979.5'004'97 75-6668
ISBN 0-07-027372-3

To my wife Julie,
invaluable helper in collecting
material for this book

ACKNOWLEDGMENTS

The author wishes to express his gratitude for their kind cooperation in supplying information to: Mrs. Bertha Johnson of Ketchikan; Joe Williams, Mayor of Saxman; Nathan Jackson, carver, of Ketchikan; Frank Collison, band manager, Masset; and Claude Davidson, carver, Masset; Allan W. Hall, assistant director, North Coast District Council, Prince Rupert; Mrs. George Leighton, Old Metlakatla; Community Development Officer Wally Liesk and his assistant, Solomon Atkinson, New Metlakatla; John Smith, manager, New Metlakatla Cannery; Ken B. Harris, hereditary chief, Gitsegyukla; Richard Benson, band manager, Glen Nowel, and Kenneth Muldoe, band manager, Kispiox; Joe Daniels, band manager, Kitwanga; Howard Wale, chief councillor, Hazelton; James Servid and William Scow, Alert Bay; Edward Moody, band manager, Bella Coola; Andy Schooner, Bella Coola; Ronald Witt, Superintendent of Indian Affairs, Bella Coola and Bella Bella; Cecil Reid, chief councillor, Bella Bella; Michael Wilson, chief constable and fire chief, Bella Bella; Judge Roderick Haig Brown and Mrs. Brown, Campbell River; Daisy Neel, Campbell River; S. J. Frye, Supervisor of Indian Affairs, Campbell River; William Roberts, chief councillor, Campbell River; Mrs. Mary Johnson, chief councillor, Gold River; Reverend Terry Whyte, Port Alberny; Superintendent of Indian Affairs William Sheppard, Nanaimo; Norman Joe, band manager, Cowichan Band, Duncan; Miss Deirdre Norman, archivist, Anthropological Museum of the University of British Columbia; and Louis Demerais, acting director, Union of British Columbia Chiefs.

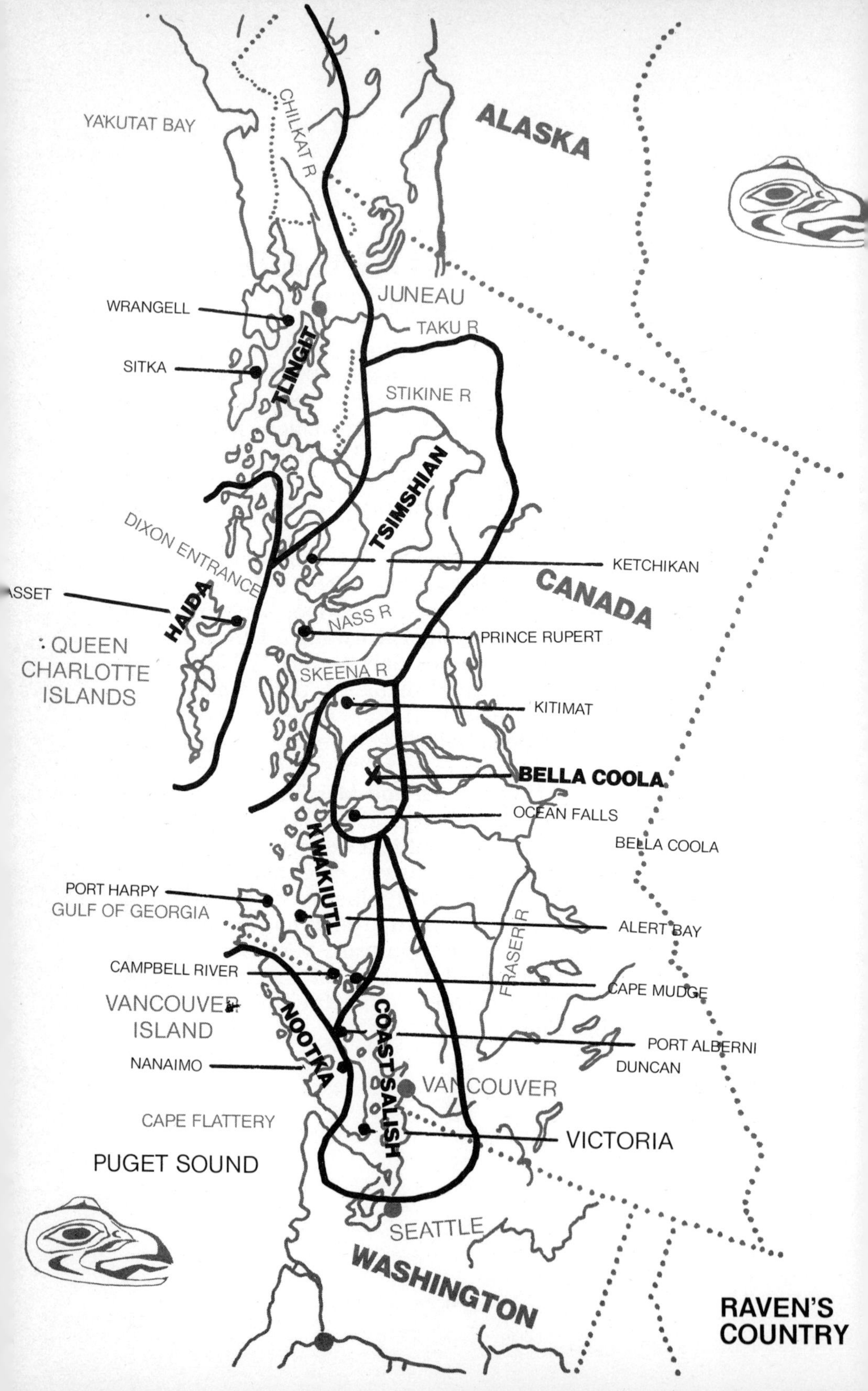

YAKUTAT BAY
CHILKAT R
ALASKA
JUNEAU
WRANGELL
TAKU R
SITKA
TLINGIT
STIKINE R
TSIMSHIAN
DIXON ENTRANCE
KETCHIKAN
CANADA
ASSET
HAIDA
NASS R
PRINCE RUPERT
QUEEN
CHARLOTTE
ISLANDS
SKEENA R
KITIMAT
BELLA COOLA
OCEAN FALLS
BELLA COOLA
KWAKIUTL
PORT HARPY
GULF OF GEORGIA
ALERT BAY
FRASER R
CAMPBELL RIVER
CAPE MUDGE
VANCOUVER
ISLAND
NOOTKA
COAST SALISH
PORT ALBERNI
NANAIMO
DUNCAN
VANCOUVER
CAPE FLATTERY
VICTORIA
PUGET SOUND
SEATTLE
WASHINGTON

RAVEN'S
COUNTRY

CONTENTS

II

THE CULTURE

III

THE NORTHWEST COAST TODAY

INTRODUCTION

A great canoe, hollowed from a single tree trunk, now stands in the entrance to the American Museum of Natural History. Its prow is handsomely decorated and it is filled with effigies of Indians, fantastically and imaginatively costumed. For many years it was tucked away in the dimly lit Hall of the Northwest Culture. Now it receives the full light of day and appropriately greets the visitor to the museum.

Similarly, in the past, the culture of the Northwest Coast Indians has remained obscure, the domain of specialists. Aside from a vague awareness of totem poles, the general public has known little of one of the richest human achievements ever created by a native group on the northern American continent. The way of life of the Plains Indians has long been a part of the American tradition. Our children grow up with some knowledge of it and for foreigners it is one of the identifying characteristics of the New World. The Southwest native group—with its katchina dolls, its adobe apartment houses, its snake and corn dances—is also a part of the American historical experience. The Northwest, however, has yet to be appreciated and properly integrated into the heritage of North America.

It is for this reason that this book has been undertaken: to tell the story of a people and to paint a picture of a culture. At a time when man himself is an endangered species, when he is uncertain of himself and his goals, when his own works tend to destroy his individuality, every scrap of color, every artistic creation of the human spirit becomes doubly precious. And there is no doubt that the adjustment to nature, the lifestyle, the imaginative expression created by the Northwest Coast Indians is an artistic triumph.

Furthermore, when I visited these people today to learn at first hand their present condition, I was delighted to discover that they have never ceased fighting to assert and preserve their identity and are actively working to maintain their heritage.

How this way of life achieved its individuality is still under discussion. It is distinct from that of the Eskimos and the Plains

Indians, and from the hunting Indians of Canada. The effect of the sea, of the coastal habitat, has been all important, and the symbols of marine fauna and of existence near the water color the mythology, art, ritual, and theater of these remarkable people.

The scope of this book is therefore defined by the boundaries of this particular cultural unit which extends to what can be called seven "nations," that is, seven groupings of many tribes, each group sharing a common language. These are—from southern Alaska to Puget Sound and the northern tip of the state of Washington—the Tlingit, the Tsimshian, the Haida, the Kwakiutl, the Bella Coola, the Nootka, and the Coast Salish.

All these nations share a highly developed ceremonial life whose symbols express the most profound social drives, and all of them cultivate aristocracies and concern themselves with distinctions of rank and lineage.

In the Northwest the art of sculpture and painting has been developed to a higher point than anywhere else in aboriginal North America and, in addition, the graphic resources of this culture have lent color to a theater which expressed a complex relation to the natural world and embodied powerful emotional concepts.

Finally, the attitude of the Northwest Indians toward property is unique. It seems to me that a society such as ours, which has formed its values on the acquisition, retention, control, and manipulation of wealth, has something to learn from a people which gains social approval by giving it away.

—H. R. Hays

I
THE HISTORY

THE RUSSIANS, SPANISH, AND ENGLISH DISCOVER AMERICA'S NORTHWEST COAST

1

According to the Haida Indians of the Northwest Coast of the American continent, long ago there was no land to be seen. There was just a little thing in the ocean. It was in the midst of the open sea and Raven sat upon it. Raven was a character, both trickster and culture hero, well known to all the tribes of this area. Raven said, "Become dust!" The little thing became earth. Then it increased and he divided it and he put this earth into the water, some on each side of him. One bit of earth he made small, but he made the one on the other side larger. The Haida had in mind the Queen Charlotte Islands where they lived; but the creator spirit did not stop once he got going, for this fabulous coast is broken, indented, and made up of many islands, large and small, surrounded by channels and inlets and the mainland, too—a ragged fringe of bays and indentations.

Wrote an early navigator:

> The eye soon finds itself checked by the steep hills and mountains, every part of the lowlands covered as well with thick woods down to the margin of the sea. The summits of the higher mountains were covered with sharp prominent ridges of rocks, which are clad in snow instead of verdure; now and then we saw a spot clear of woods but it was very rare and of small extent.

It was a land rich in animal life, particularly that of the sea, in which there was an abundance of whales, dolphins, halibut, cod, herring, salmon, the olachen or candlefish, prodigal in oil—a land whose rocks and beaches were laden with clams, mussels, crabs, and other edible marine life, including kelp, a native delicacy.

It was this plentiful supply of food which made it possible for the 100,000 or so native inhabitants (about a third of the total aboriginal population of Canada) to develop the highest type of culture, outside of Latin America, on the American continent. Until much more archeological work is done, what we know of them begins with the annals of commerce and with the convergence of three great imperialist powers—Russia, Spain, and England—upon this Indian Eden.

The first approach was by Russia through Siberia and Alaska. This was a wild world, a place of storms, gales, and snowy winters. Moreover, the Kamchatka Peninsula, the northwest tip of Asia, was populated by the Chuckchi, an indomitable semisavage people with whom the Russians fought, rather as the pioneers of the United States fought with the Plains Indians.

There had been considerable speculation in the early eighteenth century as to whether Kamchatka joined the mainland of America or not. The Russians do not seem to have been outstanding seamen. Those in Siberia, displaced Cossacks, were called *"promishchlenniki."* Eventually the energetic ruler Peter the Great dictated a memoir just before his death on January 26, 1725, to investigate the problem; and two of his explorers were Danes, Vitus Bering and Martin Spangberg, the third a Russian, Alexei Chirikov.

Bering's first voyage, as far as latitude 64, proved in his opinion that there was no land bridge to America. He did not impress his Russian employers, and only after years of pleading was he allowed to make a second voyage. In 1741 he set out again, commanding the *Saint Peter,* Chirikov, the *Saint Paul.* The ships lost each other; Bering sighted the mainland of Alaska but refused to land, turned back, and after a scurvy-ridden voyage cast away his ship on what is now Bering Island and died there on December 8, 1741. Chirikov, steering further south, entered a bay at latitude 57, sent out a longboat with 10 men which was never seen again. He sighted a canoe full of natives who shouted *"Agai! Agai!"* (Come here!), but Chirikov was turned back by bad weather and scurvy. He returned home in September 1741, having lost 21 of his men.

Chirikov and Bering had noted sea otters, which were to become the basis of the coastal fur trade. By 1745 this trade had become profitable and the first Aleut was shot. The *promishchlenniki* proved brutal enough. They attacked the natives, built small boats and wrecked them, and made money in sea otter furs. One Russian commander describes European Tlingit contacts with some objectivity: Eustrate Delarov wrote that in Prince William's Sound in 1783, "A number of canoes surrounded the vessel, one man standing up and waving his hands and chanting." This, as we shall see, was the Northwest Coast method of greeting strangers.

They came on board and I obtained 14 sea otter skins in exchange for some glass beads; they would not accept shirts or any kind of clothing; they conducted themselves in a friendly manner, and we ate and drank and slept together in the greatest harmony. The natives mentioned two other ships which had visited them from which they received beads and other articles. They also had copper kettles and knives from some trading source.

With remarkable impartiality he added

Suddenly on the 8th of September, the natives changed their attitude, making a furious attack on my people. I knew of no cause for this change until one of my boats returned, when I learned there had been quarreling and fighting between the boat's crew and the natives. I have no doubt that my people were the aggressors.

Thus ended the first Russian attempt at penetration of the West Coast. The inhabitants, however, proved to be tougher than the Aleut, and thus the developing fur imperialism of the Russians received a setback from which it took some time to recover. The Russians never made serious claims to the coast much below latitude 60 and eventually settled for Alaska.

Meanwhile the other two powers who had been eyeing the scene were not idle. The Spaniards reacted first. Their firm foothold on the coast of California provided them with bases for voyages northward. The Spanish sovereign, Charles III, laid claim to all of California and also entertained ambitions concerning the area further north. He saw to it that Bucarelli, the viceroy of Mexico, commissioned the Mallorcan Juan Pérez to sail north, take title to the country, and block the Russian penetration. He was ordered to "dislodge by persuasion or force any strangers found established on the coast up to 60 degrees latitude." In true Spanish style it was added that he should

convert the Indians, shedding upon them the light of the Scriptures . . . setting up a great wooden cross with a stone base and a flask in its interior, and sealing it with pitch for better conservation, a copy of the order laying claim to the land.

Whether he actually set up the wooden cross is doubtful, for accounts state that he did not land; but he did lay claim to the coast as far as latitude 60 and sailed to the Queen Charlotte Islands, where he made contact with the Indians who came out to the ship at Langara Island, northwest of Graham's Island.

Unfortunately, Pérez was ill most of the time with either ulcers or stomach cancer (he died the following year) and his contacts were brief. Apparently he traded with the Haida, for one of the missionary friars who went along, Juan Crespi, says

At latitude 55 Pérez treated with the Indians and saw that they were cheerful, robust, with beautiful eyes. The women were good looking with the lower lip pierced and in the incisions an oval in proportion in size to the one who wore this decoration. They bartered sea otter, bear and wolfskins for knives, glass beads and the like and were so tricky that it was necessary to give them the stipulated trinkets in advance and when they left they were accustomed to demand more, threatening not to fulfill the contract agreed upon. They saw among them half a bayonet and a fragment of a sword which Pérez believed must have belonged to the people commanded by Captain Tschirikoir [Chirikov] in the launch which set out on a mission in this area and never returned.

Actually, the Spaniards were not aware of how much trading the Russians had been carrying on—and the fact that iron implements were probably moving down the coast from tribe to tribe.

Pérez's ship, the *Santiago*, took soundings near the Nootka Peninsula in August, but, because of bad weather, then turned back and reached Monterey in November 1774. Pérez, however, had clearly preceded Cook and, according to the custom of the times—that of snatch-and-grab—had set up a legal Spanish title to the coast.

Pérez was followed by another Spanish captain, Juan Bodega y Quadra, in March 1775, who set out with the packet *Sonora* and a frigate, the *Santiago.* The first voyage merely resulted in an incipient mutiny, sternly quelled. The second, in 1779, with the ship *Princesa* and the frigate *Favorita,* resulted in Bodega's reaching the area just north of Queen Charlotte's Islands. Bodega seems to have been a good observer, for he had much to say about the Tlingit, with whom he succeeded in establishing good trading relations. He exchanged bits of iron for oysters, fish, and bearskins.

The priests took a seven- or eight-year-old girl on board and a nine- or ten-year-old boy to "Catechize them." Bodega says of the Tlingit that they were wheat-colored to almost white, their faces well made, in temperament arrogant of spirit and warlike. Some were covered with deer- or bearskin from shoulder to knees; others wore well-woven cloaks of wool. They had leather shoes, open behind and laced with a cord, and hats woven from tree bark on their heads. Their hair was worn waist long and braided into a pony tail. The women's complexions were clear, their cheeks rosy; they wore skin tunics from neck to feet belted at the waist, and over these they sometimes sported sea otter skins. He mentions the *"tablita"*—the labret inserted into the lower lip—which he thought was the adornment of married women only. In war the Tlingit wore corselets of narrow strips of wood which left the arms free, around the neck a thick piece of wood which covered them up to the eyes, and a helmet in the shape of a wild animal. From the waist down there was a wooden apron, while their rear was covered with hide. They used bow and arrow, lances, and iron knives (when they obtained iron), as well as axes of flint or greenstone. The dwellings that Bodega saw were very light—no more than four poles with bark walls. He knew, however, that they were temporary and that their houses in the interior were large affairs of thick boards.

He records that their foods were mostly salmon, haddock, sardines, hake, and various shellfish. They also hunted whales, deer, and ducks. Bodega admitted he could not learn anything about their religion.

Despite these early voyages of the Spaniards, the English were not to be outdone and sent their celebrated navigator, Captain James Cook, in 1776 to the Northwest Coast. He sailed up from Hawaii and sighted the coast at latitude 44, eventually anchoring in Nootka Sound. Indian tradition has it that he was greeted by Chief Macquinna, and, since the latter was prominent in all the contacts which followed, there is every reason to believe the chief was on hand.

The greeting ceremony generally consisted of canoes filled with warriors paddling rapidly around the ships while a chief holding a spear stood upright either speaking or sounding a note in which all joined, swelling it out in the middle and letting it die among the hills. They often wore masks of men or animals; these could be moved by strings. Sometimes they all joined in choral greeting in unison, impressing the Englishmen by their melodies.

Cook went up the sound to visit a village, where he was courteously invited into the large houses, on the floors of which mats were spread for him to sit. He noticed that the women were weaving bark fiber to make dresses in a manner similar to that of the Maori. Others were opening and smoking the small herrings which he called sardines, the catches of these being divided up. As they dried they were hung higher and higher until finished when they were baled and covered with mats. In the stream he saw weirs made of wickerwork, 20 by 12 feet placed in 3 or 4 feet of water. One chief reacted in a surly fashion, but some young women hastily dressed in their best and sang him a song.

When other strange canoes appeared, there was much singing and even dancing in platforms placed on the canoes. The local Indians, however, were careful to keep a monopoly of trade with the Europeans. Some of the visitors seem to have been Kwakiutl; from them the explorers obtained female portrait heads used in the Towhuit dance, which will be described later.

Cook summed up what he had learned of the Nootka like the pioneer ethnologist he was. He counted 95 canoes and, assuming 10 men to a canoe, a population of about 2000 is possible. Cook thought the women too broad-cheeked and bandy-legged for beauty. The men powdered their hair with the white down of birds and some of them plucked out their beards. Fur cloaks, sewn together and tied over the shoulder, reached to the knee. The men wore no lower garments and only assumed the cloaks on ceremonial occasions or for warmth. On their heads they wore conical, tightly woven straw hats. They made blankets of mixed wool and bark thread, the women manufacturing circular cloaks of the same material. They wore copper rings and earrings, for copper was available and could be hammered easily, although they did not know how to smelt it. They also wore long strips of leather or plaited material hanging from their ears to their breasts.

The elaborate masks represented human faces and also birds and animals. The Englishmen, on some of their ceremonial visits, saw them used during the singing. Songs were appropriate to both war and peace, the chorus in unison while a chief led. Sometimes they were conducted by a man "dressed in a garment of many colors to which is hung deer hooves, pieces of bone, etc., in such a manner as to strike one against the other at every movement of his body. This man is masked and shakes in his hand a rattle as do some of the others. . . ." Sometimes they beat their paddles against the side of the canoe in unison to mark rhythm of the songs.

The men wore nose rings, and both sexes painted their faces red, black, and white, mixing ocher with grease. Iron sand was also rubbed on to make the face paint glimmer.

Their only instruments were a rattle and a pea whistle, the

rattle often shaped like a bird with pebbles in the belly and the tail for a handle.

Canoes were 40 to 60 feet long, 7 broad and 3 deep, with a high stern and prow. They were not carved and only a few were painted. The large houses were made of logs and boards, many of the latter 30 feet in length. Some were floored with logs which made a sort of porch along the front of the building. The roof boards were loose, and, since movable, holes could be left for the smoke. The buildings were divided into apartments for each family, cubicle fashion, in which each group kept its possessions and provisions of dried fish in decorated boxes. Large houses had a passageway down the middle, a smaller one at the side. The fireplace was in the middle. The Indians were not disturbed by dirt. Cook said the dwellings stank of smoke, oil, and fish. The family groups all ate out of the same wooden trough, which was never washed. Cook thought they seldom washed their bodies, but many other witnesses testify to much ceremonial bathing.

Along the side of the houses were raised benches covered with mats, while at the ends the two poles supporting the roof were huge images of human beings. These were called *ack-weeks*—the same word as for "chief" or "V.I.P." Cook did not think they were gods and indeed, with some intuition, felt that they worshipped their ancestors, although he accurately added that he did not learn enough of their language to discover much about their religion.

Cook brought up the question of cannibalism, as did other voyagers. The natives sold three or four human hands which had been recently cut off. They also offered human skulls. Cook says they made signs that the hands were good eating. Another author, the astronomer of the *Discovery,* J. T. Bayley, says he bought a hand and desired the man who sold it to eat it, whereupon the man refused. He offered to pay him to eat it, but the man departed in "great contempt and anger."

Cook remarked that, with so much trading going on, it was not remarkable that iron knives and chisels were in general use. Apparently, even when there was no direct contact, metals had been penetrating either up from Spanish sources or down from Russian ones along the coast. Cook's testimony and that of voyagers to follow him indicate that the local artistic tradition and other elements of the culture, such as pride in aristocratic creasts and competitive gift-giving, had been long established.

Cook—himself a man of high principles, a fine seaman and

a great navigator, and, on the whole, humane and tolerant in his dealings with native peoples—was, of course, along with charting little known shores, serving the aims of imperialism. He had instructions to take possession of any lands that had not already been discovered and to distribute articles to indicate where he had been; but he had also been instructed not to encroach upon the pretentions of the Spaniards. We shall see, however, that the English were quite willing to use Cook's voyage to support their own claims against those of Spaniards in the events which follow.

THE FRENCH ADVENTURE

2

We have seen that by the eighteenth century the Spanish, Russians, and English had begun to make gestures toward the Northwest Coast of America. It remained for France to put in an appearance. Somewhat jealous of Cook's exploits as an explorer, that nation had sent out Louis Antoine de Bougainville, who was charmed by the South Sea Islanders. Now in 1785, in emulation of Cook, for whom he had great respect, Count Jean François de Galaup de La Perouse embarked on a voyage to the Northwest Coast, carrying with him a group of specialists including doctors, astronomers, and botanists. The French Academy of Medicine was particularly anxious for the exact physical measurements of any peoples he encountered. La Perouse himself disclaimed any vulgar motivation such as greed or the desire for territory. The Hawaiian Islands, he said, "had luckily become known in an epoch in which religion no longer serves as a pretext for violence and greed. The modern navigator by describing the customs of new peoples is setting out to complete the history of man. . . ." As we shall see, however, this admirable eighteenth-century objectivity was not maintained too consistently when it came to describing the Tlingit.

He first made port in 1786 in Yakutat Bay at the foot of Mount St. Elias and later braved the shoals and currents of the difficult entrance of Lituya Bay, which was surrounded by great glaciers which shed chunks of ice into the water, breaking the primal silence of what was almost a lake, so completely was it cut off from the sea; and indeed its name means "Lake-within-the-Lake."

We are fortunate in having an account which has been passed down for a hundred years from father to son, narrating the reactions of the Tlingit who encountered white men for the first time. The local Indians already felt an awesome respect for the entrance to the bay, which, they maintained, contained a dangerous spirit which drowned unwary canoemen. Indeed, they were still mourning the loss of four canoes when to their amazement two great black birds with far-reaching white wings entered the harbor. They immediately decided that these were emanations of Yehlh, the Raven, a creator spirit of great power. They immediately fled to the woods. Since to see Yehlh with the naked eye was to be turned to stone, they looked at the strange phenomena through the rolled-up leaves of the skunk cabbage. When the sails were furled, they thought the figures of the sailors on the yards were black crows—Yehlh's messengers, occupied in folding his wings. Finally, after much discussion, one bold group of warriors put on their leather armor and their wooden collars and helmets and armed with copper knives, spears, and bows launched a war canoe. As soon as they set out from the beach, smoke rose from the black bird, which spoke with a voice of thunder. The crew of the war canoe was so disturbed that they upset their craft, and they had to scramble ashore as best they could.

Finally, an old warrior who was nearly blind said he had not long to live and would venture to find out what Yehlh would do. He commanded his slaves to prepare several canoes; but, as he approached the strange being, all the slaves, except the two paddling the canoe, lost heart and turned back. Finally he was put aboard. Since he could scarcely see, he still thought the Frenchmen in their blue sailor's uniforms were crows. He was given some cooked rice, which he thought was worms. At last he exchanged his otter robe for a tin pan and some strange foods. When he returned to show these to his people, they could not believe he was alive; they touched him and smelled him to make sure. He was finally able to convince them that he had met men and not Raven—whereupon his people ventured to trade in otter skins for many strange new articles. (Up to this time the Tlingit had only been able to procure copper and iron from the tribes at Yakutat, who got them from the Russians.) It was at about this time that two of the strangers' small boats were capsized and the crews drowned.

The head chief came out to meet La Perouse, made a long speech, and ended by singing a melody "similar to the plain-chant of our churches." The chorus repeated it, and when the whole group came on board they danced for nearly an hour. The chief became so fond of the life on board that he spent five or six hours every day on the ship, expecting presents every time he appeared.

La Perouse's account of the Tlingit is constantly colored by his complaint that they lost no opportunity to steal. He had fired his cannon to show his strength, and he took care to fire a bullet through a number of hide corselets to show the superiority of his weapons; but these demonstrations had little effect. When he set up an observatory in tents on an island, the Tlingit slipped under the tent and stole while the Frenchmen slept. The chief offered to sell the explorer the island. Although La Perouse knew that land was held communally and the chief had no right to it, he submitted to this mild blackmail and paid a hatchet, some bars of iron, and some nails. He buried a bottle with an inscription and some French medals. He had wished to explore canals which led from the bay into the interior, with the notion that he might find a river which would lead to central Canada; however, two of the three canoes he sent out were wrecked by a sudden squall with the loss of 22 men. Even by enlisting the aid of the Indians they could not recover the bodies.

The Tlingit, La Perouse wrote, burned their dead except for their heads. These were wrapped in skins and together with the ashes were placed on little raised platforms. The food of the natives included salmon, trout, and mussels. Skins of bear, lynx, ermine, and marten proved that they also hunted these animals. Their houses were about 20 by 20 feet, divided into compartments, their belongings kept in many decorated wooden boxes. Their canoes were 24 feet long. They wove blankets of wool trimmed with otter skin. He found their sculpture of men and animals passable. Important chiefs wore sea otter cloaks; their noses and ears were pierced with ornaments and they painted their faces with ocher and black. There was some tatooing, but he disliked the wooden labret inserted in the lower lip.

On the whole, La Perouse showed no philosophical tolerance for their way of life. They never washed; their household utensils and their dwellings stank of fish. They showed no modesty about answering the call of nature—did not even move aside but went right on with their conversations. He felt that they were moved most by fear and the desire for vengeance and were easily angered. They all had a passion for gambling "as intense as that encountered in French cities," and out of this came many quarrels. He had no use for Rousseau's myth of the noble savage, close to nature, and he felt that if these Indians were given liquor it would end by destroying them. "The same dignitary whom I loaded with presents did not disdain stealing a nail or an old pair of trousers." When they smiled most amiably he could be sure they had just stolen something. Though it was probable that every society had its virtues,

I did not have the insight to perceive them; always quarreling among themselves, indifferent toward their children, real tyrants to their wives who are always condemned to the most exhausting labor; I have seen nothing of these people which permits me to soften the colors of the picture.

This was the only French contribution to Northwest Coast history. Thereafter the English and Spanish rivalry for the possession of the coastal area intensified.

THE IMPERIALIST CONFLICT

3

In the next few years a whole group of navigators visited the Northwest Coast and especially the Nootka; their voyages overlap and they have various things to say about each other. Americans, Spanish, and British were competing for the golden harvest of sea otter furs, but only the British and Spaniards actually laid claim to the area. The Indians were, of course, a pawn in the trade, since they did the actual hunting, and we find Chief Macquinna very much in evidence.

We should perhaps begin with the voyage of Captain George Dixon, a navigator and map maker of considerable stature who named the Queen Charlotte Islands and gave his own name to the sound north of them, Dixon's Entrance.

Dixon dedicated his ghost-written account to Sir Joseph Banks with a rather pretentious introduction in which he says it is well known that the Spaniards committed shocking barbarities when they encountered native peoples, while the British always labored to gain their esteem and affection. British traders were handicapped by the fact that their government had granted the South Sea Company a monopoly of trade in the Pacific; thus, Dixon's backers had to take out a license from this organization and also agree to let the East India Company control the marketing of the furs in China. Since these large organizations reaped their percentages, the Americans were in a better position than the British, for they were not hampered by any restrictions.

Dixon set out in 1785 in the *King George*, accompanied by Captain Portlock in the *Queen Charlotte*. They fell in with some Russians at Cook's River. Dixon said of them that "they frequently quarreled and fought with the natives and were at present on such terms with them that they never used to sleep without their arms ready loaded by their sides."

After some trading in skins, bad weather forced the Englishman to return to Hawaii. By April 1787 he was back at Prince William's Sound. He learned from some Indians that there was another ship nearby. This was the *Nootka* under Captain John

Meares, who was to play an important role in Spanish–British rivalries. Meares was wintering in the sound, his crew so sick with scurvy that at times Meares was the only man on his feet. Dixon said they were so drunk they had to keep to their hammocks. Actually Meares was a poacher, for he had no license from the South Sea Company. He and his mate, according to Dixon, did not tell the same story—one said they obtained 700, the other 1000, skins. From all contemporary reports Meares was an unmitigated liar in matters of trade, but his data on the Nootka are detailed and probably trustworthy.

Dixon continued to complain of stealing: he says some Indians sang and danced on the deck while their companions threw everything they could lay hands on overboard into their canoes. When they tried to steal an anchor, they were forbidden the ship.

At Mount St. Elias, Dixon was disappointed in his hopes of furs because the Russians were already exploiting the area. Like so many Europeans, he disliked the labret in the lower lips of the Tlingit women. Their houses were only a few poles stuck in the ground covered with loose boards; but he learned that their large dwellings were in the interior, those on the coast being temporary. They were full of "stinking flesh, grease, oil, etc." Dixon's ghost writer in his role of natural philosopher said they were nevertheless probably happier than "those who live under the gilded roof of a despotic monarch." In their big dugout canoes, which held 14, they bottom-fished with wooden hooks and squid for bait, using bladders as floats. They cooked with hot stones in wicker baskets.

Their burial custom was to separate the head of the corpse from the body, wrap it in furs, and place it in a square box, while the body was put in a long chest. Two stout poles were set in the ground with a timber across them; on this the headbox was fixed, decorated with rows of shells or teeth, the poles painted white.

On July 1787 some Indians endeavored to steal skins he had bought, which seemingly made Dixon nervous, for he ordered his men to fire in the air. Subsequently the Indians claimed he had killed one of their number. This was a poor introduction to the Haida of what he now named Queen Charlotte's Islands. Dixon seems to have made his peace with them, however. In this area there was an abundance of furs. Dixon thought the women showed "feeling and sensibility which perfectly astonished us." He was, however, afraid to go ashore for fear of being butchered. Dixon sometimes obtained 300 beaver skins in half an hour and once sold his whole cargo for $54,-857.

While the British were reaping a profit in furs, the Spaniards, also in 1787, sent an expedition northward under Alferez de Novia Estéban and José Martínez. The latter commanded the *Princesa* and was to play an unfortunate role in later events. On this voyage they sailed as far north as latitude 60 and contacted the Tlingit. They were glad to find wild celery growing on shore, for during the 1779 expedition they had learned it cured scurvy. They encountered a Russian fur outpost commanded by a Greek who made friends with a Greek in the Spanish crew.

This would have been Eustrate Delarov, who was born in Greece. He told them the Muscovite colony at the entrance to Cook's River consisted of 442 men and five galliots. The Russians were beginning to think about setting up a colony south at Nootka. The Spaniards hastened home on December 1788 to suggest an immediate Spanish settlement at Nootka to contain the Russians and the English.

Nootka was becoming a busy port. In the spring of 1788 Meares was back in the *Felice* accompanied by the *Iphigenia* under Captain Douglas. Meares had with him Conekela, the brother of chiefs Macquinna and Callikum. Conekela was eager to show off his cocked hat and regimental coat. He also wore a copper plate on his chest and in his hair were tied copper saucepan handles.

A party was given by the returning chief's relatives for him and the British. Meares seems to have been on good terms with the Nootka, which gives the lie to American charges that he used intimidation in extracting skins. He says of the native houses:

> Each of these mansions accommodates several families and is divided into partitions in the manner of an English stable in which all kinds of dirt, mixed with blubber, oil and filth, are discovered by more senses than one, to form a mass of undesirable filthiness.

The British put up a tent on shore and in May 1788 canoes of a war party returned with Macquinna and Callikum. In each there were 12 to eight men, their hair powdered with white down, faces painted red and black in the designs of a shark's jaw plus a kind of spiral line. The chiefs wore high, pointed straw hats, the crowns topped with a small tuft of feathers.

The chorus was in unison and strictly correct as to time and tone; nor did a dissonant tone escape them; sometimes they would make a sudden transition from high to low tones with such a melancholy turn in their variation that we could not reconcile ourselves to the manner in which they acquired or contrived this more than untaught melody of nature.

They beat time with their paddles at the ends of stanzas, pointing them north and south. Meares thought that Western orchestras could not be more effective.

Macquinna was a handsome man of thirty, Callikum about forty. They drank copiously from bladders of oil and received presents of copper and iron objects from the British. In return they made the dramatic gesture of throwing off their sea otter cloaks and stood nude on the deck until the traders, in return, gave them woolen blankets. Meares had often seen chiefs throw their furs at each other's feet in this gesture of gift-giving which we now know led to the extremes of the potlatch. All this trading took place with much ritual and shouting.

Meares built a house on shore, paying the Indian laborers in beads. He was later to claim that he bought the land, but Macquinna always denied it.

Meares had much to say about cannibalism. According to him, Callikum was averse to it, but he accuses Macquinna of eating a slave every month. The ritual consisted of singing a war song, bandaging the victim's eyes, and killing him with a club while he was blindfolded. Meares may have been exaggerating, but Bodega y Quadra repeats the same charge against Macquinna, with whom he was on the best of terms. Bodega, however, was not an eyewitness.

It is clear that the Northwest Coast people were headhunters, a custom which is often, in other parts of the world, accompanied by ritual cannibalism; and the symbolic cannibal dance also suggests that sometime in the past the custom might have been in force.

The native eagerness for copper and brass which could be shined and iron which could be used as tools was, of course, already affecting the culture as a result of trading with the whites. Macquinna on state occasions now affected a white ruffled shirt, and powdered his hair on formal visits, bowing in eighteenth-century style.

Meares went down the coast to visit Wicananish, who presided over a village of 400 people. The Britisher was anxious to acquire a monopoly of the fur trade in this area as well. The roof of the chief's house was supported by three enormous carved logs raised at the ends and in the middle—

> . . . by gigantic images carved out of huge blocks of timber; the same kind of board planks covered the whole to keep out the rain; but, they were so placed as to be removed at pleasure, either to receive light and air or to let out the smoke. In the middle of this spacious room there were several fires, and beside them large wooden vessels filled with fish soup. Large slices of whale flesh lay in a state of preparation to be put into similar machines filled with water to which women with a kind of tongs conveyed hot stones from very fierce fires in order to make it boil; heaps of fish were strewn all about, and in the central part of the place which might be very properly called a kitchen, stood large sealskins filled with oil, from whence the guests were served with that delicious beverage. . . . The trees which supported the roof were of a kind which would render the mast of a first rate man of war diminutive on a comparison with them. . . . The door by which we entered this extraordinary fabric was the mouth of one of those huge images which, large as it was supposed, was not disproportionate to this monstrous visage.

He noted raised benches on the sides where the inhabitants of the house sat and slept. The feast consisted of slices of boiled whale and fish soup served in wooden bowls with mussel shells for spoons. The women did not eat with the men. The native diet was varied and included wild onion salad, crayfish, berries, and now and then venison.

Meares's trading expedition was successful. He got 150 sea otter skins for his copper kettles and a promise of a monopoly of the fur trade with Wicananish. chief.

At this point the United States contributes to Northwest Coast history in the persons of Captain Kendrick and Captain Gray of Boston. Word was getting about that the fur trade offered great opportunities for profit and the skippers of Boston were not slow to avail themselves of the West Coast potential. They had the advantage over the British that no South Sea Company or West India Company restricted their efforts. A group of backers put Captain John Kendrick in charge of the ship *Columbia Redivivus* and Robert Gray in command of the sloop *Lady Washington* in 1787 to take part in the fur trade. On April 1, 1788, they became separated while rounding the Horn. Kendrick seems to have been a vacillating character who behaved unscrupulously toward his owners, eventually selling his ship to himself and never accounting for his operations. Gray was a better seaman but "passionate and foolhardy," and neither seems to have been successful in their relationships with the Indians.

Gray arrived first at Nootka on September 17, 1778, with a damaged *Washington,* which had to be towed into the harbor by Meares's *Felice* and the *Iphigenia.* The latter ship was registered under the Portuguese flag because the Chinese charged much lower harbor duties to this nation and China was the best market for sea otter furs. Gray had had a brush with some Indians; Kendrick had lost two men from scurvy.

Meanwhile, Meares was building a small schooner, the *West Coast of America,* and Macquinna and Callikum prepared to go north with another war party. Meares decided to give them arms so they would be sure to win; thus, his fur monopoly would be secure. He accompanied the guns with a Protestant lecture on how to be merciful in war and never to kill prisoners. The 20 canoes set out and returned with several baskets, which contained 30 heads, plus a considerable booty of sea otter skins.

The two American vessels remained in the sound until March 1789. The *Columbia* having been successfully repaired, Kendrick ordered Gray to trade up and down the coast. His mate, Robert Haswell, complained that the price of otter skins had risen from three to nine chisels. The Boston traders had not provided enough iron for these. When Gray went south to Wicananish's territory, Haswell described the houses and was struck by the house posts carved into human figures, which he says were called *klemmas* and added a few new anthropological observations. He said that some chiefs liked to purchase their wives from neighboring tribes:

> When a child is born it costs near as much to purchase a name for it and until it arrives to a considerable age they change their names every year and when he arrives of age he assumes a number of names or titles.

This is clear evidence that the accumulation of names and titles was a well-established custom. Haswell said that Wicananish's village was called Opitsitah. It was situated at Port Cox in Clayoquot Sound. He saw the chief strike a whale, which was buoyed up with 16 floats. He declined to attend the ensuing feast but was told that at the first kill of the season they sacrificed a slave and laid the body alongside a large piece of the whale's head adorned with eagle's feathers. He was told that an eagle of enormous size carries a whale high in the air and, when it drops the animal, this causes the sound of thunder. When the people went whaling they cut their tongues and painted themselves with the blood so the whale would not be afraid of them nor they afraid of it.

The *Washington* then went north, encountered the Kwakiutl, and the Haida of Queen Charlotte's Islands, and did some successful trading—indeed, Gray persuaded the Kwakiutl to sell 300 sea otter skins for one chisel apiece.

While Gray was gone things began to happen at Nootka. Don Estéban José Martínez arrived in April in the *Princesa* along with López y Haro, with instructions to take possession of the port for Spain. He first challenged the *Columbia,* but Kendrick wrote him fawning letters saying he had merely put in for repair and offered to forge iron tools for him. Martínez went ahead and fortified a small stockade at the mouth of the harbor. At the end of March, however, the *Iphigenia* under Douglas and the *North West America* under Funter, both of which had been wintering in Hawaii, appeared. Then ensued a comedy of charges and countercharges, always with the possibility of serious hostilities in the background.

Martínez demanded to see their "passports." The *Iphigenia* was arrested, it was said, on account of her dubious Portuguese registration. She was eventually let go and went north. Apparently *The North West America* bought some rigging from the Spaniards. At any rate, Martínez received what he considered to be a bill of sale for the ship, but Douglas, who knew the Spanish captain was ignorant of English, wrote some document which was carefully invalid. To add to the confusion, Martínez maintained that the *Iphigenia's* papers contained "insulting remarks." Then, to complicate matters, as a result of Meares's taking on new partners, on June 14 the *Argonaut* under Captain James Colmett and the *Princess Royal* under Thomas Hudson appeared. For some unknown reason the *Princess Royal* was allowed to proceed and even allowed to take on the skins from the *North West America,* which Martínez was now holding as a prize. Then she returned and was arrested 10 days later. Colmett, however, according to Martínez, refused to show his documents. Martínez accused him of planning to build a fort and wishing to take over the area for the British. What followed enters history in more than one version. Gray and his mate, Ingraham, who were anxious to placate the Spaniards, wrote a testimonial concerning the English mariners taken prisoner: "We presume none of them will be backward in confessing that Don E. J. Martínez always treated them very kindly, and all his officers, consistent with the character of a gentleman." And Gray, in a July letter to his owner, Joseph Barrel, described the event as follows:

> We are now in good friendship with the Spanish Commodore, and expect to sail in a few days, who has taken possession here and erected a fine fort and claims this coast, who, I think, has the best right of any Nation. They have stopped three English vessels here that came from Macao in China, to take possession of this coast and fortification, but they being of very little force are obliged to give themselves up and go to San Blass for a Tryal.

Captain Vancouver was to recount Colmett's version of the story at a later date. According to him, when Colmett protested at the *Argonaut's* not being allowed to sail:

> Martínez quitted the cabin in an apparent rage, and instantly dispatched an armed party on deck who, after knocking Captain Colmett down, arrested him and detained him as a prisoner aboard the *Princesa.* Martínez then captured Captain Hudson of the *Princess Royal,* when that ship appeared, and ordered Hudson to hand over the *Princess.*
>
> At the yardarm was rove a rope, with which Mr. Hudson was threatened to be hanged if he declined signing the letter, or if the sloop under his command should fire. [The letter was to his second in command ordering him to give up the *Princess.*] The treatment which Captain Colmett received whilst on board the *Princesa* has nearly proved fatal to him; he was seized with a violent fever, attended with delirium which did not abate until he was removed on board his own vessel. . . .

There is proof, however, that Martínez, who was the Mexican viceroy's nephew, was a violent and disagreeable man. In July 1789, Chief Callikum had brought a present of fish which was rudely snatched from him. He began to protest at such treatment and, to quote Martínez's diary, "Irritated by such abusive language, I took a gun from among those my men had carried over when they went to bring the sloop in—and I took another and fired it, killing Kaleken."

The Indians, naturally, had no use for Martínez and moved their camp inland. The *Argonaut* and the *Princess Royal* were manned with Spanish crews, their skins confiscated, the ships themselves being sent south to California. Thus ended Meares's dreams of monopoly.

The British crews were at times well treated and at times severely handled. Colmett ended up in Mexico where Viceroy

Revilla Gigedo returned his ship and cargo. He claimed he had been cheated. Spain endeavored to be moderate but demanded that those who ordered Colmett to found a colony in Spanish domains should be punished. England took the attitude that her subjects had lost money. Captain Meares jumped into the act with a long memorial to the British government claiming he had been defrauded of half a million dollars. Dixon challenged his figures. The Spaniards announced that they would not tolerate encroachment on their domains and warned Russia. Russia agreed to keep out—above latitude 60. Britain demanded reparations for the property of her subjects. On May 25, 1899, the affair was turned over to Parliament by George IV.

By this time Spain was preparing for war and Charles V appealed to France for help. Louis XIV was ready to provide it, but the National Assembly vetoed the idea. The Spanish ambassador was demanding absolute sovereignty up to latitude 50, while Britain was suggesting latitude 40. France threw her weight into a negotiated settlement which resulted in the Nootka Convention, ratified in Madrid on November 22, 1790.

Any land taken from the British was to be restored (Meares's blockhouse, which he never owned), and the Northwest Coast was to be free to all nationals. Meares settled for $200,000; Martínez was recalled and Macquinna moved back to the coast when Francisco Elisa took over. The situation had looked dangerous, but in the end the European powers were not ready to go to war over the fur trade.

VANCOUVER TAKES OVER

4

The American traders were, of course, not concerned with quarrels over annexation. Gray and Kendrick returned in June of 1789 and learned what Martínez had done. They continued to trade but once more took a chief hostage to get back a Hawaiian deserter—another action which was to help destroy the relations between the Europeans and the Indians. By September they put into Clayoquot Harbor to winter. They had managed to provoke the Haida chief, Coyah, who attempted unsuccessfully to capture Kendrick's vessel.

John Box Hoskins, who was a clerk sent on the voyage to check on Gray, describes some of his experience at Opitsitah, Wicananish's village. When the chief's son became ill, the witch doctors were—

> Pressing on his belly and breast, others sucking his throat, making, at times, a most hideous noise which was answered by the voice of a great multitude . . . and then those men would pretend to scoop up something (as though it was water) with their hands and blow it away.

On his second visit to the sick man 200 men and women were singing and shaking rattles in the shape of birds. A woman did a comic pantomine dance. The sick boy said he had had a dream that there must be a great deal of singing or he would die. Hoskins spent the night in Wicananish's house, for on the following day an important dance was planned.

In the morning the men all bathed and oiled and painted their bodies. They came dancing slowly along the beach, led by Wicananish. There were four women musicians with copper instruments containing pebbles. Then about 600 crowded into the young chief's house; double that number stood outside. Singing went on, then bundles of laths were brought to start a fire. More singing and dancing took place. When they danced the Indians squatted on their hams, then leapt up and twirled. One acted wildly and tore the robes of the others with his teeth.

The faces were painted white, black, or red with eagle tail feathers on their heads.

When Hoskins returned to the ship it was to learn of a threatened tragedy. Ottoo, the Hawaiian deserter, had been urged by the Indians to wet the priming of the firearms so that they could not be used. An attack was to be led by a chief with whom Hoskins had just dined. It is not clear how deeply Wicananish was involved, but the Indians wished to be revenged for the taking of another chief as hostage the previous June. Gray scolded all the chiefs and sent them away, forbidding them to board the ship on pain of death.

Gray spent the winter building a small ship, the *Adventure,* of which his mate, Haswell, was put in command. In May, Gray sailed south and gave the name of his ship to the Columbia River. Then he and Haswell cruised north together.

Meanwhile, Bodega y Quadra had been made commissioner of the coast and arrived in Nootka in March 1792 to take over the port and to build himself a house. (In this year 28 vesssels visited the Northwest Coast.) Of Bodega everyone had flattering things to say. He treated all nationalities considerately, was well liked by the Indians, and indeed in all situations maintained his courteous Castilian cool. Some of his notes on the Nootka add a few more bits of anthropological data:

> Their heads are large and flattened in front so that the opposite side forms a conical elevation. This occurs because they put them in a mould or narrow cradle of wood whose edges are so placed that they cause this shape and they stay thus until a year and a half.

He goes on to mention other details:

> Each village has two chiefs who have charge of their internal government [Meares said Macquinna ruled over 7000] and see to it that they have plenty of provisions for the winter. In the course of the year they sometimes change their dwelling, depending upon the abundance of seeds, fruit and fish. It appears that women prisoners of war are their only prostitutes and these are paid.

Meares testified that many of the women refused to accommodate the sailors for money. Bodega went on to say that they could travel 16 leagues a day in their canoes (they were now using sails) and that they treated their prisoners of war humanely, cutting their hair short to set them apart. They were very fond of the roe of the small herring of the area, leaving purse-shaped nets in the water and drawing them up every two or three days full of fish eggs. Bodega evinced some interest in their imaginative life:

They adore the sun, as far as can be made out and they pray to it to preserve them from other tribes and to give them the superiority over them which they need. The figures sculptured in wood which they call klemmas are reproductions of their defunct ancestors. Macquinna asserted that the one he had in his house was in memory of his daughter who had just died. They believe in the immortality of the soul which exists within the body in the form of a bird which descends immediately after death to a profound depth below the sea where there is a beautiful city destined to receive them, where they remain knowing and known by their ancestors who preceed them, with only the memory of having left the territory in which they used to dwell and the friends who survive them. They believe that the good, bad and indifferent go to the same place and consequently their future hopes should not influence the moral aspect of their actions. Despite this we saw them very fervent in their prayers to the Supreme Being, in this way wishing to avoid their sorrows and to be provided with relief.

He pointed out that important people did not marry within the tribe but sought relationships with distant groups. Children were engaged in their infancy and did not see their future partners until the time arrived for marriage. Adultery was punished with death, the bodies being thrown out to be eaten by wild animals. Bodega also observed:

When a father wishes to give a name or title to his son, he pays a considerable sum to the chief and to the godfathers of a celebrated person. Curiously, Dahi has six of these titles and Macquinna has ten and in a word the distinctions of nobility have been introduced into Nootka and are not in proportion to men's merit but according to their wealth, inherited by son from father and thus the son of Honaree is called Kooskukomuk. . . .

While Bodega was initiating a regime of peaceful coexistence between all groups, the last act of the Spanish–British rivalry was to take place. The famous navigator and protege of Cook, George Vancouver, appeared on the scene. He first cruised along the coast below Nootka, exploring and charting. He then sailed north and spent some time near Cheslakee's village at Johnstone's Straits, observing the customs of the Kwakiutl. He saw them making mats and baskets so closely woven that they would hold water. The houses, 34 in all, were small temporary dwellings arranged in streets; the larger ones, in which the principal chiefs lived, were decorated with paintings forming various figures—"apparently the rude designs of fancy; though it was by no means improbable they might annex some meaning to the figures described too remote or hieroglyphical for our comprehension." Vancouver found that they no longer wanted iron beads or trinkets for their sea otter furs but fire-arms. They were finally persuaded to accept sheets of copper and bolts of blue cloth.

Vancouver arrived at Nootka in August. He was very ceremonially received by Bodega y Quadra, who explained and elaborated the Spanish version of the Colmett affair. He insisted that Captain Hudson had incurred debts to the Spanish crown and for this reason the *North West Coast of America* had been seized as indemnity for bills of exchange. He said that Hudson had been well treated, but Colmett had arrived and announced that he had come to hoist the British flag and set up a blockhouse and a colony. Martínez had insisted he had taken possession for Spain. Colmett had said he was an officer of the king; Martínez had replied that he was only so on half pay, and had boasted he was the viceroy's nephew. According to Bodega the capture of the *Argonaut* and *Princess Royal* was all very formal with much courtesy and gentlemanly treatment of the British.

Vancouver listened and then announced that he was taking over the port for the British in accordance with the terms of the convention. Bodega politely agreed to return the port provisionally but pointed out that the convention made it a free port and did not hand it over to the British (which was correct). Bodega agreed to bow out while the dispute was arbitrated. Vancouver had a record as an annexer. He had once negotiated a treaty annexing Hawaii for the British crown in which he had not been sustained by Parliament.

Meanwhile, Macquinna had come out to Vancouver's ship, apparently without the soldiers' chorus, and, what with British class consciousness, was mistaken for a mere Indian. He was indignant and went to the Spaniards to complain. Finally, Vancouver and Macquinna were invited to dinner at Bodega's house with the Spaniard's five changes of silver plate (Captain Gray's mate counted 170 dishes). Macquinna, doubtless in his ruffled shirt, was given a silk handkerchief and drank wine with the two officers. He complained that he wished they would make up their minds who controlled the port, for he found it all very unsettling. Both commanders were now on terms of stately friendship. (When Bodega died a year later, Vancouver paid a tribute to his memory.)

No one seems to have asked Macquinna if he had sold land or granted rights to the British. He later denied that he did. The Spaniards believed, however, that he had sold the harbor to Meares for several sheets of copper and some blue cloth. Actually, the British simply remained in possession. Viceroy Gigedo had apparently decided that the fur trade was coming to an end and did not feel like insisting on the actual terms of the convention.

At Bodega's suggestion, Vancouver made a ceremonial visit to Macquinna at his village of Tasheis. He was received with ceremony, visited many houses, and ended up at Macquinna's. Bodega had brought dinner; Vancouver made suitable presents.

Then a war dance was performed in which 18 men with 16 foot lances carried out a pantomime of attack and defense. Vancouver was given two fine sea otter skins. Not to be outdone, the British commander had his sailors perform country dances and reels to drum and fife music. On Macquinna's return visit, Vancouver had his men shoot off fireworks, an entertainment he often provided for the Hawaiians.

Vancouver continued to cruise about, and in May 1794 he came back to Nootka. Macquinna was celebrating the engagement of his daughter and heir to a son of Wicananish. After more northward cruising in June 1794, the British commander investigated a Russian fur station at latitude 60. By this time Alexander Baranov was in charge at Kodiak Island. The settlement at Cook's Inlet was an outpost, and Vancouver observed that the traders lived, much like the natives, on oil and fish and seemed on good terms with the Tlingit. He remarked that they were neither studious nor learned; apparently they were real *promishchlenniki* barbarians.

Back in Nootka in September 1794 he made another state visit to Macquinna. After a war dance Macquinna did a solo—

> in which he with great address frequently and almost imperceptibly changed his mask. . . . The masks he made choice of did credit to his imagination in point of whimsical effect, his dress was different from that worn by the other performers, consisting of a short apron, covered with hollow shells and small piece of copper so placed as to strike each other, being accompanied by the music before described [box drums] as a substitute for a drum and some vocal exertions, produced a savage discordant noise.

With a last exchange of presents, Vancouver was ready to return home.

Meanwhile, the rest of Captain Gray's voyage seems to have been a catalogue of disasters. According to the log of John Boit (fifth mate on the Columbia), Gray fell out with Wicananish and sent Boit with three boats to destroy the village of Opitsitah, thus initiating a form of reprisal against the Indians which was to repeated numerous times by the Canadian government. The settlement was burned to the ground, including all the carvings. Boit said he was sorry that Gray allowed his passions to go so far. The Americans had built a sloop—the *Adventure,* commanded by Robert Haswell—as they sailed north in the spring of 1792. At the entrance to Queen Charlotte's Sound, Boit was sent out with a boat's crew to cut a mizzen topmast, at which time they were attacked by 200 Haida. They shot some of these and fought their way back to the ship, which fired a round of grapeshot. When a number of canoes approached them farther up the sound, singing, the ship's guns were fired over their heads. A chief was shot for ordering an attack and another as he threw a spear at the ship. Captain Gray's passionate disposition seems to have interfered with the kind of public relations necessary for trading. The *Columbia* struck a rock near Milbank Sound and returned to Nootka for repairs. These were speedily taken care of, to the admiration of the Spaniards. Gray, having sold the Spaniards the *Adventure,* returned home in the *Columbia* by way of China, where he sold his skins, and reached Boston on July 29, 1793.

After Bodega left Nootka, no European settlement remained. In the first decade of the nineteenth century, during John Jewitt's captivity, Jewitt remarks that the foundations of the Spanish governor's house were still visible.

The Spaniards, however, seem to have left in high favor with the natives, thanks to the character of Bodega y Quadra. Hoskins wrote what could serve as Bodega's epitaph: "A gentleman and a friend to all the human race, a father to the Indians who all love him and a good friend to the Americans in general."

MACKENSIE MEETS THE BELLA COOLA

5

In the meantime, Sir Alexander Mackensie, as an explorer and advance man of the North West Fur Company, embarked in June 1789 from Fort Chippewayan on the Peace River, which flowed toward Hudson's Bay from the Rockies. He, too, was in search of a northwest passage for the discovery of which a reward of £200,000 was offered by Parliament. He traveled partly by canoe, partly overland with French *coureurs de bois* and Algonquin Indians. Admittedly the fur trade, for some decades, had created a situation in which the *coureurs* had quarreled and fought with the Indians of the East, fed them liquor for skins, and in general had not created an atmosphere in which much intelligent observation and report on their customs took place. Mackensie, although himself a temperate and intelligent man, seemed only too often to be suffering from the expectation of being attacked and, as he was continually on the move and anxious about weather and provisions, he did not have much leisure to take notes. He first met the Bella Coola Indians on their river, which leads down to the sea, after having crossed the Rockies in July 1793.

At the first village he came to, the chief and all the principal people embraced him and the chief's son broke the thong of his sea otter robe and flung it over the explorer. He was taken to a large house and fed roast salmon and cakes made from the inner rind of hemlock soaked in oil. There was a weir in the river to catch the salmon, which were running, and thousands of these fish were strung on cords fastened to stakes in the river. During the whole of the period Mackensie stayed on the coast, the salmon were running and the natives ate nothing else. Taboos and magic surrounded these fish from the beginning: the explorers were kept away from the river, and the Indians took away their iron kettle, for they said the salmon did not like the smell of iron.

In this village were seven elevated houses and four built on the ground. The former had floor posts about 12 feet above the ground. The houses were compartmental, as usual, and here had as many as four or five separate hearths. Roast fish hung from the roof poles, and the roof itself, except for smoke holes at the ridge, was covered with bark and boards.

At the end out of the house was a narrow scaffolding ascended to by a piece of timber with steps cut in it and at each corner of this erection there are openings for the inhabitants to ease nature. As it does not appear to be the custom with them to remove these heaps of excremental filth, it may be supposed that the effluvia does not annoy them.

Mackensie insisted that the chief offered him his wife for the night, an invitation which he resisted. He described interesting ceremonial objects:

Near the house of the chief I observed several oblong squares of about twenty feet by eight. They were made of thick cedar boards which were joined with so much neatness that I at first thought they were one piece. They were painted with hieroglyphics and figures of different animals with a degree of correctness that was not to be expected from such an uncultivated people. I could not learn the use of them but they appeared to be calculated for occasional acts of devotion or sacrifice, which all these tribes perform at lease twice a year, at the spring and fall. I was confirmed in this opinion by a large building in the middle of the village, which I at first took for the half finished frame of a house.

This was about 50 by 45 feet, the corners formed by large posts supporting a beam along which were three center props. Those at each end supporting two ridge poles on their heads were 2½ feet in diameter carved into human figures 12 feet tall:

The figures on the upper parts of this square represent two persons with their hands up on their knees, as if they supported the weight with pain and difficulty; the others opposite them stand at their ease with their hands resting on their hips.

In the central area of the building, which did not seem to be roofed or sided, there were the remains of several fires. The posts, poles, and figures were painted red and black.

Mackensie was asked to treat a couple of patients, including the chief's son, who was suffering from infected wounds. He gave the young man some patent medicine and described the actions of the native medicine men who "blew on him and then whistled." They sometimes pressed their extended fingers into his stomach with all their strength. They put their doubled forefingers into his mouth and spouted water from their own mouths with great violence into his face. The patient's belly and breast were covered with scars which the explorer learned had come from applying lighted touchwood to the flesh to relieve pain. One of the practitioners scarified the boy's ulcered back with a blunt instrument.

The chief had two coats with brass buttons which seemed to be Spanish. There was considerable copper in evidence, some pieces cut from old stills. The Indians also had acquired iron daggers.

The chief asked Mackensie not to use his navigating instruments for fear they might affect the salmon. He also managed to explain that he had met white men in two ships on the sea coast 10 winters before, which Mackensie surmised to be the Cook party. Mackensie pointed out that both Cook and Meares were wrong in thinking that the canoes were adorned with human teeth; instead, those of the sea otter, which looked similar, were used.

Further down the river the party was entertained by a chief in another village. They were given a wooden trencher of blueberries and large white berries, larger than blackberries. Mackensie saw the women spinning the inner cedar bark, which looked like flax, with a distaff and spindle. They then wove it with a mixture of strips of sea otter skin in a loom placed against the side of the house. Men fished the river with a dragnet and two canoes.

They soon reached the sea through a narrow arm of the river and saw a large number of sea otters, porpoise, a bald eagle, and some ducks. They took observations which indicate that they had reached Cape Menzies of Vancouver. They met some Indians who spoke a different tongue and who said that, when a large ship had recently been in the bay, one of the white men, whom he called "Macubah," had fired on him and his friends and that "Bensins" had struck him in the back with the flat of his sword. (Vancouver's sailing master had fired on the Indians.) From this point on the Indian continued to make trouble, insisting that Mackensie go to his village and at the same time demanding presents. The explorers collected a few skins, heard more talk of Macubah; but by now Mackensie's apprehensions had got the better of him and until he left the coast he went about expecting hostility. He met Indians who did not speak the language of his Bella Coola guide; wrote his name and date on a large rock; and checked on his latitude, which was 52.

His guide was afraid of the alien Indians—Macubah's victim continued to behave threateningly—so the explorers returned up the river to reach Fort Chippewayan on the twenty-fourth of May 1893, having added more proof to the now fairly well-established belief that there was no practical northwest passage through the continent of North America.

THE YANKEE PRISONER

6

The last important document dealing with the coastal fur trade is the narrative of John Rodgers Jewitt, who was a prisoner among the Nootka from 1803 to 1806. Jewitt was born in Boston, England, and in 1783 had a better-than-average education, for he was sent to a private school in which he did well (except for the study of Latin). His family moved to Hull, England, where he heard stories of the exploits of Captain Cook. It so happened that the American ship *Boston,* engaged in the West Coast trade, put into this port for repairs. Captain John Saltar, evidently aware of the young man's interest, suggested he sign on as a smith, a trade in which young Jewitt was proficient. In September 1802 the *Boston* sailed with a cargo of English cloth, beads, knives, razors, 3000 muskets, and 20 hogsheads of rum. The last two items significantly indicate what direction the coastal fur trade had taken in the last decade of the eighteenth century.

On the voyage Jewitt worked at making hatchets and knives for the purpose of barter. Captain Saltar, he said, was a good seaman and a man of mild temper who treated his crew well. On Saturday night a band played for their edification. When the vessel anchored in Nootka Sound five miles north of Friendly Cove, Chief Macquinna came on board in a cordial mood. Jewitt describes him as six feet tall, dark copper in color, his features distinguished by a large Roman nose. He wore his hair in a bunch on top of his head, powdered with the ever-present ceremonial white down. A mantle of black sea otter hung down to his knees, belted at the waist. By this time he spoke a fair amount of English and expected presents whenever he came on board a ship, even when he had no goods to trade.

Indeed, by now the Nootka area had been so exploited that there were very few furs available, and consequently Saltar concentrated on getting supplies of water on board and repairing the spars and rigging. The inhabitants of Nootka Sound had a history of pacific relations with strangers, while the Indians of the north were considered "more ferocious."

Macquinna and some of the lesser chiefs came on board to dinners, at which time Jewitt noted they pulled up their legs and squatted in their chairs like Turks. They adored molasses on bread and refused to eat salt. Saltar apparently gave them the run of the ship, for they crowded around Jewitt's forge, fascinated by his techniques for making weapons. It was to this that he later owed his life.

Some time later Macquinna came on board with a present of some ducks. He brought with him a fowling piece, given him by Saltar, of which he had broken the lock. He gave it back, calling it "bad." Saltar was angry and made some remarks to the effect that Macquinna did not know how to treat it and tossed it over to Jewitt to be repaired. Macquinna, who understood very well what the captain had said, was furious. He kept rubbing his throat and chest with his hand, as he told Jewitt "to keep his heart down."

Nevertheless, the next day he came on board wearing a wooden animal mask and danced for some time, marking the rhythm with blasts on a whistle. He told the captain that since he liked salmon he should send a group of men with a seine to a spot where the Indians would show them how to catch them. The first mate and nine men therefore went off in the jollyboat and the yawl. Jewitt was working below at his forge when he heard a disturbance above. Clearly Saltar had been very lax about security, for when Jewitt ran up on deck an Indian grabbed him by the hair and cut a gash in his forehead with an ax. Later he was dropped into the steerage. While the massacre went on above, the hatch of the steerage was kept closed by Macquinna, who had his own plans for the smith. Jewitt heard songs of triumph. After a time the chief ordered him up on deck, where he was greeted by a bloody sight—the heads of the captain and twenty-four crew members. Macquinna asked Jewitt if he would work for him and be his slave, which the young man agreed to, kissing Macquinna's hands and feet as a token of submission.

Jewitt learned later that the captain had been so careless that the Indians had been able to break open the arms chest and thus take over the ship. Subsequently they ambushed the group fishing for salmon and destroyed them as well.

Although Jewitt was weak from his wound, he was ordered to get the ship into Friendly Cove, which he did by cutting the lines and directing the Indians on how to operate the sails until the vessel was beached.

The young man was then taken to Macquinna's house, where

the chief's nine wives were kind to him and exhibited a good deal of pity for his wound. The natives carried on their victory celebration and most of them, including some of the chiefs, wanted Jewitt killed. They argued that, if he were left alive, news of the massacre might reach his compatriots and no one would come to trade at Nootka. The argument reached a climax with Macquinna still refusing to kill his prisoner and finally chasing the dissenting councillors out of his house. Although he had the practical intent of making use of Jewitt's talent, he seems also to have taken a fancy to the young man.

Jewitt, on his part, tried in every way to satisfy his captors. He made friends with the chief's son, cut the buttons off his own coat, and made the boy a necklace from them. The smith now recollected that there was one white man still about the ship—Johnson, the sailmaker, who had hidden below. Since he was older than Jewitt, the latter concocted the story that Johnson was his father and begged Macquinna to spare his life. This the chief did in the face of considerable opposition. Johnson was a brute of a man who did not make life any easier for Jewitt, for he never relaxed his bitter hostility toward the Indians, all of whom he felt should be exterminated.

Indians from 20 neighboring tribes visited Nootka to help celebrate the capture of the *Boston*. The local Indians dressed in stolen finery. Macquinna got up on the roof of his house to drum his triumph and ordered his followers to fire off muskets and captured cannon with songs of victory. Unfortunately, while the Nootkans were plundering the ship of its rigging they inadvertently set fire to it, thus depriving themselves of much of its cargo. Jewitt managed to save a Bible and a Church of England prayerbook, along with an account book which he was to use as a diary.

Among the festivities there was a feast of whale blubber and smoked herring roe plus dried fish and plenty of oil, which was drunk like wine. During the dancing, bags full of down were scattered about. The king's young son was dressed in yellow, his mantle trimmed with small bells, while the chief danced behind him in a sea otter's skin, accompanying himself with a rattle and a whistle. Many of the steps consisted of springing into the air from squatting position or turning fast on the heels in a narrow circle. To the sound of drumming on a hollow box, this went on for two hours. Then there was choral singing led by Macquinna, as the chief gave away many presents in the name of his son—among his largesse were 100 muskets, 100 mirrors, 100 yards of cloth, and 20 casks of powder. All this indicates that something like the potlatch was already an institution among the Indians of the coast. The men got so drunk on the captured rum that the women became alarmed and left the house. Jewitt felt it was fortunate so much of the rum was burned or there would have been no end to the debauchery.

Jewitt was kept busy repairing muskets and making copper jewelry for Macquinna and his wives. No one would feed Johnson, who took no pains to hide his hatred for everything pertaining to Indians. Jewitt was allowed to share his provisions with him and was even allowed to sell some of his work to visiting tribesmen. He was continually distressed because he was not allowed to cook his own meals but was forced to bathe everything in oil. He managed to contrive to make ink from blackberry juice and quills from crow feathers, with which he wrote in his diary. Jewitt attempted to please his captors and gained a fair knowledge of the Nootkan language.

The village consisted of about 20 houses spread along the shore of friendly cove. Macquinna's, the largest, was about 40 by 150 feet with a ridge pole 8 feet in circumference, painted with red and black circles. The posts supporting it ended in huge sculptured heads. The loose boards of the roof had to be anchored with stones during storms. Belongings were kept in decorated wooden boxes and tubs. Commoners wore bark cloth mantles, important personages otter cloaks. The Indians ate from bark trays a foot wide and 3 feet long and from 6 to 18 inches deep. Four to six people used one tray, while the chief had his own. It was a great mark of favor to be offered food from the chief's tray. Formal feasts were for men only; visitors took leftover food home with them. The men, as well as painting their faces on formal occasions, also sprinkled mica on their skins to make them shine.

Except for sea otter, now become shy and scarce, little hunting was done, but fishing was carried on with wooden hooks which the Nootka abandoned when Jewitt made them iron ones. In whaling they used a detachable harpoon and a line with floats. Whales were considered solely the sport of chiefs, Macquinna pursuing them in a 42-foot canoe.

In felling trees for canoes the natives originally had used flint chisels, but now they shifted to iron, still using stone for mallets. The vessels were decorated with designs of eagles, whales, and human faces.

Jewitt noted that war songs were composed in a style different from that of ordinary speech. The plaintive melodies were accompanied by box drums, rattles, and whistles.

When Macquinna caught Jewitt writing in his diary the chief accused him of writing bad things in it. After that he wrote on the sly.

In September the tribe moved about 30 miles up the bay to another campsite. There the frames of buildings were ready to receive the wooden planks which they brought with them. Here they collected herring roe and took salmon in pointed weirs woven of flexible twigs. They split the fish and hung them to dry for the winter. The salmon roe was allowed to putrify, in which condition they ate it with pleasure. Jewitt was revolted.

About this time Johnson gained a little favor for himself by making a patchwork coat of many-colored European cloths for Macquinna, decorating it with brass buttons.

In talking with Macquinna, Jewitt gained some insight into the reason for his bloody attack upon the *Boston.* Macquinna had never forgotten the series of injuries done him by foreigners which demanded vengeance. The Spaniard, Martínez, had killed four chiefs (as we know, one of them was Macquinna's brother). An American had stolen skins. Captain Hannah of the *Sea Otter* had fired on his people and killed several in a clash over a stolen chisel. Captain Saltar's insults were added to the list. It was clear that Macquinna's vengeance was a kind of impersonal eye-for-an-eye in which the innocent contributed their heads, which were then considered war trophies.

Jewitt records some interesting facts concerning bear hunting. Bears were caught by baiting a heavy deadfall with salmon, the trap crushing the bear's head. The animal was then carefully cleaned of blood and dirt and seated opposite the chief with the chief's hat on its head and its fur ceremonially powdered with white down. Food was set before it and it was invited to eat. This is, of course, the identical propitiation rite used by most circumpolar peoples. After the ceremony was over, the bear was cooked and eaten. Interestingly enough, those who had eaten bear's meat were not allowed to eat fish for two months: if they did so, the fish would not allow themselves to be caught.

Jewitt described a ceremonial during which the two whites were exiled from the village for 21 days. On their return three men with bayonets stuck into their ribs were singing war songs, apparently disregarding the pain. There were other such trials of stoicism—in one, 20 men came singing and boasting into the chief's house with arrows run through the flesh of their sides.

This seems to have been an ordeal similar to the Plains Indian sun dance practices.

Jewitt also noted that Macquinna passed a whole day singing and praying before going whaling. There was much ceremonial bathing, and sexual activity was forbidden before beginning the hunt.

The burial of a chief who had died in a pathological mental state involved wrapping the body in a sea otter skin and placing it in a coffin ornamented outside with two rows of white shells. Jewitt noted that 24 fine sea otter skins were buried with him in a cavern in the side of a hill. At Macquinna's house numerous articles owned by the dead man were burned. The observances ended with a feast, during which Macquinna covered his head with down. A speech was made by a kind of court jester who was attached to Macquinna and was a great favorite. The dead man had suffered from hallucinations concerning the two members of the *Boston's* crew he had killed. This event seemed to have disturbed the psyche of the village. Macquinna was blamed for the massacre when the fishing was poor.

The prisoners were commanded to take part in a raiding party attacking a neighboring tribe. Before the raid took place, the Nootka warriors went in for ritual bathing and the scrubbing of their skins with brambles until they were bloody. This was to harden themselves. They also deprived themselves of sex and took very little food. The group attacked at dawn. Jewitt stayed on the outskirts of the village, but Johnson cheerfully killed seven of the enemy, which raised him in the estimation of his captors. After the raid there was a feast and a victory dance.

When the group migrated inland during the second September, Jewitt was told it was considered to have become a member of the tribe and must behave like one and marry. Jewitt was against this, for he feared he would never be allowed to leave; but he was finally forced to choose the pretty daughter of a neighboring chief. Macquinna brought presents for the father-in-law and made a speech praising Jewitt, indicating that except for his white skin he was almost human. At this point the captive was forced to wear Indian dress. Although his wife was amiable and intelligent, Jewitt continued to be unhappy and was cold in Indian clothes. He finally had an attack of colic and complained so much that Macquinna allowed him to send his wife home and resume European dress.

Early in the third year a vessel came into the harbor. Jewitt pretended to show no interest. A council was held in which some wanted the prisoners put to death, some were willing to release them, and some wished to hide them in the interior. Macquinna asked Jewitt if he should go aboard the ship. Jewitt urged him to and gave him a letter, supposedly of recommendation. Actually the letter urged the skipper to hold Macquinna as a hostage, which he did.

The Nootka were furious, but at length the two white men were released. Jewitt made his peace with Macquinna, but the latter said he would never put trust in a letter again.

The experiences of Jewitt bring up the whole question of the relationships between West Coast Indians and foreigners during the era of active coastal fur trade. F. W. Howay, who has analyzed these relations up to 1805, lists numerous incidents of attempted capture of smaller vessels, some of which were prevented, while others resulted in bloody massacres. For instance, Captain John Kendrick of the *Washington*, who has been discussed earlier, annoyed by native stealing, captured the Haida chief Coyah, threatened to kill him, "tied a rope around his neck, whipped him, painted his face, cut off his hair, took away from him a great many skins and then turned him ashore." It is not surprising that Coyah later tried to attack the *Columbia* and took a British ship and killed the crew. He also captured Captain Metcalf's brig and massacred the crew.

In most cases on record the clashes were preceded by high-handed behavior on the part of the ships' captains, who too often held important chiefs as hostages because of stealing or in order to reclaim deserters. Sometimes it was done to extort skins without payment.

The desire for good intercultural relations was weak on the part of close-fisted captains out to extract a profit from the fur trade. Such men had no understanding of the fierce pride of important chiefs, whose crests and lineages entitled them—in their own eyes and those of their fellows—to the highest respect. Howay says that, in the case of Saltar and the *Boston* incident, the captain had said Macquinna was a low fellow and that he did not look like a chief. Macquinna, who had been treated like royalty by governors and visiting captains, was furious and answered back. Saltar threatened him with a gun. The result we have seen.

Shame and prestige were the two poles of Northwest culture. Warfare was meant to inspire terror, which was equated with proof of prestige, or it was used as revenge against a rival.

Clearly, from their point of view, Coyah, Macquinna, and also Wicananish had suffered intolerable shame at the hands of the whites. As Franz Boas has pointed out, preliterate ethics consist of respecting one's neighbors, relatives, and fellow tribesmen, while outsiders are considered fair game and not human.

Most of the incidents of slaughter occurred in the last decade of the eighteenth century when the traders were competing for the now scarce furs. They had taught the natives how to use firearms and how to drink rum so that these became the most desired articles of commerce. Captain Saltar's cargo of rum and muskets was asking for trouble. Unfortunately when two cultures come in contact it is seldom the wisest and most tolerant in each who meet. If many native customs were violent and bloody, neither did the so-called civilized white men hesitate to use violent methods in pursuit of profit.

A COLONY IS BORN

7

From 1805 up until almost the middle of the nineteenth century, data on the condition of the Indians of the Northwest Coast is scanty. The history of central and western Canada coincides with the expansionist aims of and the hostilities between the Northwest Fur Company and the Hudson's Bay Fur Company. As we have already indicated, it was Alexander Mackensie of the Northwest Company who first made the overland trip, once again in search of an illusory northwest passage, proved there was none and made contact with the Bella Coola Indians. His company—which was formed in 1779 by Simon MacTavish, who was to bring in his nephew William Macgillivray—was effectually prevented from using the water access of Hudson's Bay because the older organization had monopolized that area since its formation in 1670. The Northwest Company tried unsuccessfully to maintain a monopoly of the fur trade in Western Canada. Both companies depended upon the half-wild French *voyageurs* to make contact with the Indians. Many of these—and even such important figures in the fur trade as Mackensie himself—took Indian wives; yet, on the whole, they seem to have been incurious concerning the natives' way of life and only too often became involved in hostile clashes with them.

Mackensie eventually withdrew from the Northwest Company, formed his own company, and carried on a civil war with his former associates which resulted in the death of a clerk. His principal opponent died in 1804; peace was arrived at and the two organizations merged. In the region of the Columbia River, the Northwest Company competed with John Jacob Astor's Pacific Fur Company. In 1814 Astor sold out Astoria to his rival, who changed the name of the settlement to Fort George. This left the coastal area from San Francisco to Alaska technically a Northwest monopoly. In this era of capitalist buccaneering, however, two such giants as the Northwest and the Hudson's Bay Company could not live peaceably together. After various hostile episodes the two organizations, both on the verge of bankruptcy, had sense enough to unite, with the Hudson's Bay Company dominant thus giving it control of all of Canada except the eastern maritime provinces.

At Vancouver the fort was commanded by John McLoughlin, who had formerly been important in the Northwest Company. Shortly before the merger, however, he had made a deal with its rival and emerged as a top official of the new company—in fact, he was now dubbed "the Emperor of the West." Second in command was James Douglas, who was subsequently to become the governor of British Columbia.

McLoughlin's letters from the fort describe an incident of 1828 which illustrates the punitive methods used by the Hudson's Bay Company against the Indians, this time probably the Coast Salish. A group of Hudson's Bay people had been killed and one woman taken prisoner. McLoughlin sent four clerks and 59 servants to punish the Indians. They killed eight members of "a party of the tribe of murderers." They negotiated for the return of the woman prisoner, attempting to hold a council which broke down. The Hudson's Bay people fired on the Indians, killed one, and wounded one. Lieutenant Aemilius Simpson, whose gunboat was nearby, was invited to fire a few cannon shots into the village—which he obligingly did—and "under cover of cannon burnt the village with all the property of 46 canoes, the third day after this the natives gave up the woman and we gave up the wounded Indian." McLoughlin notes that not a man of the Hudson's Bay Company was hurt and the expedition "was most judicially conducted." Although the Indian losses were high, the chief factor stated that this did not trouble them: "They are so devoid of feeling that this does not affect them so much as the burning of their village and property and the destruction of their canoes." The pattern set by Captain Gray was still being followed and would be for decades.

In the journal of a singularly obtuse missionary who traveled on the Northwest Coast in 1829 with an American fur trader, we get an insight into what was happening in the extreme north. The ship had nets of strong cord around its decks to prevent the Indians from coming on board. The Tlingit were encountered at the entrance to the Nass River. Jonathan Green, a Protestant, made no effort to learn anything about these Indians but merely exercised his talent for physiognomical analysis:

The Nass men seem to combine the "man-brute" with the "man-devil." They appear more dirty and degraded than any Indians whom I have yet seen while at the same time they exhibit an intelligence strongly marked. This intellectual strength without one softening feature assumes the aspect of a desperate fierceness.

Nevertheless, the Reverend Green, through an interpreter, treated their chief to a discourse on a deity above and informed him that the Bible forbade murder, stealing, quarreling, and drunkenness. The chief displayed his intellectual strength by inquiring, "Why then is rum brought hither?"

To do him justice Green was full of indignation against the traders, who were teaching the Indians the worst habits of white culture. Green accused them of encouraging the Indian women to come on board for the purpose of prostitution.

When the ship anchored in Masset Inlet, Green asked the Haida who made the world. They replied "Raven."

Apparently, despite his nets, the Captain was not careful about letting Indians on board. Several Indians got into a quarrel with the traders which developed into a fight. Shots were exchanged, some natives killed, and when the Reverend Green perceived an Indian approaching him with a knife he ran below, seized the captain's pistol, and knelt in prayer, holding the pistol in his shaking hand.

For many years no other missionary attempted to convert the natives, and the Hudson's Bay Company continued to reign supreme.

Roderick Finlayson, who was apprenticed to the company as a clerk in 1837, left some notes concerning his residence on the Northwest Coast which reveal something of the fur company's relations with the Tlingit. In 1840, when the Russian American Fur Company leased Fort Stikine and the area around it to the Hudson's Bay Company, Finlayson took over. The Russians, when they gave over the fort, said they could not hold it because the Indians were warlike and had many slaves they forced to fight on pain of being shot. Finlayson and his companions were sure they could hold it with 18 men. The territory was being leased to the British for 10 years in return for European goods and agricultural products. Finlayson tells us that the New York and Boston ships' captains had continued the bartering of arms and liquor, which was already causing trouble in Jewitt's day, and had now so demoralized the Indians that it was dangerous to venture outside of the 18-foot stockade—built to this height so that the Indians could not scale it.

Profit knowing no moderation, the Hudson's Bay Company determined to undersell the Yankees, using liquor to lure the Indians away from the maritime traders. (By 1825 more than 230 vessels were trading yearly along the coast.) Hudson's Bay at this point continued the trade in firearms as well as liquor. Finlayson maintained that the Americans frequently quarreled with the natives and fired upon them. By now the ships had steel netting placed around their decks to prevent the Indians from coming on board.

In the stockade a watch was kept day and night, and Finlayson was careful never to let more than two or three natives in at a time:

> One day several Indians forced themselves in at the gate which was fully opened to allow those who had traded to go out, when I had to go to the rescue in attempting to put a strong fellow out, he struck me a severe blow, which enraged me so much that I imprudently followed him out. I was at once seized by 50 of the wild savages, dragged by the hair, my clothes torn off and carried away towards the harbor where their canoes were.

The commander of the fort fired blanks from his cannon, which frightened the Indians into letting Finlayson escape. This was indeed a far cry from the amiable dinners and visits to the Indians' houses in which the early traders participated at Nootka. Contact with so-called civilized cultures had resulted only in bringing out the worst in both groups.

Finlayson gives an early description of a potlatch. Each of two chiefs had 90 to 100 slaves, mostly purchased from the Haida of Queen Charlotte's Islands, who captured slaves all along the coast, even venturing as far south as Cape Mendocino to obtain them. The Tlingit were willing to sell slaves to the traders for $10 apiece.

At the potlatch one chief made a speech boasting of the amount of property he owned. He then shot one of his slaves. The rival also boasted and did likewise. Eventually 10 were killed and left lying on the beach, for it was considered degrading to touch them. Finlayson had the bodies of these victims of "these fiends in human form" burned. He then made a speech through an interpreter announcing that there was "a God in heaven who would punish such evil deeds." The Tlingit, naturally, were not convinced.

Although Finlayson was an unsympathetic observer, he substantiates this brutal practice, which the missionaries cited repeatedly in opposing the institution of potlatch.

Finlayson was transferred to the fort on the Stikine River early in 1841. He says the Indians tried to capture it and in the ensuing hostilities a chief was taken captive and used as a hostage to bargain for peace. Finlayson's assistant was John McLoughlin, the half-breed son of the chief factor at Vancouver. The young man was a dropout from medical school and had a spendthrift record during a period when he lived in Montreal. Finlayson was transferred to Fort Simpson in September 1841, leaving McLoughlin in charge of Fort Stikine; in April he was murdered by his subordinates. George Simpson, head of the Hudson's Bay Company, arrived at the fort shortly afterward, but, receiving an account of the affair in which the young man was branded as a drunkard and a tyrant, his attitude was that the episode should be forgotten. McLoughlin senior was naturally enraged and did not cease to investigate until he got an account of the facts from one of the conspirators, who admitted that he had never seen the young man drunk. In a letter to George Simpson of July 1842, the chief factor wrote that Douglas had questioned Pierre Kanaquasse, who stated:

> In consequence of Mr. McLoughlin's not allowing the men to take Indian wives or bring Indian women into the fort and not allowing them to go out at night to go after Indian women and his flogging the men who had given away their wearing apparel to the Indian women, all of the men of the fort except Pouhow, a Sandwich Islander, had signed an agreement, which had been written by James MacPherson before last Christmas, to murder the late John McLoughlin.

McLoughlin blamed the death of his son on Finlayson's transfer. Although he discovered who had fired the shot and arrested the ringleaders, nothing was done because the killing had taken place on Russian soil and the Russians would not prosecute.

The episode adds a few more details to the picture of trading company relations with the Indians. On the one hand, the forts were in a state of semi-siege and, on the other, nothing was allowed to interfere with the sexual relations between Hudson's Bay employees and Tlingit women. And somehow business went on as usual.

Indeed, it went on so well that Finlayson wrote that "we managed to drive off other fur traders of the coast so that we had entire control of the trade." At first this was accomplished by supplying liquor, but eventually the Hudson's Bay Company and the Russian American Fur Company made an agreement not to deal in liquor for 10 years and to drive all vessels which arrived with liquor from the coast. The merchants had finally come to the conclusion that liquor made the Indians unsafe to deal with. At first the natives went on strike and refused to trade, but when it was made clear that no one would provide whiskey they agreed to accept blankets.

The liquor problem was no less significant in Canada than in the United States, where Henry Rowe Schoolcraft, America's first anthropologist, valiantly fought to preserve the Chippewa from its demoralizing effect. None of the Northwest Coast tribes had intoxicants before the coming of the whites. The Russians brought liquor to the Aleutians as early as 1741. When whiskey was first offered to the Tlingit, they refused it, very intelligently believing it made them vulnerable to their enemies. By 1790 the English and American traders had succeeded in arousing a taste for alcoholic spirits, and by 1800 liquor was a basic item of the coastal trade. It must be admitted that in this connection U.S. skippers played a miserable role. The inland fur traders sometimes looked ahead to some continuity of business relations with the natives, but the Americans, mostly from Boston, seldom made more than three voyages and consequently could not have cared less about the effects of their actions. As Finlayson records, the Hudson's Bay Company made a pact with the Russians, but this stipulated they would not sell liquor unless compelled to—by U.S. competition.

As the Indian's addiction to liquor grew, it became another reason for the concentrations of Indian settlements around the trader's forts. That, despite the laws passed against the sale of liquor, much bootlegging went on in the later nineteenth century is evidenced by the fact that from 1858 to 1864 there were 336 court cases concerning infractions of this prohibition. Worse still, the unsuspecting natives were sold all sorts of wretched adulterations at extravagant prices. Camphor and tobacco water flavored with whiskey was purveyed, whiskey itself was generally adulterated with three to ten parts of water, and both vanilla extract and cologne were drunk when nothing else could be obtained. When Alaska became a part of the United States in 1867, the American troops sent in to occupy it bootlegged liquor across the border to the British Columbia Indians; in fact, it was an American soldier at Fort Wrangell who taught the natives how to make *hoochino*—molasses, flour, dried apples, salmonberries, or blackberries with water added to make a thin batter. After fermentation a sour muddy liquid with a violent kick was achieved.

Why was liquor felt to be a special Indian problem? In most

cases the addiction of the natives coincided with the awareness, conscious or unconscious, that their lifestyle was threatened by the whites and very soon they realized that they were doomed to be dominated by the alien civilization. It is no wonder that they took to heavy drinking, which sometimes allowed them to express their repressed hostilities and sometimes helped them to forget the fading away of their former glories. Likewise it must not be forgotten that, in the case of the Northwest Coast Indians, theirs was a society which prized ecstatic experience highly. The whites taught them how to obtain it—from a bottle.

Finlayson founded a fort on the Straits of Juan de Fuca, and finally Fort Misqually on Puget Sound came under his command. Here a farm for cattle and sheep was established. Unfortunately, relations with the Coast Salish were such that the latter killed and ate the cattle. Finlayson demanded reparations, but the Indians in 1844 responded by combining with other tribes to attack the fort. He fired on them, intimidated them, and extracted damages. This minor skirmish was to be cited as evidence of conquest by the Canadian government in 1927, as we shall see.

Finlayson's dismal narrative brings out clearly that to the fur traders the Indians were of interest as providers of furs, the women as sexual objects, and no responsibility was felt toward these original inhabitants of the land. The general policy of the Hudson's Bay Company was more than once criticized as anticolonist. Occupation of the land meant restriction of the hunting grounds and thus threatened the fur industry. The fur traders preferred that the Indians be kept in a more or less wild state. Yet the goods the traders brought, including liquor, were already changing the habits of the natives. Actually, the newly acquired riches and improved techniques resulting from the use of iron caused the native culture to develop a kind of hectic efflorescence during the nineteenth century.

Change was inevitable. The settlement of the Oregon boundary dispute with the United States in 1846 at the 49th parallel meant that the territory north of this latitude became Crown Land. The Hudson's Bay Company wanted to govern all of the territory north of Rupert's Land, most of central and western Canada; it finally got a grant giving it control of Vancouver Island with the understanding that it would assume responsibility for colonization. In 1849 land was selling for a pound an acre.

Finlayson's former superior, James Douglas, the chief factor of the fur company in 1849, became governor pro tem. Then Richard Blanchard, a lawyer, was appointed in 1850. There was to be an elected assembly. By November 1851, Blanchard resigned, alleging that the only settlers were company people and that the fur organization was assigning itself the best land free of charge. He also implied that the company wanted to maintain the area as a mere trading post. Apparently, although the British government was in favor of colonization, it was not prepared to spend money to encourage it.

James Douglas returned to replace Blanchard as governor. He seems, in the years that followed, to have been a capable administrator. He was accused of being too indulgent toward the Indians and of bribing chiefs to keep the peace. This may have been to his credit. He did nothing about setting up a police force to maintain the white man's law and order. In his personal attitude toward the Indians he never seems to have freed himself from fur company philosophy. Still, in comparison with later administrations, he did endeavor to give them fair treatment.

Governor Douglas installed customs and decreed three ports of entry. Newcomers could settle in any area not inhabited by the Indians, but the Indians were not allowed to take up land. Douglas had some respect for native territorial rights. His attitude was that it was necessary to make treaties with the Indians (he made 14) and to pay them £2/10 a family per acre, whereupon the land passed to the whites forever. It was understood that the Indians retained the right to unoccupied land and the right to maintain their fisheries.

The Kwakiutl who lived north of Victoria, the capitol of Vancouver, were sharp businessmen. A traveler noticing some small cannon in Fort Rupert remarked that they seemed rusty, dusty, and probably useless. The officer in charge said there was a tradition that they had been fired once to impress the Kwakiutl—who shrewdly ran after the balls, retrieved them, and offered to sell them back at a good price to be used again.

It was the same Kwakiutl who again became a thorn in the flesh of the Establishment when coal was discovered in their territory near Fort Rupert in 1836. The Northwest Coast had been importing it exclusively from Wales. It was believed there would be a good market to the south in the United States settlements. When negotiations were begun with the natives, according to one of Finlayson's letters, "they informed us they would not permit us to work the coals as they were valuable but that they would labor in the mines themselves and would sell us the product of their exertions." The always hostile Finlayson wrote: "But we know from the indolent habits of the Indians, even if the material for working for it were in their hands that in six months they would not furnish a sufficient quantity for the consumption of a day."

Since by 1859 the Hudson's Bay Company monopoly was to end, its officials pushed for a bill to renew it. Their spokesmen maintained they had suppressed the liquor trade with the Indians, by whom they were loved, that they had been successful in maintaining peace, and that their monopoly should be renewed for 21 years. Although British sentiment was becoming anticompany and the head of the organization was reputed to be anticolonist, his spokesmen came up with the argument that its monopoly should be maintained because competition would demoralize the Indians.

By midcentury the fur trade was no longer important in Vancouver and its center had shifted to the Frazer River, Thompson's River, and Sitka. (The agreement with the Russians continued until Alaska was bought by the United States.)

After ten years of argument, the Crown took back Vancouver, reimbursing the company. In 1858 an act created a government in British Columbia, which now included the island itself, the Queen Charlotte Islands, and those near them. Douglas was made governor, and by the following year the era of domination by the fur company was over. The period of colonization had truly begun—by now the area had a population of 10,600 whites.

ABOVE: Spanish engraving of Chief Macquinna, left, and his brother Callikum, right. Note otter fur cloaks worn by aristocrats. *(Provincial Archives, Victoria.)*

BELOW: Interior of Nootka dwelling as drawn by Webber, James Cook's artist, 1778, at Nootka Sound. *(Provincial Archives, Victoria.)*

ABOVE: View of houses, Nootka Sound, by Webber. *(Provincial Archives, Victoria.)*

CENTER: Puberty ceremony of Macquinna's daughters, from a Spanish engraving of 1792. *(Provincial Archives, Victoria.)*

BELOW: Seizure of Captain Colmett, left, from the Argonaut by Don Estéban Martinez, right, the Spanish Commandant at Nootka Sound in 1789. *(Provincial Archives, Victoria.)*

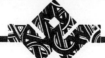

ABOVE: Hudson's Bay trading post, Fort Rupert, late nineteenth century. Note stockade defense against the Tsimshian. *(Provincial Archives, Victoria.)*

CENTER: The Reverend William Duncan. *(Provincial Archives, Victoria.)*

BELOW: Duncan's Indian village of Old Metlakatla as it looked in the mid-nineteenth century. *(Provincial Archives, Victoria.)*

ABOVE: Nootka female shaman at Clayoquot engaged in ritual bathing. *(E. S. Curtis photo, 1915, Provincial Archives, Victoria.)*

BELOW: Coast Salish (Cowichan) basket maker. *(E. S. Curtis photo, 1912, Provincial Archives, Victoria.)*

ABOVE: A turn-of-the-century potlatch at Alert Bay, given by a Kwakiutl chief. *(National Museums of Canada, Ottawa.)*

BELOW LEFT: Nootka spearing fish. *(E. S. Curtis photo, Provincial Archives, Victoria.)*

BELOW RIGHT: Nootka woman digging roots at Clayoquot. *(E. S. Curtis photo, 1915, Provincial Archives, Victoria.)*

ABOVE: Nootka halibut fishermen cleaning their catch. *(E. S. Curtis photo, 1915, Provincial Archives, Victoria.)*

BELOW: Kwakiutl warrior. *(E. S. Curtis photo, 1914, Provincial Archives, Victoria.)*

RUSSIAN BEARS AND TLINGIT RAVENS

8

The history of the Tlingit, one of the ethnic groups which shares the culture with which we are concerned, began with Russian contacts; and, since the Russians established their control over the coastal area of Alaska down to latitude 55, the contacts of this group of Indians were with the Russians until the sale of Alaska to the United States in 1867.

It was Grigorii Shelikov, aided by his wife, Grisha, who built up an important fur trading company and founded the first significant settlement on Kodiak Island off the coast of Alaska in 1784. Shelikov succeeded in negotiating with the Aleut and getting them to work for him. He tried to obtain a monopoly of the fur trade, with government backing, from Catherine the Great, but at the last moment she refused it. His son-in-law, Nicolai Petrovitch Rezanov, became involved in the company and, when its founder died, worked with Grisha to protect it from unbalanced Czar Paul. The latter promoted a kind of xenophobia—no Russian was allowed to leave the country and he even interfered with trade for he feared all foreign contacts. Rezanov succeeded in persuading the Czar to amalgamate all the fur traders into one organization with a loose connection with the Russian government, more or less on the Hudson's Bay model. The Russian-American company could maintain its own armed forces, treat with neighboring powers, and trade where it wished. It was supposed to control the coast from the Arctic to latitude 55. Needless to say the Shelikov interests were the majority stockholders. Meanwhile, the colony had been existing as a stepchild. For two years no ship had visited it, supplies were urgently needed. Eustrate Delarov, who by now was manager, was due to be replaced.

The replacement arrived in a native sea lion hide sailboat in the person of little Alexander Andreevich Baranov. This small, blond, balding administrator, who was destined to become the Czar of Alaska, arrived delirious with pneumonia. The ship in which he had set out from Okhotsk had been wrecked at Unalaska, where he had wintered, and he finally had managed to build skin boats to transport himself and his crew to the Kodiak settlement much the worse for wear.

Baranov, who was the son of a storekeeper and already forty-four years old, was scorned by the rough seamen because he had not weathered six weeks in an open boat (subsisting on raw fish) too well. But all winter at Unalaska he had been busy learning how to hunt and cultivating the Aleut, whose language he had learned.

He was intelligently self-educated, fond of science, and had learned German when he worked for a German merchant. He had left a wife and daughter in Russia when he went to Siberia to deal in sable with the Chuckchi. At Okhotsk he met Shelikov, who recognized his ability. He accepted the post in Alaska because it enabled him to escape from the Russian caste system which frustrated men of nonaristocratic birth.

Baranov put the inefficient, demoralized colony on its feet, set up strict discipline and ordered the men to live monogamously with their native women. He was able to make friends with the Aleut, thanks to his study of their language. He investigated Prince William's Sound and, as a result of his negotiating with the natives, married the handsome daughter of an Aleut chief. Years later when his Russian wife had died and he was enobled, his wife Ann and his half-breed family were also elevated to the Russian nobility.

Baranov helped a British trader which put into port with a broken mast and established trading relations and a friendship with its skipper and mate, despite the Russian rule of avoidance of relations with foreigners. This was to be of use, seeing that the supplies from Okhotsk were uncertain and the voyage hazardous.

The territory to the south was controlled by the Tlingit, who were in no mood to allow foreigners to exploit it. Baranov encountered, in Yschugat Bay in 1793, a raiding party which was in search of slaves. The natives apparently attacked first. They wore armored waistcoats, consisting of wooden rods bound together by rawhide, which were capable of turning bullets; on their heads, wooden hats also a protection against firearms. They had already acquired muskets from the Americans. The Tlingit, when in battle, also sported masks of bear, dogfish, and other animals. In the end the Russians killed twelve, themselves losing two men and nine Aleut. More than fifteen were wounded.

Baranov was furious when ships arrived lacking the provisions he had asked for. More than once he demanded to be replaced.

His troubles were increased by a contingent of missionaries, whom Shelikov had conned into setting out for Alaska with stories of a church already built. The Russian clergymen did not take to digging clams and catching fish. Some of them became Baranov's bitter enemies. Shelikov had also sent a number of serfs, many of whom were exiled criminals, who were supposed to set up an agricultural colony. Baranov did not know what to do with them. He sent an emissary to attempt to negotiate with the Tlingit at what is now Yakutat on the mainland. He was told the natives would not allow the Russians to hunt sea otter for nothing. No agreement seems to have been made, but in 1794 Baranov appeared with the Russian flag and founded a settlement of 80 people.

Once more Baranov asked to be replaced, but it was at this point that Shelikov died. Grisha urged the little administrator to carry on.

This he agreed to do, despite his troubles with the missionaries, who blamed him for everything, and some officers from the naval academy sent as navigators, who, because they were nobles, resisted his authority. Baranov's chief enemy, Father Iosaf, however, was lost at sea on the voyage home to become Bishop of Russian America. If he had undertaken his assignment he would have undoubtedly succeeded in having Baranov dismissed.

Sitka continued to be a Tlingit stronghold and—to Baranov, who was expansionist-minded—Russian influence had to be established along the coast. In the spring of 1799 he set out with 100 Russian, 700 Aleut, and 300 mainlanders in skin boats. A number of canoes were swamped, and in consequence the party wearily settled down to sleep on a mainland beach near a dense forest. In the middle of the night they were roused by Tlingit war cries. Some of the Aleut ran into the woods—into the arms of the war party. The rest of the party fought, the darkness favoring them, since it was impossible to distinguish friend from enemy. The following morning it was discovered that 26 men were missing, either killed or captured.

Baranov continued to attempt negotiations with the Sitka Tlingit. What he could not know was that the Tlingit were still furious at the behavior of an English captain, Henry Barber, who had invited natives aboard his ship, then held them for ransom, sometimes murdering them when payment in skins was not made quickly enough to suit him. It was the same old story that had been happening all along to the south. Finally Baranov succeeded in obtaining permission for a fort a few miles from the Tlingit settlement. All did not go smoothly, however, for the chief was criticized by his own people and throughout the Tlingit Confederation for allowing the foreigners to obtain a foothold.

Baranov returned to learn that the newly formed Russian-American company had appointed him governor and also to face more undermining by his Russian clergy, who tried to turn his Aleutian wife against him. He arrested them; they forbade him to attend services. There was still a lack of supplies and no ship from Russia. Fortunately, one of his British friends arrived with much-needed supplies which they were ready to trade for skins.

In 1802 the same Captain Henry Barber who had fomented trouble with the Tlingit in the first place arrived with 23 survivors of the Sitka fort. While some of the garrison were out hunting, a strong force of several Tlingit clans had attacked, taken the fort, burned it to ashes, and destroyed 20 Russians and 30 Aleut, some of whose heads were impaled on stakes. The delightful Henry Barber demanded a ransom of 50,000 rubles before he would release the Sitka survivors. If he did not get the money he would bombard the Kodiak settlement. He extracted 10,000 rubles' worth of furs.

Baranov was by now obsessed with the retaking of Sitka, even though Yakutat had barely escaped attack, and only then because it was warned by a traitor to the Tlingit. Baranov, as usual, lacked supplies, in this case arms for his expedition. His English friend, Joseph O'Cain, however, turned up with a ship he now owned in partnership with a Massachusetts merchant. He brought greetings from King Kamehameha of Hawaii, arms, and ship-building tools. Baranov had no furs, but he solved his problem by arranging with O'Cain to let him hunt sea otter on the shores of the California coast—technically poaching, because the coast was closed by the Spanish who, however, did not patrol it well. The project worked excellently: O'Cain got his skins and the Russian company also made a handsome profit. O'Cain went off with the company's furs to sell them in Canton, while Baranov in 1804, with four ships and 300 skin boats, set out for Sitka. Fortunately for Baranov, a Russian frigate, the *Neva,* with Rezanov on board bound for Japan, turned up at this point. Rezanov had heard of the Sitka affair in Hawaii.

The *Neva* somewhat intimidated the Tlingit, who agreed to a parley. Baranov demanded permission to build a fort and ordered the natives to evacuate the island. The Tlingit refused. The conflict of interests was simple. The natives did not believe the Russians had the right to exploit the country in which the Indians lived for nothing. They were, after all, as property-conscious as the invaders. They also had no wish to be dominated by the foreigners. The Russians, of course, subscribed to the European tradition that any land explored by a so-called civilized man belonged to him if he saw it first. This difference in point of view is only just being resolved to the satisfaction of the Northwest Indians.

By this time the Tlingit had built their own stockade. Baranov sent a landing party to attack it. The natives made a sortie from the fort in which they killed 14 Russians and wounded two. Finally, after more negotiations which failed, the Tlingit evacuated the fort after it had been pounded by the *Neva*'s guns and the defenders had run out of ammunition. Before the Russians burned the stockade, they ascertained that it was a square fortification containing 14 houses and two cannon. The island now bears Baranov's name.

The Russians founded a port in 1804, naming it New Archangel. Despite his successes with the Aleut, Baranov never seems to have learned the Tlingit language, nor to have penetrated the culture of these natives. In 1804 when they attacked and took Yakutat, except for ten men, the garrison was either wiped out or enslaved. The fort at Prince William Sound was also under attack, but this time the Aleut defenders won. Even the outpost at Cook's Inlet called for reinforcements. At New Archangel no one went out without a gun.

In 1807 Baranov, ill with arthritis and weary, again wanted to retire but stayed on because Rezanov had just died. Then in 1809 a group of new arrivals, who decided Baranov was a tyrant, plotted to overthrow him, seize a ship and all the women of the community, with the intent to found a republic on Easter Island. The conspiracy was easily crushed, but so was Baranov. He made his will, sent his family to Kodiak Island, and stayed drunk all winter.

An expedition he sent south was shipwrecked, the survivors ending up captives of the Nootka. They were finally ransomed by a Boston trader who took them back to Archangel. Seven of the crew had died. Thus ended the last Russian attempt to gain a foothold on the coast south of Alaska.

Behind Baranov's back the company voted to dismiss their indefatigable servant who had so often begged to be replaced. After Baranov was lied to and in general shabbily treated, he was replaced by a young naval officer who had just married his daughter. Baranov died on the way home to Russia in 1818.

His replacement was eased out after two years. At this time the company got a new charter and appointed Captain Matvei Muraviev as governor of Russian America. He instituted a social regime with music, charades, whist, and balls—but no foreigners were entertained. Alexander I, no longer a liberal, had instituted a new version of xenophobia: no trading, no socializing, and Russian waters were to be closed to strangers. The governor initiated a new policy with the Tlingit, allowing them to camp near New Archangel. Nevertheless, he strengthened his defenses and it continued to be true that Russians did not dare to go 50 feet from their fortifications unarmed.

When Alexander died in 1825 he was succeeded by another reactionary, Czar Nicholas, his brother. A group of younger aristocrats and intellectuals had been plotting a revolution against Alexander's despotism. When they continued to plot against Nicholas, he shot down the leaders of a demonstration and put the rest in jail. The head of this Decembrist conspiracy was employed by the Russian–American company, and a number of other members of the organization were sympathetic. The ensuing investigations nearly wrecked the organization. It was given a shot in the arm by the appointment of Baron Ferdinand von Wrangell, who had been an explorer and a scientist. He terminated the clause allowing American whalers and traders access to the shoreline waters, chiefly to put an end to the rum trade. Wrangell instituted better social services, and by this time a few of the natives had been converted to the Russian Orthodox Church. The Tlingit were beginning to dress up in discarded military or naval uniforms, a stage which always took place in European preliterate relations. There was little trading in furs from the fort. The maritime traders had placed nets around their decks as they did in the British Columbia area; these allowed only one man to come on board at a time. The cannons were kept loaded and the crew lined up armed. The chiefs were then taken aboard and shown these preparations. They were told that no Indian would be allowed more than 10 steps from the rail—and if this rule was breached the offender would be shot. Such an event would not be considered a breach of the peace.

Wrangell went on the board of directors of the fur company by 1836, and it was he who negotiated the final deal with Sir George Simpson of Hudson's Bay, leasing the southern portion of the colony to the British. The British were competing in the fur trade in the neighborhood of the Stikine River, an area on which the Russian had only a tenuous hold. Wrangell made the best of a difficult situation. The British, however, were also making the best of a difficult situation. In 1834 McLoughlin sent an expedition under Duncan Finlayson to the mouth of the Stikine River with instructions to travel some distance up it and build a fort. They were stopped by the Russians at the mouth and told they could not proceed. The Russians agreed to communicate with Wrangell, who was still at New Archangel. The answer was no. The British cited international agreements to no avail; the Russians threatened to stop them by force. Added to this was an announcement by a group of Tlingit chiefs who told the British they could build on the sound but they could not ascend the river, since the Tlingit intended to continue to be the middlemen between the Europeans and the interior tribes.

The British desisted, McLoughlin feeling that it was wise to cooperate with the Russians in order to combat American penetration. Nevertheless, when James Douglas was sent up to New Archangel in 1839 to settle the details of the lease, he had secret instructions that, if the deal did not come off, he was to use force to open the Stikine River. Douglas, however, was diplomatic, never showing the iron fist. All went well, but by 1841 the situation on the Stikine River was so tense that the Russians were glad to turn their fort over to the British, for they feared they could not hold it. And indeed, when the Hudson's Bay agents became involved in the fatal quarrel in which John McLoughlin, Jr., was killed, the Tlingit were about to attack and were only checked by the arrival of Sir George Simpson on the Russian gunboat. Simpson subscribed to McLoughlin's thesis of combining with the Russians against the Americans. He even came and paid a courtesy visit to New Archangel.

Something was done, however, during Wrangell's administration in the way of Russianizing the Tlingit because of the arrival of a cultivated man of genius. Ivan Veniaminov (born Ivan Popov) was a handsome, 6 foot 3 inch giant, the son of a sacristan, who went to Unalaska in 1821 as a missionary. He was a skillful artisan, able to do anything from carpentry to clock making. He was also interested in and well read in the science of the period. When he came to Unalaska at the age of twenty-seven with his mother, wife, and son, he found no living quarters, no school, nothing but a tumbledown chapel not worth repairing. Veniaminov plunged into what grew into an anthropological study of the Aleut language and customs. A tireless worker, he made friends with the natives and easily persuaded them to build a church, a parish house, and a school. In ten years of preaching, teaching, composing a dictionary and grammar of the Aleut language, organizing, making general scientific observations, he accomplished wonders. In 1834 Wrangell persuaded him to move to New Archangel to work with the Tlingit, on whom Russian culture had made little impression; understandably, from the modern point of view, the Tlingit valued their own. They were not proof against the personality of the untiring, sympathetic priest. The Hudson's Bay Company chief, Sir George Simpson, testified that at first Veniaminov's gigantic figure inspired awe, but then "the gentleness which characterizes his every word and deed insensibly moulds reverence to love."

The industrious missionary soon learned the Tlingit language and plunged into a study of their culture, the first Russian who had showed any interest in it. Their conversion did not follow automatically. The first great epidemic of smallpox which struck in 1836 brought out the best in the dedicated priest and the local doctor. Despite their efforts to bring serum to the natives, between a quarter and a half of the Indian population died. Since it was evident that those who took the white man's serum survived, some of the Tlingit faith in their shamans was weakened.

Still no great number of conversions followed. Veniaminov, however, was an honorable exception to the bigoted missionary type to whom everything Indian was bad. He exhibited a broad-minded tolerance, respecting and continuing his interest in those who remained pagan. The officials complained that the *promishchlenniki* bankrupted themselves to buy finery for their Tlingit mistresses. Veniaminov wrote tolerantly of the same women: "In their housekeeping they are efficient and industrious, and very much concerned with the welfare of their men." He even, on a visit to Fort Ross, took the trouble to push on to the Roman Catholic mission of San José, where he conversed with the Spanish priests in Latin, attended their services, and, when he went home, sent them some barrel organs he had made with his own hands.

In 1836 New Archangel had a new governor, Captain Adolf Etolin, who had known Baranov. Illegitimate himself, half Finnish and half Russian, he was a self-made man. He continued the era of good relations with the Indians and other natives and cooperated well with Veniaminov.

At the prompting of Baron Wrangell, who became the power on the board, the Holy Synod had decided to set up a bishopric in Russian America. Czar Nicholas had to approve the election of Veniaminov as bishop. One interview was enough; even the reactionary Nicholas was captivated. Veniaminov, however, had to join the black or celibate order of the church.

Since his wife had died in 1839, the choice was made easier, but the giving up of his children was a wrench. Nevertheless he obeyed orders and took over the new diocese, which included the coast of Siberia.

In 1841 Nicholas extended the company's franchise for another 20 years. Several provisions in this document were evidently inspired by Veniaminov. Natives who did not profess the Christian rites "shall be permitted to carry on their devotions according to their own rites." In converting, missionaries should use conciliatory and persuasive measures, "in no case resorting to coercion." Also, Christian natives who transgressed ecclesiastic regulations were not to be punished but simply instructed.

The same year saw the colony's first locally built steamboat, a sternwheeler, the *Beaver.* The Tlingit and Aleut were gradually replacing the *promishchlenniki,* and there was a growing number of half-breeds, who were mostly Russianized. With this new labor force the shipyard was manned and a 40-bed hospital, a playground for children, and a clubhouse for the company personnel were being built.

Etolin continued to do well with the pagan Tlingit. He had pressured the Hudson's Bay Company, with whom there was peaceful cooperation, thanks to the Stikine area lease, to go along with his complete ban of liquor even for whites on the frontier. This achieved, he instituted an annual fair at New Archangel where the natives came to feast, sing and dance, and sell their goods.

Veniaminov planned a cathedral and set up a new school. By ship, skin boat, or dog team, he visited every part of his huge diocese. He had translated some of the church service into Tlingit and wherever he went he noted the local dialect with the intention of supplying school texts and vernacular liturgies.

In the 1850s, despite the presence of the bishop, who remained until 1854 when he left for Siberia, relations with the Tlingit declined under the governorship of a man named Rosenberg. He maintained so little control over the area that he allowed the Sitkans to ambush and murder a large group of Stikine Tlingit. His successor was even more powerless, and once more, in 1854, the Tlingit moved against New Archangel. After considerable fighting with losses on both sides (the Tlingit lost 60) peace was negotiated with a new exchange of hostages.

By the time a competent governor, Dimitrii Petrovich Maksutov, was appointed in 1864, there were rumors of the sale of the colony, but no one took them seriously.

It happened, however, that the secretary of the Russian legation in Washington, Eduard de Stoeckl, was a careerist. Impressed by the manifest destiny oratory, he was convinced that the United States would take Alaska by infiltration and dedicated himself to the project of selling it. Stoeckl had a pipeline to President Buchanan through Senator William Gwin of California. In 1860 an offer of five million dollars was made and refused.

Meanwhile, the new charter of the fur company was being hotly debated by its friends and foes. Apparently the Civil War had so unsettled matters that Alaska was off the market, and Grand Duke Constantine, now President of the Imperial Council, had promised the company a new charter.

When Stoeckl was withdrawn and returned to St. Petersburg, he continued to talk about the possible sale. Suddenly a meeting was called with the Czar and various notables who were for and against the idea. In the end the Czar sent Stoeckl back to Washington to negotiate a deal. Senator Gwin was no longer in office, but William Seward, Secretary of State, was strongly in favor. When Seward and Stoeckl wrote a bill, various senators expressed opposition. Then Senator Charles Sumner made a long speech in favor, and the bill passed by a two-thirds majority. The problem of getting a bill authorizing the payment of $7,200,000 through Congress, however, nearly drove Stoeckl to distraction. After a violent fight the bill was passed in 1868. Seward told President Johnson, in confidence, that bribery had been used. No one was happy about the result. The fur company officials who lost money were furious. The Russian press supported them and spread the impression that the affair was shameful. The U.S. press and general public censured Seward, calling the Alaskan continent "Seward's ice-box." The area was generally considered unfit for human habitation. Stoeckl himself returned to St. Petersburg, where he was refused another post and pensioned off. Alaska had been handed over by a nation which did not particularly want to sell to a nation that did not particularly want to buy. The aborigines were scarcely mentioned.

On October 18, 1867, the town of New Archangel was officially transferred. Since the Tlingit were not allowed in the town, they had a view of the proceedings from their canoes in the harbor. They watched the lowering and raising of the flags, listened to the thunder of the cannon, and then quietly withdrew.

If the Russian achievement had been uneven and their history in America often stained with blood, the early American regime was on the whole a period of disgrace. The American commander who took over, named Jefferson C. Davis, was—aside from the first mayor of the city, William S. Dodge—the only representative of government. Instead of territorial status all Alaska got was more soldiers, all under the command of Davis.

The mayor went about trying to protect the inhabitants from the American soldiers who drank, raped, and looted, even pillaging the cathedral.

Syphilis and drunkenness were their gift to the Tlingit, who were now introduced to *hoochino.* Davis himself got one of their chiefs drunk, dressed him up in a cast-off uniform, then had a guard send him on his way with a kick. Four people were eventually shot; then Davis "restored peace" by firing on the Tlingit village.

The Russian inhabitants, who had been promised peace and prosperity, left in large numbers. What little civilized activity took place was carried on by the newly formed Alaskan Commercial Company, which took over the facilities of its Russian predecessor, and the Russian Orthodox missionary society. The new fur company did pay for schooling and provide medical services for its native employees. The Russian missionary society was spending more money for schools for the natives than the United States did on education for the entire territory 20 years after it had become a U.S. possession.

THE ATTACK ON THE INDIAN WAY OF LIFE

9

Northwest Coast Indian history in the second half of the nineteenth century is the story of the intervention of missionaries and Indian agents in the lives of the people and of the efforts of the Indians to preserve their heritage and identity. To run ahead a little, when Governor Douglas retired in 1862 his fairly benevolent regime gave way to the pressures of colonists who saw in Indians nothing but obstacles to the exploitation of the land. Already, as Commander R. C. Mayne had pointed out in his 1861 volume, the germs of hostility were present. Of the Vancouver area Mayne wrote:

> This valley is the most extensive yet discovered on the island, and it is reported by the colonial officers who surveyed it to contain 30,000 to 40,000 acres of good land. It is peopled by the Cowichin [Coast Salish] tribe of Indians who are considered a badly disposed set, and have shown no favor to those settlers who have visited their valley. Although it has been surveyed, it cannot yet be settled, as the Indians are unwilling to sell, still less to be ousted from their land.

He also mentioned an incident in which a party went to prospect on Queen Charlotte's Island. Near Skidegate a group of Indians wanted to attack them, convinced they were about to rob them of their land. The whites were protected by one of the chiefs, although several shots were fired after them. However, "the fear of loaded cannons pointed at the village" near what is now Port Alberni made the Indians in that region more amenable.

The man who controlled Indian policy after Douglas's retirement in 1864 was Joseph Trutch, chief commissioner of lands and works. His point of view dramatized an attitude which is only officially changing today:

> The Indians have really no right to the lands they claim, nor are they of any actual value or utility to them, and I cannot see why they should either retain these lands to the prejudice of the general interests of

the colony, or be allowed to make a market of them either to the government or individuals.

Thus, on the one hand there was a drive to obtain the land claimed by the Indians, while on the other the attack on the Indian way of life was initiated in British Columbia—with supposedly the best of intentions, by a remarkable lay preacher by the name of William Duncan. Born in Beverly, Yorkshire, in 1832, by 1853 Duncan had decided he wished to become a missionary. It so happened that a certain Captain Prevost operated a steamer which plied between Victoria and Fort Simpson. Prevost, who was of a religious turn of mind, was well aware that the Hudson's Bay Company was doing nothing constructive for the Tsimshian Indians, but rather, by selling them liquor, was hastening their demoralization. He felt the answer was to convert them to Protestantism and sought for a missionary. The young Duncan was ready and willing. He arrived at Victoria in 1856 and had an interview with Sir James Douglas, the governor. The latter's first reaction was straight Hudson's Bay Company. Before bringing in a missionary the company should have been consulted because company officials knew all about the condition of the Indians. Sir James proceeded to demonstrate that he himself knew very little, for he went on to tell Duncan that he would speedily be killed by the "savage and bloodthirsty natives."

Duncan, however, was undaunted and won the governor over. The latter finally said, "Well, young man, if you are to be killed and eaten, I suppose you are the one most vitally interested." Transportation, however, was not immediately available, which meant that the eager missionary had to wait three months in Victoria, where he at least found a Tsimshian with whom he could begin the study of the language.

On his voyage north, he saw on the beach the bodies of some Haida Indians who had been killed in a night raid because they had broken some rule of etiquette important to the local natives.

In October 1857 he had his first view of Fort Simpson, built of palisades 32 feet high, with huge iron-bound gates, which were kept bolted while a smaller door within them was protected by a sentinel. The situation is the same as that described by Finlayson 10 years earlier: only two Indians were allowed in the fort at the same time. There were bastions at the four corners upon which cannons were mounted. Goods for barter and the bartered furs were kept within the 32-foot walls, protected by a garrison of soldiers. The Tsimshian, who had formerly resided 17 miles up the Skeena River (their name meant "on the Skeena"), had moved into settlements alongside the fort. There were 2300 living in 140 houses. Other tribes lived 45 miles to the north on the Nass River. The most important chief at Fort Simpson—whose authority was largely based on the fact that he had given away the greatest amount of property—was Legaic. But Legaic was also notable in that he had achieved some cohesion among the tribes that lived near Fort Simpson, bordering on a loose confederacy. He was therefore a man of some distinction, although Duncan only saw him as an obstacle to his aims.

A brutal episode took place almost immediately. Legaic, because he felt his rank had been slighted, shot a visiting Haida. The man was finished off by the chief's slaves. No one in the fort took any notice—in fact none of the garrison even knew the Tsimshian language; they made out with "Chinook," a pidgin trader's dialect. Chinook had by 1840 about 250 words; 18 of these were Nootka, 41 English, 34 French, 111 Chinook, the speech of a tribe of the Columbia River.

Duncan got hold of an intelligent Indian who knew no English and the two taught each other. Interestingly enough, the Tsimshian had passed down the story of the first visit of the white men, in all probability Cook's party.

Four halibut fishermen suddenly saw a great monster coming up from the sea through the mist. The Indians paddled to shore:

> When they came near the shore, the fog lifted and then they saw a big round monster swimming in the sea. Trees were growing out of its back and the heads of men were hung on the branches of the trees [the blocks]. Then a baby monster came out of the belly of the sea monster and there were heads of many white ghosts sticking up from the back of it and they had long sticks and they pushed the water back with them. The baby monster fled toward the shore. When it came to the beach the white ghosts lifted up the sticks and the tears of salt water crawled down the sticks and fell in the water with a great drip-drip. Then the white ghosts went on shore. When the Indians saw them they were afraid but the white ghosts pointed to the halibut and the Indians gave them one and they cut it up and threw the pieces in a round black box. Then they wanted fire and the Indians brought sticks to make a fire and commenced to rub them together. But the white ghosts laughed and one of them took a little dry grass and something from his pocket and made a big noise and a flash and fire came right away in the wood. When the Indians saw that they "died"

[were amazed]. . . . After that the white ghosts emptied a sack of maggots in the box. After a while they took the maggots out and put them in a dish and they poured over the maggots "grease of dead men" [molasses]. Then they wanted the Indians to eat the maggots but this the Indians would not do. Then the Indians ran away behind the rocks and the white ghosts eat the maggots and the grease themselves. . . . But the chief and his slaves came down to the beach. And the chief was painted black and red. And he stood up right before the white ghosts and he looks wild at them. And the blood of many men makes his eyes very red. And when the white ghosts see his red eyes, then the white ghosts "die." And when the chief dances and sings the war song, hard and high, then the white ghosts "die" again.

The Tsimshian were sharp traders in that they insisted on being the middlemen between the whites and the tribes of the interior. Duncan said the women had the deciding voice in making a deal. He felt the Hudson's Bay Company got exorbitant profits. A blanket worth $2.50 or a piece of soap as thick as a man's finger cost four marten or 50 mink skins. Sea otter skins worth $700 brought $2 to $4 in company goods.

The staples of Indian food were salmon, halibut, clams, crabs, and cuttlefish cooked in olachen oil. In March the natives traveled 45 miles up the Nass River to catch olachen, which were so filled with oil that they melted in a pan like butter. The oil of one of these, after boiling the fish, was pressed out against the bare breasts of the women—any other method would "shame" the fish. "You are all chiefs," the Indians cried as they netted them. The Indians already had sails on their canoes. When they caught salmon, these fish had to boiled in wooden kettles—again, any other utensil would shame them.

At puberty the girls were segregated for three months and the slit was cut in the lower lip for the labret. The higher the rank, the larger the labret; slaves were denied it entirely.

The Tsimshian cremated their dead and placed the ashes in a box behind the deceased's totem pole, if he rated one. The nine tribes at Fort Simpson were all made up of the same four clans, a more important division than the tribal one. Lineage was seldom illustrated by totem poles, but totem animals were painted on the front wall of the houses. The Tsimshian had three dance societies: the cannibals, the dog eaters, and the singers and dancers.

Duncan maintained that members of a tribe contributed goods to a chief so that he could dominate his rivals at the potlatch. The day before one of these was given, the goods were exhibited. By now such trade goods as calico were given and yards of this material fluttered in the breeze as blankets and skins were carried along the beach. Duncan was highly critical of the traders, whom he accused of bringing drunkenness and prostitution to the Indians.

After eight months of study, Duncan preached his first sermon in Tsimshian, going from house to house to the important chiefs and repeating it. He then persuaded the Indians to build a schoolhouse which housed 140 children and 50 adults.

When Legaic's daughter was away during her puberty segregation, Legaic wanted school recessed. The chief threatened to kill the missionary, who was protected by his interpreter. The school was kept open—and finally even Legaic came.

Duncan was still not ordained, but by 1861 he had considerable influence over a number of Indians. Somehow by means of preaching he made them forsake their cultural heritage. By now they knew they were a minority among the growing number of whites in whom political and military power resided. Up to now no one had taken a sympathetic interest in them; the fur traders had merely exploited them. Duncan, if narrow-minded, was a man of goodwill. At this time he decided that the good Indians must be removed from the wild ones and from the low ethical standards manifested by the Hudson's Bay people at the fort. On May 27, 1861, he moved with about 350 followers to the sight of old Metlakatla. All had to subscribe to his rules—no medicine men, no potlatch giving, no painting of faces, no drinking, no working on Sunday. All must become Christians and all the children must go to school. The Indians must be clean, peaceful, honest in trade, build neat houses, and pay a village tax.

It was a complete statement of the attitude which was to prevail in official quarters from then on. Everything Indian was bad; the only approved values were those of the white Protestant culture. There were to be no chiefs. Wrote his biographer: "The government of the village was and of course had to be in the hands of Mr. Duncan. He could brook no chiefs beside him, certainly no one above him."

Later, when he was to have dissidents, they were mostly demoted chiefs. Duncan, with his benevolent dictatorship, reminds us somewhat of Father Rapp and his Indiana religious colony, though on the whole Duncan was much less of a fanatic than the German leader. Duncan did appoint 12 natives constables to keep order, the number later expanded to 30. He finally also set up a village council. Shortly after the move, smallpox was brought to Fort Simpson, where one third of the Indians died. Metlakatla fortunately only lost five members.

Legaic came to the new colony but continually returned to Fort Simpson to preside at potlatches and take part in the old customs. Duncan finally told him he must choose one side or the other and since he could not make up his mind he had better leave. Legaic left and was back in three days, wanting to be baptized. He also wanted to be a constable because he liked the idea of a badge. When he found that it involved work, he gave up the office.

Duncan encouraged the Indians to plant garden plots and started a soap factory. He felt that Fort Simpson and the trading schooners were nothing but grog shops and in consequence he wanted the Hudson's Bay Company and other suppliers to set up shops in the village on his terms. The fur company attempted to organize a boycott unsuccessfully. Duncan decided that Metlakatla should have its own schooner. He put up some of the capital himself and raised the rest with $5 shares bought by the Indians. This enterprise was a success, as the Indians got good prices for their furs in Victoria. After the first year the Indian stockholders got a $5 dividend on their shares. Hudson's Bay Company finally gave in and agreed to ship the furs in their own schooners. Duncan also set up a forge, a carpentry shop, a sawmill, and a brick kiln. Presumably these were cooperative enterprises.

The council was finally organized on the basis of male suffrage (it would never have occurred to Duncan to let women vote). The council was an advisory body, with Duncan as the final authority. This authority was often self-assumed.

When a Russian trader arrived in a schooner carrying liquor, Duncan threatened to incite his Indians to beach the schooner and burn it. The trader complained to Governor Douglas, but the latter, by now Duncan's supporter, merely sent the missionary a commission of justice of the peace. Duncan's judiciary methods were also of the do-it-yourself variety. Wife beaters were kept in jail until their wives requested that they be let out. For other crimes he instituted flogging.

Duncan's high-handed methods earned him the hostility of many of his contemporaries. Aside from the fact that he used the lash freely in his sentences he went out of his way to be provocative when it came to infractions of the law against selling liquor. In 1870 he sent an Indian constable to Fort Simpson with a beaver skin, with which he offered to buy a bottle of liquor. Apparently the director of the trading post, Hans Brenzten, sold him a bottle of rum. Duncan immediately got out a warrant for the arrest of the overseer of the fort, Robert Cunningham, and had him brought into court. The fact that Cunningham had not sold the liquor made little impression on Duncan, who merely arrested Brenzten as well. Eventually Metlakatla's dictator fined Cunningham $500 and Brenzten $100.

In 1870 the missionary visited England. He persuaded a wealthy manufacturer, who had bought instruments for a brass band only to have them rejected by his workers, to donate the horns and trumpets to Metlakatla. The obedient Indians were soon taught to use them. Somehow the spectacle of the magnificent choral traditions of the Indians—which had impressed all the traders, as the natives sang and paddled about their ships—being replaced by the dismal strains of Protestant hymns played out of tune on brasses is one of the most painful aspects of the conversion of the Tsimshian.

There is no doubt, however, that Duncan was a staunch defender of the Indians when it came to the land question. Although Governor Seymor, who succeeded Douglas, gave away 100 canes with silver tops on the Queen's birthday to leading Indians and assured them their reserves would remain undisturbed, in actuality he gave Trutch a free hand. After repeated complaints, Indians of the lower Frazer Valley sent him a petition, probably written with missionary help:

> Some days ago came a new man who told us that by order of the Chief they have to curtail our small reservation, and so did to our greater grief; not only they shortened our land but by their new paper they set aside our best land, some of our gardens, and gave us in place some hilly and some sandy land, where it is next to impossible to grow potatoes. . . .

The missionaries taught the Indians to use petitions, but over the years they were to learn that petitions to government officials, without political power, go in one ear and out the other. More effective was a Cowichan chief who told a government official that Governor Seymor could not take the land from him and that if the governor sent his gunboats he would fetch his friends from all parts and hold the land against him. He added that the governor was a liar and had not paid for land that had been already taken. This bold confrontation worked, for the governor met with the chiefs, interviewed the surveyor who had reduced the reserve, and ordered the land returned.

The Indians, however, were on the whole peaceable and, in any case there was a long history of the gunboats pointing their artillery at the villages.

In 1871 the colony of British Columbia became a province of Canada. Joseph Trutch became lieutenant governor and requested the Prime Minister to let him continue to direct the Indian Administration. He was still singing the same song:

> We have never bought out any Indian claims or lands, nor do they expect we should. . . . If you now commence to buy out title to the lands of B.C. you would go back on all that has been done here for 30 years past and would be equitably bound to compensate the tribes who inhabited the districts now settled and farmed by white people equally with those in remote and uncultivated portions.

In 1874 a number of chiefs were petitioning against the curtailment of their tribal land.

In 1875 Duncan himself, who now had a following of from 900 to 1000 Tsimshian, went to Ottawa to protest legislation which was meant to restrict each Indian family to 10 acres. He succeeded in persuading the governor general, Lord Dufferin, to visit some Indian villages and make speeches, but Trutch simply adhered to the 10-acre policy in practice—even though Douglas, from retirement, wrote that he had never considered setting such a maximum. Over this issue the federal and provincial government disputed for some years, the federal government being inclined to allow a more generous allotment.

For Duncan, however, the land was a minor issue; the important goal was de-Indianizing the natives. All this time Duncan had refused to be ordained, despite pressure from the Mission Society. Actually, he could not bear any interference in his benevolent dictatorship and had been avoiding the jurisdiction of the Episcopal Church all along. At one point he was ready to hand over his village to the Reverend A. J. Hall. He had already left when he heard that Hall was countenancing an emotional style of preaching which resulted in revivalism, the Indians beginning to have visions of angels and devils. Duncan rushed back and took over once more, and Hall was transferred.

In the eighties a struggle began between Duncan and the ecclesiastical authorities. When the diocese was split into three parts, Bishop William Ridley, who had been stationed in India, took over the area which had Metlakatla as its seat. Ridley seems to have been overemotional, high-handed, and high church. Duncan hated everything that smacked of high church ritual. He was, moreover, somewhat of an individualist in his interpretation of how the Christian services should be conducted. He did not give the Indians communion because he believed they had been cannibals and he thought this ceremony might revive their old enthusiasm for human flesh. (Apparently he never saw the irony in this.) In addition, he did not approve of wine being used in the church service for fear it would weaken his ban against liquor. And, finally, he did not believe in baptizing his converts without a long probationary period; Ridley was ready to baptize wholesale. These matters were all irritants, but the long and the short of it was that the two men were struggling for supreme power in the little community. For several years Duncan had had an ordained assistant, the Reverend R. Tomlinson, who was working in the Nass River area. Ridley wished to transfer him elsewhere. He also transferred Hall from Fort Rupert to Alert Bay. Duncan wrote to the Mission Society and had these changes overruled. Ridley initiated a conference of the other missionaries who had come into the area; the bishop did not attend, but he provoked a vote as to whether Duncan should go or stay. The vote, including that of William Collison (of whom we shall hear more later), who was pro-bishop, went in Duncan's favor, including the provision that the village be left in his hands without clerical supervision. The bishop wrote to the Mission Society to complain, and that body, on September 1881, requested that Duncan should come to London for a conference. Since Duncan was at the point of setting up a salmon canning factory, he wrote that he would have to come later. Ridley, however, had exacted a letter from the Mission Society saying that if Duncan refused to come to England he was to hand the village over to the bishop. Ridley handed this to Duncan, remarking that now they would see who was in charge. Duncan did not remain to fight, however, but deputized Collison and returned to England. Meanwhile, the Indians passed a unanimous resolution in their council demanding that Shinaugel ("the chief"—Duncan) remain as their leader. The Mission Society then wrote another letter relieving Duncan of the necessity of going to England; Ridley was told to get him and the mission back into the fold.

Then followed a period of disturbances. The bishop got up an opposition party led by some demoted chiefs. There was an argument over the ownership of a drum; scuffles took place. The bishop, claiming there had been a riot, called for a warship.

The provincial government of British Columbia denied that

the Indians had any right to the land on which the village stood. The bishop sided with the government and announced that the land on which the mission buildings stood belonged to the Mission Society. Duncan and a delegation went to Sir John MacDonald, the governor of the province. The latter agreed to make Duncan superintendent of the Indians for a year and persuade the Mission Society to withdraw its claims. Later, after talking with representatives of the Mission Society, the governor reversed himself and called Duncan an "intolerable dictator." Government surveyors came to check on the land. The Indians sabotaged their work by pulling up their stakes. Finally a warship arrived and the leading Indians were given three to six months in jail in Victoria.

The situation had reached a point where the Indians either would have to fight for their land or go elsewhere. The Canadian government, which had never worked out a sensible policy toward its Indians, claimed they had no rights. Duncan decided to move. He succeeded in getting the support of such public figures in the United States as Henry Ward Beecher. He was also received by President Grover Cleveland. Cleveland said the United States would welcome the colony and promised land. On March 30, 1891, the U.S. Congress passed a special bill granting land in Annette Island of Southern Alaska as a reservation under the supervision of the Secretary of the Interior.

Out of 948 residents of Old Metlakatla, 323 followed Duncan to Port Chester on Annette Island. By 1908, in spite of a government-endowed school, Old Metlakatla faded away in importance.

The Alaskan village, however, prospered, although in 1908 the death rate was alarmingly high. Duncan's biographer admits cautiously that white man's food and lifestyle seemed to have had an unfortunate effect.

In New Metlakatla everything was communally owned, except for the houses and the land on which they stood, which could only change hands with community approval. Duncan designed identical five-room houses which, when placed in rows, rivaled modern Levittowns in their conformity. The Metlakatla leader, however, was destined never to escape from ecclesiastical encroachments. The Presbyterians of Alaska educated young students, who were used to infiltrate Duncan's village. While the old man was away on a visit to England they managed to get a majority of signatures to a petition urging the U.S. government to take over Annette Island. Duncan fought the move unsuccessfully, for New Metlakatla was made an Indian reserve under the supervision of the United States Department of Education. The government also built a cannery with the understanding that the Indians would be allowed to buy it, which they did.

Duncan had thoughtfully arranged that the inhabitants of the village should get a percentage on every salmon caught near Annette Island. With this the Indians were able to buy the cannery. Eventually the competing churches made peace. Duncan was a power until his death in 1918.

By 1958 the village had its own church and its own power plant. The young people had so far lost their old culture that they could not speak the Tsimshian language fluently.

Duncan differed from the other missionaries of his era in that he was not content to merely destroy the old culture and to leave the Indians at sea in that of the white man. His communal projects and his encouragement of industries to make the natives self-supporting, and above all his organizing ability, were a more important contribution than his religious proselytizing.

PIONEER PREACHERS AMONG THE HAIDA, TSIMSHIAN, AND SALISH

10

The Reverend William Collison, who was sent to British Columbia by the Mission Society in 1873 along with his wife, was a medical missionary. At Metlakatla he was received by Duncan and remarked that the latter's Indians were "a pleasing contrast to the tribes we had seen in their paint and blankets along the route." Collison never wavered from the platform that everything Indian was bad and the only values were those of white Protestantism. He began working among the Tsimshian, but in 1874 a Haida fleet of 40 canoes, each with two snow-white sails, visited the area. Apparently Collison's interest was awakened in this group of tribes. The canoes looked like "immense birds or butterflies with wings outspread." Collison was to know them intimately, for he risked his life many times in storms on journeys to the north.

He became friendly with a Haida, married to a Tsimshian woman, who urged him to do something about the northern tribes. Accordingly in 1876 he got permission from the Mission Society to go on a canoe trip of 100 miles to the area north of Graham Island. The main crests of these Haida were the eagle, bear, wolf, and finback whale; the beaver and eagle; wolf and heron; bear and sun; rainbow and owl; frog and raven. From a distance the village looked like a port because of the forest of totem poles. Collison was entertained by a chief of the bear clan who sat in a seat made from a carved section of a tree while slaves prepared food. Many of the men and women who gathered around the fire had their faces painted red or black. At night Collison was disturbed by the odor of decay which emanated from the remains of the dead. These were placed in grease boxes or wrapped in cedar mats and left behind the house. Many of the wrappings had fallen apart, scattering the bones.

The center of the house was a pit dug about 12 feet into the earth, while halfway down was a ledge on which the residents sat.

After Collison had preached at the chief, the latter answered him saying that his people had been twice decimated by smallpox and were now suffering from the introduction of alcohol. He did not think the white men's ways were particularly good. Although Collison had the grace to be ashamed of the Canadians, he continued to talk about Jesus.

A chief answered him stoutly:

> Yes, you can lead our children in the new way but we do not desire to abandon the customs of our fathers. We cannot give up the old customs. The spirit of our medicine men is strong, stronger than the words of the great chief above, so you will have no power to change them. It would not be good for you to try.

The meeting ended with a heated discussion, while the medicine men glared at Collison.

Despite his prejudice against Indian culture, Collison was obviously moved by the ceremonies which took place during a state visit of members of a neighboring tribe.

The strangers arrived chanting their brave deeds. They were answered by chanting from the shore. The musicians moved their heads and bodies in time to the beat of a drum made of a cedar box, painted and covered with skin. A naked slave then cast the large pieces of copper, with designs on them, which now served more or less as bills of large denomination in Indian economy, into the water to honor the guests and show the riches of the hosts. The visiting chief was then led to his host's house by a group of dancers. The host wore a headdress of sea lions' bristles. His head was covered with white bird's down. He bowed before his visitors and showered them with this down, which was a gesture of peace. The visitor's name was Edenshaw, of whom it was said that he had captured and enslaved the crew of the American schooner *Susan Sturges.* The ship was pillaged and burned, but the crew was finally ransomed with blankets by the Hudson's Bay Company. It is interesting to note that Charles Edenshaw was one of the most notable modern Haida carvers.

Collison continued to proselytize but found that one reason why the chiefs did not wish to embrace Christianity was their disinclination to give up their slaves. The missionary felt that Masset, on Graham's Island, was a strategic spot for a mission because from it both Queen Charlotte's Island and Alaska were easily reached. The return canoe trip almost resulted in a catastrophe for a squall nearly capsized the vessel.

The missionary finally persuaded a schooner to transport him and his wife and children to Graham's Island. The skipper told him he would be murdered, for the captain himself had more than once put up his boarding nets to keep off attacks of Indians.

Collison set up housekeeping in a little 10 by 12 storehouse, which was always filled with curious Indians. Visitors who came to view the missionary arrived in canoes dancing, singing, and wearing masks representing their crests.

Then there were feasts in which small canoes filled with berries mixed with grease and snow were offered. The wooden trenches were carved and inlaid with mother-of-pearl. Dried salmon and halibut were boiled in olachen grease. Boiled kelp with bitter berries were beaten to a froth with water and eaten with long narrow wooden spoons.

When a Haida gave a potlatch the first thing he did was to erect a totem pole on which was carved the legends of the ancestors of the chief. The rough work was done with an ax, the finer detail with an adze, then the sculpture was polished with dogfish skin.

Before a potlatch many Haida had themselves tatooed on the chest, arms, and back with their own crests. Collison says they sometimes sacrificed a slave, throwing the body into the hole in which the totem pole was erected. Collison attacked the potlatch on the grounds that it was wasteful and that "It tends to demoralize and degrade its followers."

The Haida were notable for the totem poles and their canoes, the latter being built up to 50 feet long and 6½ feet wide. Although these Indians were now adept at using sails, like all vessels without keels the canoes could easily be capsized, and on the stormy West Coast navigation was often dangerous. Canoes were originally made with stone hammers, chisels, and adzes, but in Collison's time iron was generally in use. There was always the danger of their being smashed in the heaving surf, for the great hollow log could split from the force of the water. The Haida had the advantage of the especially big cedars which grew on Queen Charlotte's Island, and the fame of their vessels was such that they sold them to other tribes.

About the time Collison moved to Graham's Island, miners had begun to arrive in the neighborhood of Fort Simpson and contact with them did not improve the condition of the Indians. Collison, however, thought that bits of old uniforms and patchwork European dress were preferable to skin cloaks or the wearing of blankets.

The Haida, like all coastal Indians, were ardent gamblers. For this activity they used 80 sticks kept in a pack. Each had a name, some were inlaid with abalone shells, and some were carved like miniature totem poles. Sometimes an Indian would gamble away all his goods and at times quarrels arose with fatal results.

Collison, being a doctor, was especially hostile to Indian practitioners, and it never occurred to him that their efforts might have psychological value. He tells a self-righteous story of saving a slave accused of making a chief sick by causing him to be possessed of an evil spirit.

Haida tombs were H-shaped, two solid posts with a hollow crosspiece in which the coffin of a chief was placed. Sometimes it was decorated with the effigy of the dead man's crest—a frog, for example.

As the Hudson's Bay traders were becoming more active, Collison asked the government for a justice of the peace. He himself had been more or less acting as one. Eventually some young chiefs were sworn in as constables. Collison had also succeeded in vaccinating many of his contacts against smallpox, which was once more a threat.

The Haida were warlike, chiefly raiding the Tsimshian on the lower Skeena River and also those on the Nass River. According to Collison, it was thanks to missionary influence that warfare began to die out.

Collison's taste in music was similar to Duncan's. After his years of activity, when strangers came to visit, instead of warrior's choruses and black-painted naked slaves rushing into the water to cast presents before the visitors, Collison assembled his young people to sing *How Beautiful upon the Mountain.*

On the whole, Collison, who became a bishop, did not possess Duncan's administrative initiative and insight into the importance of economic independence. One other missionary, Robert Tomplinson, who had been Duncan's assistant for a time, worked in the Kispiox area, where Bishop Ridley sent an opposition missionary to compete with him. He finally resigned from the Mission Society and went to work on the Skeena River. Imitating Duncan's methods, he set up a sawmill and, eventually, a brick factory.

As the Church of England's influence waned in the Fort Simpson area and that of the Frazer River, the Methodists moved into the gap. The Reverend Thomas Crosby, who had first worked among the Flatheads, moved in among the Tsimshian in 1873. He wrote that Duncan first thought the Methodists were encroaching on him, but time showed there was room for both, especially since their missions were 15 to 20 miles apart.

Crosby went to Fort Rupert on the Hudson's Bay Company steamer *Otter,* taking with him his new wife. The steamer did not stop at the fort but put them off in an Indian canoe, promising to drop off their baggage on the return trip from Fort Wrangell. Fortunately, an old Indian woman went ashore with them, steering while the missionaries paddled. They were waylaid by some Indians who persuaded them to stop on an island until an adequate welcome could be prepared. The fort was the same as it had been for over 20 years before, 18-foot stockades with cannon, which were always under lock and key, outside the gates.

Apparently the Indians had expected practical benefits from the Methodist Missionary Society, but Crosby soon undeceived them and set about extracting money from the poverty-stricken natives themselves. He seemed to think it a great achievement when he succeeded in collecting a last blanket or a single gold ring in order to build a church. Depending almost entirely on Indian resources, he built a mission house in the winter and the following summer a church. It seemed there was nothing left of Duncan's original installations. Later Crosby managed to accumulate some outside contributions to build a schoolhouse.

Crosby's proselytizing seems to have been more emotional and sentimental than that of Duncan. He speaks of a wave of revivalism which went through the community in which the Indians fell on their faces and cried to God for mercy. He admits, however, that many of these conversions did not take.

Like other missionaries, the Methodists set up their own government structure, in the absence of such activity on the part of the province. Crosby called together a council and drew up a series of blue laws against gambling, Sabbath breaking, whiskey drinking, and fighting. Likewise, dancing and heathen marriages were forbidden. A scale of fines was established, with Crosby a self-appointed justice of the peace. The Methodists set up schools and orphanages (especially to save girls from a "sinful life") and carried on medical and social services—as most frontier clergymen did, since there was no one else who took any interest in the natives.

Crosby does not show much interest or insight into Indian culture, aside from a few myths, collected by his daughter, and a few artifacts which he subsequently gave to a museum. His judgment on the imaginative life of the Tsimshian was that "it was not apparently a coherent system of beliefs on a high order either intellectually or morally."

Crosby describes his peacemaking. An old Tlingit chief came

to him and said that he had a grudge against a certain Haida which made it very difficult for him to keep the peace. Would the missionary arbitrate at a formal peace council? This Crosby was happy to do, especially as the Haida had the reputation of being extremely warlike and conducting slave raids all up and down the coast. The council went on for many nights and many speeches were made on both sides. Often these became inflammatory as the orators recalled old massacres and the death of kinsmen. In such cases Crosby had to jump in and calm the speakers down. He persisted, closing each meeting with hymns and prayers, and appealing to the Christian law of forgiveness. Finally, on June 16, 1878, both sides signed a treaty agreeing all claims were satisfied. When this was done, the chiefs embraced emotionally.

Crosby complained that, from the U.S. bases established in Alaska, the soldiers bootlegged liquor across the border to the British Columbia Indians; he attributed the name "Hoochino" to that of a village called "Hoot-son-o."

Apparently when Crosby scouted the settlement of Bella Bella, he was entertained by a Kwakiutl chief, who pointed to a great heap of blankets and said that if he could have a missionary at once he would donate them toward building a church —but, if the Methodists did not come at once, he would convert them into firearms and go to war with his neighbor. Crosby got him a missionary in short order.

Crosby's descriptions of Indian customs are not very detailed. Like most men of his type, he was highly antagonistic toward the shaman who went through the theatrical act of extracting the disease-causing object from the patient's body. "His deceptions are so well carried out that not one in fifty suspects that he and his friends have been duped."

By 1886 the Nass River converts had a brass band, an institution which every missionary seemed to cherish, for when we turn to the Catholic settlement among the Salish of the Gulf of Georgia we find that these Indians were also inducted into the joys of playing brass wind instruments.

The Oblate fathers first contacted the Salish in 1866 and were driven away because the Indians "knew what white men are." Two years later, however, the Sechelt tribe of the Salish came back in a repentant mood and asked the French priests to establish a mission. What this highly dedicated group achieved parallels the labors of Father Duncan on the one hand and is also somewhat reminiscent of the methods of the Jesuits in seventeenth-century Paraguay.

By 1871 the whole Sechelt tribe had been confirmed and a chapel had been built. Work was also being done among three other divisions of the Salish. The guiding spirit was Father B. Durieu, who later was made bishop. He set up a theocratic dictatorship—which, in effect, was an Indian state ruled over by the bishop, missionaries, and one or two resident priests acting through tribal appointees. The Frenchmen retained chiefs, subchiefs, captains, watchmen, and policemen whom they established in office. The Sechelt had four chiefs, each with his full quota of subordinates. The watchmen served as truant officers to insure attendance at religious services by both children and adults. They also reported small misdemeanors, for the Oblate rule was even more strict than that of Father Duncan. There was a catechist for boys and also one for girls. A community inventory of sins was read aloud before confession. The sexton doubled as bellringer. The native chiefs acted as justices of the peace, while the native watchmen carried out punishments. The final authority was, of course, Father Durieu.

In the religious sphere all the natives had to learn the catechism and also hymns and prayers. The priests continued to enforce such old taboos as early marriages, incest rules, and respect for elders.

On the secular side, the priests encouraged the building of churches and frame houses. The houses were to be kept painted, washed, and disinfected. The natives planted gardens and fruit trees. Eventually there were white churches all along this part of the coast and, later on, water and lighting plants. All old customs which competed with Catholic dogma and ritual had to be dropped, including dancing, potlatching, the activities of shamans, drinking, and gambling. *"La tempérance"* was the watchword of the community, with the greatly extended meaning that it excluded everything the priests disapproved of.

Since the local chiefs were somewhat vacillating and weak authoritarians (such activities were not in their traditional roles), the ecclesiastics imposed their own sanctions. A sort of semi-excommunication consisted of refusing to visit whole villages, sometimes for as long as 2 years. Real excommunication was also used. In addition, the secular arm imposed fines and sentences of hard labor, such as clearing rocks from fields. Adultery and failure to attend church warranted 40 lashes. In addition, adulterers were shamed in public gatherings. The sermons of the Oblate brothers were reminiscent of Cotton Mather. The natives were told firmly that disease was evidence of a judgment from God. Since there was plenty of disease communicated by the whites, this increased the power of the priests. Tightly disciplined and fiercely dedicated, the Oblates ruled with an iron hand and were able to display a model community which drew praise from traveling Indian agents and other white observers. Newspaper editors labelled the community "moral" and "industrious."

Actually, at the peak of the later fur trade, with the growing dominance of the whites, the Indians were in a cultural crisis. Epidemics of smallpox, before which the shamans were helpless, weakened belief in the old institutions. They were also somewhat demoralized by the wealth they had accumulated from the fur trade.

The relentless discipline and the medical and social service activities of the Oblate brothers showed the Indians that there were some whites who cared. The building program and community activities gave the Indians goals.

As with Catholics elsewhere, there was some skillful adapting of their own aims to old traditions. The retaining of the chiefs as puppet rulers prevented disruption. Hereditary titles and status differences were kept alive by special distinctions and titles given for unusual piety. The donating of wealth was given a new meaning, for it was channeled toward the building of churches, schools, and their upkeep. The giving of gifts at marriages was allowed, apparently because it was similar to the French dowry system.

Above all, the Frenchmen encourage pageantry—so long as it was connected with the Church's admitting openly that it was necessary "to capitalize on the Indian's love of display." This was the greatest difference between Duncan's approach and that of the French priests for Duncan even had avoided confirmation, fearing it might remind his flock of their past ceremonials. The Oblates allowed decorated altars, processions at night with lanterns and banners, and displays of fireworks. There were tableaux and scenes of the Passion Play with Indian actors. The Salish, being natural actors, amazed the spectators and even the priests.

Not all the Salish were satisfied with the Oblate fathers' rule. The northern groups were infected with the spirit of resistance which had inspired the Kwakiutl for so long. The loss of distinction of the great chiefs also caused dissatisfaction. The crisis came with the arrest and conviction of a highly regarded priest for countenancing the flogging of a woman and her lover for adultery. That the secular power could intervene so drastically was a shock. By the early decades of the twentieth century with the growth of public schools the Oblates were losing their influence, and many moved back to Europe. When Edwin Lemert visited the area in the 1950s, he found a fairly strong current of anticlericalism. The middle-aged Indians, who remembered something of the old regime, said, "The priests filled suitcases with dollars to hoard and take back to France."

It is doubtful if the French Catholicism of the Oblate brothers penetrated very deeply into the Indian psyche. The attitude toward shame in their culture made it almost impossible for them to admit guilt and sin. The priests admitted that the Indians lied during confession. And as far as understanding the meaning of Catholic ritual, Father Durieu himself admitted ruefully that the Indians looked upon communion as a pleasant experience and would take it every day if it were offered.

There is no doubt that the missionaries filled the gap between the almost vacuum of fur company control and the coming of provincial and Dominion government. They did not realize, however, that merely changing one set of myths for another did not mean that the Indian became a part of white society. In most cases they merely confused the process of acculturation. In the long run, preparing the Indians to become members of the lowest-earning income group in Canada does not seem to be an outstanding accomplishment.

THE WAR AGAINST THE POTLATCH

11

The struggle of white Protestant Canadians, initiated by the missionaries and government officials, against the West Coast Indian way of life finally centered around the question of the potlatch. This institution stemmed from a surplus economy which had made possible a preliterate class society. In the pursuit of prestige and the avoidance of shame, the West Coast group rose to artistic and imaginative heights of ceremony. At the same time the culture exhibited elements of paranoia and, in strange ways, parodied some of the least sensible aspects of the white man's social system. Yet those who felt that the potlatch system was wasteful and demoralizing and criticized the Indians for not pursuing the white man's goals never for one moment asked themselves if the pursuit of profit and the indifference to human welfare which have resulted from capitalist culture are worthy of uncritical admiration.

The justification for a class aristocracy among the natives (as among white men) was ultimately religious. That is, a supernatural power, in the case of the Indians, had granted benefits both spiritual and material to some individual, and these, in turn, he was able to pass these down to his descendants. They were symbolized by dances, legends, crests. In Europe a similar institution was labeled "the divine right of kings." Likewise among the whites a hereditary aristocracy, in terms of a similar ancestor worship, got its crests from the divine monarch and thus justified its possession of land and other property.

Although there was family ownership of such areas as fishing stations and clam beds (often far from village locations, which had been moved about), the most highly regarded "property" among the Indians were the myths, songs, dances, and above all the privileges of nobility. (Even the early explorers were aware that only a great chief had the right to hunt whales, for instance.) The right of nobility involved not one but a series of titles which could be bought, inherited as a result of a potlatch, or acquired by killing the owner. These titles were personal names which, according to Ruth Benedict, "had not been added to nor subtracted from since the origin of the world." Such titles were only inherited by the eldest born:

When a person took such a name he assumed in his own person all the greatness of his ancestors who had in their lifetime borne the name, and when he gave it to his heir he necessarily laid aside all right to use it as his own.

Great lineage resulted in great responsibility. Involving as it did the basic motivation of prestige, this prestige had to be continually maintained by public proof of riches and liberality. Since, as has been often stressed, this was a group of people to whom nature had granted a surplus of goods, the most ingrained aspect of Northwest Coast social life was the organization of great feasts accompanied by the giving of gifts—in short a public liberality known as the potlatch (from the Chinook trader's jargon *patshall,* "a giving").

Moreover, this liberality was further complicated by a system of credit in which the recipient of gifts was supposed to pay them back within a year, with often as high as 100 percent interest.

Of course, this strangely mounting credit could not be sustained by a single individual, and often it involved the efforts of a whole family or tribal group, as William Duncan noted. Aside from tally sticks (a primitive type of abacus ciphering), the Indians used large sheets of copper, on which they etched or hammered designs; and these, like promissory notes or bills of large denomination, stood for huge quantities of goods which were exchanged. Of course, this credit system, which has been compared to a kind of life insurance, would have reached astronomical heights if, at times, goods were not destroyed, thereby reducing the whole structure.

It is important to realize, however, how the potlatch activity was woven into the whole social system. Every child of an important family, male or female, entered this economic maze as a small child. When a baby, his name merely indicated the place where he was born. When it was time for him to assume a prestige name, the adults in his group gave him blankets to distribute among his relatives at the ceremony of obtaining a second name. Bodega noted accurately that one way of gaining a name was achieved by the father's paying a sum to a celebrated person. The child's gift then had to be repaid promptly with a large sum of interest. This the boy then had to repay with interest—and the cycle kept going until he was ready to give his first potlatch.

Then, too, in the case of marriage (the Kwakiutl and the northern tribes were matriarchal in that property was inherited through the female line) a man lent his privileges to the man who married his daughter. They were held in trust for whatever children were born. There was also a large bride price given at the time of the marriage which involved a potlatch. And this had to be returned with interest by the family of the bride, usually at the birth of the first child, with another potlatch.

The religious dance societies were also organized into lineages which possess titles of nobility. During the winter rituals, men were ranked according to the importance of the spirits which had initiated them into the society. But these titles could also be inherited or gained by marriage. Involvement in these prestige activities was fascinating and engrossing to the Indians. As Benedict wrote:

> They saw life as a ladder of which the rungs were the titular names with the owned prerogatives that were vested in them. Each new step up on the ladder called for the distribution of great amounts of wealth, which nevertheless were returned with usury to make possible the next elevation to which the climber might aspire.

Curiously enough, as the number of the Indians was reduced by two smallpox epidemics (at the same time the establishment of Canada attacked the potlatch) and because the former prevalence of raids and symbolic head hunting had been stopped by the government, potlatching actually increased in the latter half of the nineteenth century.

Helen Codere, who studied the situation among the Kwakiutl (and what happened in this group is similar to what occurred elsewhere), explains how murderous raiding was transformed into fighting with property.

As it appears in the earliest reports, Northwest Coast warfare was psychologically symbolical. (Indeed, we wonder why the psychology of warfare among primitives has not been studied comparatively and related to that of war in modern society. The forms which hostility takes in its integration into society are curiously baroque and unrelated to logical motivation.) Among the Kwakiutl, at any rate, the psychic impulses were fantastic. As Codere writes, "Kwakiutl warfare was not valorous. It was waged out of feelings of grief and shame, the desire to retaliate, or above all to acquire or maintain the prestige of being considered utterly terrifying."

In other words when relatives died, a raid against another tribe with subsequent head taking compensated for the shame and grief of the personal loss. It was a defense against death by causing other deaths. Hence any victim would do, and sometimes a single head was symbolically sufficient.

The other motive, that of striking terror in the world and thus gaining prestige, is particularly well illustrated in the dance and dance songs which were allied to the ceremonial side of warfare:

You are swooping down from heaven pouncing upon a whole tribe,
You are swooping down from heaven, burning villages, killing everything before you and the remains of the tribe are like the rest of your food,
Great Thunderbird, great thunderer of our world.
You are swooping down from heaven, going from one tribe to another,
You seize with your talons the chiefs of the tribes.

The violence and ferocity of much of these ceremonies (and indeed the art, too), which is meant to be impressive and frightening), clearly reveal that, as far back as the earliest outside contacts, the ceremonies and poetic dramatizations were as important as the actual hostile actions. This is indeed the story of human culture in general. In the case of the Kwakiutl and related groups it is easy to see that when actual warfare was inhibited by the sending of warships and the threat of jail sentences, the ceremonial type of hostility took over and became a substitute for actual killing.

In the effort to shame a rival and gain prestige for oneself the almost psychotic side of the potlatch was developed. The prodigality of gift-giving knew no bounds and, added to it, the conspicuous destruction of property was a way of competing with wealth and establishing a megalomaniac superiority.

One of the Kwakiutl dances was called "Bringing Blood into the House." The hemlock wreaths the performers carried were supposed to represent heads taken in warfare. These they threw into the fire, calling out the names of the enemies they represented. But these wreaths also represented coppers given away and the names were those of individuals whom the potlatch giver had put to shame by the distribution of property. This dance, therefore, appears to be a kind of transitional form clearly showing the transformation of warfare. Needless to say, the killing of slaves, which the missionaries were accustomed to use as evidence against the potlatch, died out with the establishment of government sanctions against violence. Codere feels that the shift from overt hostility to symbolic representation took place about 1849.

In competitive destruction of property, Benedict cites feasts at which large amounts of olachen oil were poured on the fire, causing it to blaze up so fiercely that sometimes the roof boards caught on fire. Sometimes valuable coppers were cut in pieces or canoes were broken up and flung on the fire along with heaps of blankets.

Codere believes that the inverse relation between declining population and increase in potlatching resulted from the fact that more positions of prestige were left open to be competed for—a situation which seems to have stimulated the gift-giving rivalry. As European goods became more available, they, too, were used in potlatching. At first blankets, which were often taken as wages from the Hudson's Bay Company, replaced furs and bark cloth; later such things as silver bracelets, calico, kitchen ware, or zinc wash boilers were used in ceremonial exchanges.

From all of the foregoing, it should be clear that the custom of potlatching was correlated with the deepest psychological motivations in Northwest Coast culture. It permeated all the more important social activities and, when warfare was outlawed, it provided the major expression of shame and prestige, emotions which characterized the Indians' lifestyle.

The missionaries and government agents sensed the importance of the potlatch as an obstacle in transforming the natives into potential white Protestant capitalist-oriented citizens. Since they never stopped to consider (or were indifferent to) the damage that forcible eradication of the institution might do to the Indian psyche and to the social coherence of the culture, they soon decided to concentrate their attack upon it and thus initiated a struggle which went on into the twentieth century.

We have seen how William Duncan, by the strength of his personality, simply divorced his followers wholesale from all of their former customs. Other missionaries who were less successful began petitioning for a law forbidding the potlatch.

By 1871, with the Confederation of the Dominion of Canada, the federal government took over the wardship of the Indians. Anthropology, however, was still too young a science to affect governments. (Franz Boas tried to explain the institution of potlatch in 1896 in the Canadian press, but even then he was not listened to.) Indian agents were, therefore, without special qualifications and often even without much sympathy for the Indians; they were merely politicians with the usual prejudices of the era. The government report of 1872 talks of "elevating the condition" of the Indians because they were "depraved" and potlatching "encouraged idleness." It is hard to see how this institution encouraged idleness when the hard-working Indians had to be ceaselessly active in order to keep it going.

Actually, the fact that food and the basic necessities of life were still plentiful was somewhat of an embarrassment to officials. The Kwakiutl, for instance, were doing reasonably well economically and saw no reason to work for the white man's goals. Hence, agents such as William Halliday labeled them unprogressive. But Deputy Superintendent of Indian Affairs Hayter Reed wrote in 1895 that these Indians were neither degraded nor backward: "In fact many of them appear to be in better circumstances than a large percentage of white settlers resident in this country."

That they could thus maintain themselves without losing their own religious and potlatch tradition showed that they were capable of exploiting the majority cultural situation and at the same time rejecting those elements in it which would transform them into non-Indians. This fact was highly irritating to those who clung to the traditional belief that everything Indian was bad and only white Protestant values were good.

Despite the missionary agitation and the support of the superintendent of Indian Affairs in Victoria, the anti-potlatch movement did not result in prohibiting the institution until 1884. The resulting consternation of the Indians can be imagined. They were all deeply involved in their complicated system of credit and it would take years to pay off their debts. They protested and signed petitions which were ignored.

Finally an Indian was arrested for potlatching. The justice, Matthew B. Begbie, a distinguished jurist acting as attorney general for Canada, discovered that potlatch was not even defined by the law and that the prisoner didn't speak English and had pleaded guilty without knowing what he was doing. Very sensibly the justice, on August 1889, threw out the case.

Actually, there were not enough deputies or jails to enforce the law in any case. Some more sensible agents suggested the measure be repealed; the missionaries responded by demanding more teeth in it. An amendment making it stronger was passed in 1895. The Reverend A. J. Hall wrote a public letter demanding that the law be supported. The Indians of Nass River petitioned furiously, insisting they had a right to their customs. The Reverend J. A. McCullough had two of them arrested and put in jail. Another Indian from the Frazer River was given two months at the instigation of a missionary.

Chief Macquinna of Nootka (evidently a descendant of the eighteenth-century Macquinna) published a letter in the *Daily Colonist* defending the potlatch as a kind of banking operation. It was in this same year, 1896, that Franz Boas, who was now deeply committed to the study of the Northwest Coast Indians, published an article in *The Daily Province of Vancouver* pointing out that the old ceremonial warfare had already died out and that if the potlatch were let alone it, too, would gradually fade. He stigmatized outlawing of potlatching as a demoralizing attack on the Indian culture. good!

While not many Indians suffered jail sentences, just enough did to keep the issue alive, to deepen their sense of injustice, and to strengthen their unity and their determination to retain something of their culture.

When Boas first came to a Kwakiutl council to ask permission to study the group, a chief made a moving speech:

> Do you see yon woods? Do you see yon trees? We shall cut them down and build new houses and live as our fathers did. We will dance when our laws command us to dance, we will feast when our hearts command us to feast. Do we ask the white man "Do as the Indian does"? No, we do not. Why then do you ask us "Do as the white man does"? It is a strict law that bids us dance. It is a strict law that bids us distribute our property among our friends and neighbors. It is a good law. Let the white man observe his law, we shall observe ours. And now if you are come to forbid us, begone, if not, you will be welcome to us.

The reference to rebuilding their houses was an allusion to the government's punitive measure, in the past, of burning villages. Boas promised to support the Indians and did so in articles and lectures. The Nootka sent petitions asking the repeal of the law. Boas's associate Edward Sapir wrote to the deputy superintendent general in defense of the Indians. But agent William Halliday continued to order arrests. In 1920 Charles Nowell, who had spent time in jail, wrote to a member of Parliament to use his influence in putting an end to the arrests. The Indians hired lawyers, sent more petitions. By now the potlatch had become a symbol of all that was Indian.

The natives had become adept at hiding their activities, giving their potlatches suddenly before they could be stopped, and developing private potlatching, which meant that they exchanged money and kept a record. Nevertheless, 1921–1922 seem to have been peak years in the persecution of the Kwakiutl. In 1921, five Indians were tried and convicted. In 1922, 29 were tried and convicted; four got suspended sentences; the rest were penalized 2 to 12 months. Chief William Scow, convicted the same year, several times president of the Native Brotherhood of British Columbia, said, "When you took the potlatch away from us you gave us nothing in its place."

By this time, however, even some missionaries were beginning to see the irrationality of the struggle. John Antle, Missionary Captain of British Columbia, wrote in 1931: "The Indian is asking for a modification of the law which will allow him to use such of his old customs which are not contrary to what we call our civilization and I am on the side of the Indian."

Between 1947 and 1949 the issue was officially dropped. In 1951 it was left out of the revision of the laws of Canada. It was never, however, repealed. The white man had decided to forget all about it, but the Indian remembered.

INDIAN AGENT TO THE KWAKIUTL

12

We have so far sketched the attitudes of the missionaries and something of their activities as a minority of indigenous people was gradually engulfed by the burgeoning white population. Actually, with so much against them and with so much indifference to what they had been and what they were, we are amazed at the toughness of the natives that allowed them to preserve their integrity as a group for so long. As we pointed out earlier, the attack on their culture was carried on by both the missionaries and government officials. Of the latter group the Indian agent, William Halliday, is a conveniently representative figure. History comes alive through individuals and Halliday put himself on record by writing his book, his apologia.

Halliday was born in 1873 in British Columbia. His father was a schoolteacher at Yale on the Frazer River. In 1888 the family moved to Victoria after having spent some years among the Coast Salish in the Comox district. Thus, Halliday had been exposed to Indians from boyhood—though this seems not to have made the slightest impression upon the prejudices of his class and culture.

The family eventually moved to Kingcome Inlet in the Kwakiutl area. There was a residential school at Alert Bay, started by Duncan's protege, the Reverend A. J. Hall, in Halliday's boyhood run by A. W. Corker. Halliday recounts a scuffle between white boys and Indians which ended with the whites beating the Indians with switches. The head chief was angry, but the whites were arrogant—a feeling which was echoed by their parents.

An anecdote concerning this same school related by the Kwakiutl chief Charles Nowell in his autobiography is illustrative of the conflict between native and British education. In 1880 the boys in residence lived in Hall's house. Nowell, who was about ten, had been a pupil for four years. When he and another boy were told by Mrs. Hall to clean out the box in the toilet containing excrement, they looked for a pole to put through the handles since the odor was disagreeable. Mrs. Hall told them to put their handkerchiefs over their mouths and pick up the box. Charles, angered by her tone, cried out, "You come and do it yourself, God damn you!"

This caused a scandal. Hall announced he would make an example of the boy. Charley refused to allow himself to be caned, broke loose, and ran along the beach where he found his grandfather unloading wood from a canoe. The old man faced Hall and asked, "What are you doing to my grandson? You'd better go back before I hit you with this stick." After considerable argument and the intervention of the agent, Hall promised never to punish the boys again unless something very serious took place. Indians were permissive toward children; the Europeans caned them. Thanks to the supportive action of his grandfather, Nowell was turned back toward the old customs after this crisis.

The anecdote is one more illustration of the unenlightened attempt to turn the Northwest Coast Indians into replicas of the white men, a program which Halliday wholly supported. In his book he admits that his stand on potlatching made him unpopular while he was agent for the Kwakiutl. Numerous petitions were sent to the government by Indians and their sympathizers, with the result that Halliday was investigated twice. He was sustained by Inspector W. E. Ditchburn, who was later to become Indian commissioner for all of British Columbia.

Halliday was made justice of the peace in Kingcome Inlet in 1894. In 1897 British Columbia passed a law concerning stray dogs. Any found worrying domestic animals off their owner's premises could be killed. As in so many cases, trivial causes set off an incident which revealed the typical attitudes of the opposing cultures. Halliday says the settlers appealed to him to do something about the Indian dogs, of which there were many which ran about and caused trouble.

A certain Granville Landsdowne shot three dogs, which, he said, had been worrying cattle. Their owner, an Indian, insisted they were valuable bear dogs and threatened trouble. Two Indian policemen came to arrest Landsdowne. His neighbors told him that no white man should allow such a thing to happen. A fight ensued which might have resulted in serious injuries if Landsdowne had not finally agreed to go to jail. When he arrived, the white constable announced that the Indians had no warrant, so Halliday put *them* in jail.

When the anti-potlatch law went through in 1884, Halliday visited every village and told them he was going to enforce the prohibition. The first two men arrested pleaded guilty and were reprimanded. Then four from Kingcome Inlet got four months each. Then 80 were arrested but got off by signing an agreement to give up their masks, regalia, and coppers, which would be sold to museums. Those who did not sign got two months in jail.

What the Indians thought about this can be learned from Charles Nowell's autobiography as he describes the funeral of his brother in 1920. The Indian ceremony is touching and dignified: the young men first arranged the body, dressed the deceased in a suit of clothes, and wrapped it in four new blankets. It was taken out through a window—if it went out through the door, it was believed his family would soon follow him. They put the body in a little house back of the church.

Then the rest of the Fort Ruperts told the people that they are going to call this chief that has died to come and see them. They say they will call him by all his crests, because we don't know which crest he has returned to. They say, if he does come, be stronghearted when you see him, so that you don't cry because it is a very sad thing to see which crest he has returned to. One of them spoke in a loud voice, saying, "Chief, come back and look at all these people that look upon you as their chief!" This he says four times. The fourth time we hear a whistle in the woods coming from the right side of the community house. The chiefs go out and come in again and tell the people they have seen which way the chief has gone and say they are going to bring him in. They come in surrounding a mask that a man has on his head covering his face. He comes to the door where all can see the mask. The people open a path so that everybody can see him, and they see it is the Thunderbird Man. He keeps on dancing inside the front of the house. Finally the Thunderbird opens his beak in four places and it becomes a sun mask, which is another of my brother's crests. All the points are sticking out in four places, showing inside it a man's face—a wooden face all ornamented with abalone shells. The parts close again and he dances to the back end of the house. The chiefs follow him with eagle down feathers in their hands and keep blowing them toward the mask when it moves. When it gets to the back end of the house, it opens up and lets the people see the face. From there he comes round to the other side of the house to go out. . . . The chiefs watch and tell the people that they have seen the way he is going and now we all know which crest he has gone to. The Thunderbird has come to fetch him to his own, what he was before he became a man.

There was a potlatch in connection with the funeral resulting in Charley's arrest. He was sentenced to three months and later paroled. On the economic side, Nowell explained that his brother had given a thousand blankets to other people, mentioning his name because Charles had given him a copper to sell and the returns from the blankets would pay for it. Charley's loss was about $3000—and what went on throughout the whole Indian economy as a result of this unthinking piece of legislation can be imagined.

James Sewid, a Kwakiutl, although younger, also has memories of the drive on potlatching in the early 1920s:

One day in 1922 when I was eight years old, George Luther [the schoolmaster] told the kids that there wasn't going to be any school for a few days because they were going to use the school for a courthouse. The law against potlatch had been passed and the mounted police were going to enforce it. The government had sent out the word that if the people would give up their masks and coppers and regalia and everything they owned in connection with the potlatch they wouldn't be put in jail. There were only people from three villages who did what they were ordered, Cape Mudge, Village Island and Alert Bay. They gave all their masks and regalia and everything they owned from the Indian way and they put it all in a big building behind the Indian office. That was just full of masks and things from these 3 tribes and they took them away. And the people who had refused to give up their things were brought to Alert Bay and put on trial and they used that schoolroom for a courthouse. And some of them from Fort Rupert, Kingcome, New Vancouver, Turnour Island and from all over the Kwakiutl nation were brought there. After some people had been tried on a certain day the ones who had been sentenced were just kept in the schoolroom and had to sleep on the floor. The mounted police would lock the place up and guard it at night. After they were sentenced they were sent down south to jail for about two–six months. I heard some of my relatives had been sentenced, so I crept around back of the schoolroom and looked through the window. . . . I felt very badly about it because they told me they were all going to be in jail.

Halliday's attitude toward the issue of Indian title to land, which began to be discussed when he was appointed agent, was that the natives were being stirred up and "fancied that the government of British Columbia had stolen their lands." This stirring up was done by white people, "who either expected to gain financially or achieve notoriety."

In a heavily slanted attempt to discredit the institution of potlatch Halliday gives a description which, allowing for his bias, is of interest in that it testifies to what went on at the turn of the century when the potlatch had assumed exaggerated form. He describes how the chief who gives the potlatch in order to gain a higher position in his clan sends out an announcement that he is going to give away 1500 sacks of flour as well as blankets, dishes, glassware and even the newly popular aluminum pots, while his wife is repaying her dowry—at 200 percent interest.

The canoes arrive and their occupants are assigned to hosts. They are greeted with formal speeches. The first night the host may do the dance of the bear, one of his crests. In the next three days there is feasting and the guests do the dances of their crests. A copper is auctioned off; the wife repays her dowry. A Hamatsa cannibal dancer is initiated in a ceremony which goes on for several nights with much blowing of whistles and working up of emotion because evil spirits are abroad. The stage with the curtain at the end of the room is used for bear and raven dances and, on the climactic night, the initiate drops through a hole in the roof naked. He goes through the routine of biting people and is eventually tamed. White down is put on everyone's head to pacify the rebellious blood which might prompt to evil actions. The gift-giving then goes on for days; everything is carefully apportioned according to clan membership and rank, all such data being kept in mind by the host's speaker. The host then announces his new rank and dedicates a totem pole.

This description shows how the event satisfies many impulses in the Indian culture which are perfectly understandable—once the shame–prestige motivation is accepted. In the first place the formal gathering of clans and neighbors strengthens the social bonds and lends interest and excitement to daily life. There is an opportunity for much formal speechmaking, an activity which preliterates (and some civilized people) enjoy. Much of the oral literature of tribal society goes into such efforts, for it is a way of preserving history in terms of ancestry. Masked and costumed dances are certainly an art form and another outlet for creative expression. The skillful working up of emotion and excitement during the Hamatsa are an example of the dramatic sense of the Northwest Coast peoples. Finally, there is an element of the ecstatic in such ceremonies, particularly "possession" by the Hamatsa initiate—a quality important to this particular group.

Granted that the gift-giving had reached awesome proportions by the time Halliday described it, it seems possible to go a little farther than Professor Codere in interpreting what was happening to the Indian psyche. In many cases when a preliterate people finds itself dominated and demoralized by a more technically advanced and generally overpowering European culture, hostility, desire to reassert its former greatness, and a reaction against acculturation is expressed, often in a neoreligious and exaggerated form. The famous ghost dance of the Plains Indians was mainly nostalgic, but it did include the belief that its adherents would be proof against the white man's bullets and by magic the old ways would be restored. The cargo cult of the South Sea was oriented somewhat differently in that it accepted the new, but it returned to traditional ways of thinking in that the all-powerful ancestors were by magic to bestow all the benefits of the strangers upon their descendants without the latter making any effort for themselves.

It seems possible that there is a certain parallel in the increased intensity of potlatching as the Indian culture found itself frustrated in conflict with that of the whites. It was certainly a stubborn affirmation of the old ways, and some of its emotional extravagance could be seen as desperation, an outcry against the death of all that was Indian.

IN UNION THERE IS STRENGTH

13

The next important episode in the history of the Northwest Coast Indians involves organization. The Tlingit of Alaska, because of their special position in relation to U.S. culture and government, were the first group to set up a practical organization for self-defense and to assert their aspirations as Indians.

Alaska, after the purchase, continued to be a stepchild of the Union. Although the military were withdrawn in 1877 the area got no sort of government until 1891, being run by customs inspectors.

The natives were afraid of the Tlingit and succeeded in having gunboats patrol the coastline for years. Fort Wrangell, on the mainland, was bombarded in 1877 because a trader was killed in a quarrel. An Indian village was in the process of being destroyed, until the American Navy got (and hanged) its man. Another village was partially destroyed because the Indians tried to avenge the accidental death of one of its members who was employed by the Northwest Fur Company.

The Northwest Fur Company had replaced the Russian institution and by 1898 salmon fishing became a major industry with fifty-five canneries. In 1881 gold was discovered and the Gold Rush was on. The fur and canning interests did not want a government because they felt it would mean taxes.

The Tlingit adapted to the new situation. They worked for the miners as carriers, woodcutters, or diggers, earning $2 a day. The Chilkat group rented their slaves to the whites as pack carriers at $9 to $12 a load. Some used their big canoes to haul freight, underselling the steamers at $30 instead of $40 a ton. Of course many fished for salmon and also worked in the canneries.

By now most were wearing clothes made from store-bought fabrics. The big clan house was dying out and small frame houses took their place. The labret was on its way out and the traders' wool blankets were used everywhere—and also passed as currency at $3 a piece.

Many customs, however, persisted. Slavery, potlatching, and

shamanism were current up to the end of the century. Matrilineal marriage regulated inheritance and established precedence in ceremonies.

Although English-language schooling was made compulsory from the age of fifteen in the 1890s, Chinook was the general means of communication. By the nineties there were a number of public schools for whites and half-breeds who lived in a "civilized" way. Mission schools founded by the Methodists in 1876 continued to serve the Indians. As the younger generation came out of the schools and as the missionary influence increased, the majority of the Tlingit became Christians (at least nominally) and by 1912 most of them spoke English with varying degrees of fluency.

It was at this time that the Alaskan Native Brotherhood was founded with, at first, ten members. These had probably had missionary advice and had learned how to organize from membership in missionary groups but, from the start, the society was Indian-controlled. Its influence was spread by forming camps (locals) outside the Sitka area. New Metlakatla, notably, never joined. Delegates were elected on the local level from both men's and women's groups. These elected officers. An executive committee often consisted of officers or former officers. Many high-ranking Indians were involved in the early leadership. Some feeling of clanship persisted in the local groups. A certain sense of the obligations of chieftaincy inspired the delegates. The local groups soon built halls for meetings which served as social centers.

The tone of the organization varied from conservative to progressive. Its very existence was a progressive step, but the dead weight of missionary training had made the Indians almost ashamed of their own culture. Hence, one of its aims was the abolition of "unprogressive customs." It did, however, come out strongly for citizenship for Alaskan Indians and more and better education.

Actually, neither the Russians nor the Americans had ever taken a formal stand on the position of the Tlingit. This group, and the smaller one of Haida, simply insisted they were citizens. The Alaskans said they were not. They had never been offered any official "wardship." Also though it was prohibited to sell them liquor, they were technically under the jurisdiction of the U.S. Bureau of Education, not that of Indian Affairs. The natives were not (until 1931) allowed to file mining claims. The double school system was, in effect, segregation, for who was to judge whether a man "had adopted the habits of civilization"? On the question of voting, the attitude was vague. An act of 1924 included Alaskan natives. Some had voted before that, when they were known personally to the election officials. This resulted in an Indian's being allowed to vote one year and arrested the next for committing a felony. When this was made a test cast and the right to vote was established, William Paull, the leader of the brotherhood, who had legal training, was elected to the territorial legislature in 1926 and served ably.

One senses a certain parallel to the N.A.A.C.P. in the United States as the brotherhood banded together for protection and solidarity. We could also say that the missionaries had inculcated a certain amount of Uncle Tomism evidenced, in the early years of the organization, in the attitude that the closer the natives approached white ideals and standards, the better treatment they would receive.

The organization fought school segregation. One case was lost because the parents of the child "did not lead a civilized type of life." Another, however, in 1929, upset the earlier decision. Eventually the public schools took over the whole educational system.

In 1936 the question of reservations was brought up by U.S. authorities. In Alaska there had been none (actually the Alaskan Indians were spared much of what the U.S. Indians are now protesting against). Many natives reacted against the idea, feeling it would result in second-class citizenship. There was the example of New Metlakatla, in which the Indians controlled their own land. Other Indians thought that reservations would give them medical care and welfare services and would relieve them of the burden of capitalist competition. The brotherhood finally decided to encourage decision by local option but, by 1953, the situation was unresolved. The Haida–Tlingit Land Claims Association was formed outside the brotherhood; their platform was to obtain a community fund. Some clans filed individual claims.

Since the Indians were working people, the brotherhood eventually found itself involved in labor relations. There were two unions in 1939, the Alaska Marine Workers Union and the Purse Seiners and Cannery Workers Union. The brotherhood, apparently because much of its membership belonged to these groups, at times served as a bargaining agency with the canneries.

As time passed, its attitude changed toward potlatching. There began to be a revival of clan houses and an interest in traditional customs. One Indian, who had opposed the potlatch, finally decided the missionaries had been wrong in calling it ancestor worship (as indeed they were). He assumed his traditional name as chief of his clan, rebuilt his clan house, and revived the old customs. He based his changed point of view on the statement that "What the potlatch is really about is history. It tells the history of the Tlingit Indians."

Finally—and here the parallel with Black organizations is strong—the brotherhood took up the issue of racial discrimination. Some stores, hotels, and restaurants would not serve Indians; some movie houses would only seat them in the balcony. The group boycotted a movie house belonging to a large chain and began to suggest that other institutions also be boycotted. The chain gave in. Eventually, in 1946, an antidiscrimination law was passed.

All in all, the brotherhood showed that Indians were capable of working together and using the white man's methods to protect themselves. Thus it was an example and a stimulus to other groups of natives in other areas, particularly in British Columbia.

Ethnic group action among the Indians of British Columbia began with the issue of land. The question of Indian title has always been an embarrassment to both the United States and Canada ever since the imperialist powers—Britain, Spain, Russia, and eventually the United States—settled the matter of sovereignty among themselves without consulting the Indians. Still, Canada, as Wilson Duff points out, has felt a variously defined "Indian title" as a burden on its sovereignty. The whole matter has been one involving controversy and confusion.

Douglas, the first governor of the province, had a fairly liberal approach. He felt that if a generous amount of territory were allotted to the Indians they could eventually be assimilated. When he made treaties it was with the provision that the Indians would be paid for the land they relinquished. Nevertheless, in lower Vancouver, the government never appropriated the money to compensate the Salish—but the land was taken anyway. Douglas did set aside reserves on the Frazer River.

In 1867 the commissioner of land and works in British Columbia announced that the Indians had no title whatever to land they were not using. By 1870 the government was insisting that the Indians never had any title at all.

Then in 1871, with the granting of dominion status to Canada, the Indians were caught in a crossfire between conflicting Dominion and provincial policies which lasted for years. At that point only 28,437 acres were set aside as reserves. The Dominion wanted to make more land available, the Province refused. There was Indian unrest, focused partly as a result of the Duncan–Ridley feud and the question of the missionary installations at Old Metlakatla. A commission set up to study the matter disagreed and disbanded. Another committee of inquiry in 1887 came out against missionary control and Indian self-government. The Dominion and the province resolved their conflicts sufficiently to appoint Indian agents but education and health remained a missionary concern with the aid of some public subsidy.

Duncan, in the seventies, had avocated 80 acres for an average Indian family of five, but he also suggested, if the reserve were abandoned or the Indians decreased in number, the land should revert to the Province.

In 1887 the Nass River Tsimshian, the Nishga, sent a delegation of chiefs (encouraged by Methodist missionaries) to Victoria to talk to the provincial government. They made a dignified statement demanding the return of their lands and a treaty:

> What we don't like about this government is their saying this: we will give you this much land. We cannot understand it. They have never bought it from our forefathers. They have never fought and conquered our people and taken the land that way, and yet they now say they will give us so much land—our own land.

This has been the Indian position ever since. A commission took it all down—and nothing happened except that the Indians were told that there was no such thing as a treaty with the Indians and they should be thankful for what they had. Nevertheless the claims of the Nishga have continued to be a rallying point up until today.

Actually, in contrast to the many nomadic groups in the United States whose territories were vague, the Northwest Coast Indians had fairly clear notions of title, particularly to hunting and fishing areas, which were passed down by means of potlatch in terms of traditional lineages. Meanwhile, surveyors were cutting down Indian holdings, reducing them to small campsite and fishing stations. As a result a delegation of Coast Salish in 1906 went to England to present a petition to the Crown. Edward VII paid no attention. Another petition in 1909 elicited from Richard McBride, the premier of British Columbia, the statement, "Of course it would be madness to think of conceding to the Indians' demands. It is too late to discuss the equity of dispossessing the red man in America." It was in 1910 that Peter Kelly, a young Haida schoolteacher, after leading 100 Indians to Victoria and being told that the Indians had no title to any public lands, experienced a rebuff which evidently set him thinking of other ways of proceeding.

The Nishga had never ceased to press their claims, forming a Land Committee in the 1890s and raising money to hire lawyers and draw up petitions. A joint federal–provincial committee was set up to investigate. The Nishga continued to be active, sending a petition to the judicial committee of the Imperial Privy Council in 1913 (they had been told to do so by the provincial government); which insisted the Nishga must first get a local decision before they could appeal.

It was not until 1915 that a number of Interior Salish groups met to form an organization to support the Nishga. Peter Kelly, now a clergyman, and Andrew Paull were leaders of the first attempt to unite the Indians of British Columbia. Although they had sparked it, the Nishga did not join though they agreed to cooperate with what was to be the Allied Tribes of British Columbia. Peter Kelly became chairman, and the first important meeting in 1916 included representatives from the Haida, Tsimshian, Bella Coola, Kwakiutl, Coast Salish, and Interior Salish. Although the executive committee elected its chairman and secretary from its own members, its delegates were elected from the various villages. The meetings were conducted in English because of the diversity of languages. At first there was a tendency to elect hereditary chiefs, but the natives soon learned that the more acculturated were their best representatives. The first secretary of the executive committee was a white man, a former trader named James Teit who had married a Salish woman and become an anthropologist. On his death in 1922 he was replaced by Andrew Paull, and Arthur O'Meara, a not very accomplished lawyer who had represented the Nishga group, became counsel for the organization. The Allied Tribes immediately opposed the royal commission of 1912–1916, saying that it merely allowed the government to take Indian lands without their consent. Another bill amending the Indian Act to give franchise to the Indians was also opposed, but it, and an act giving the government power to diminish the Indian reserves, were passed over the native protest.

In 1923 the Allies Tribes presented a set of demands to the minister of Indian Affairs, Charles Stewart. These included an increase in the reserves and recognition of Indian title and suggested a cash settlement of $250,000, plus increased educational and medical benefits. Finally, in 1927 a special joint committee of the Senate and the House of Canada was appointed. The Indians made their usual demands for recognition of aboriginal title, but the deputy superintendent of Indian Affairs defended his department and insisted that the Indians had already been fairly compensated. There was disunity among the Indians, since the lawyer for the interior tribes did not support O'Meara—who in turn did not present the Indian case competently. Kelly and Paull made a good impression, but the commission appears to have been prejudiced. It brought up the skirmish of 1844 when Finlayson threatened to burn an Indian village near Victoria to prove that Indian lands had been taken by conquest. The commission, for its part, insisted that the natives had no tradition which stated there was an aboriginal title to the land and maintained that the Indians had been consenting parties to the policy of the government concerning reserves, and other benefits "they had accepted for years without demur."

After this quaint conclusion, the commission formulated the final rebuff in what has been called "the great settlement of 1927":

> Having given full and final consideration to all that was adduced before your committee, it is the unanimous opinion of the members thereof that the petitioners have not established any claim to the land of British Columbia based on original or any other title . . . it is the further opinion of your committee that the matter should be finally closed.

The final recommendation, making it illegal for the Indians to raise funds to further present their claims, spelled the death of the Allied Tribes and effectually prevented further action on the land issue until 1951.

Yet for all the finality of the commission's finding, which immediately became an amendment to the Indian Act, a sense of guilt remained for the $100,000 annual grant, which was tacked on to it, as Peter Kelly remarked, "deviously admits the actuality of the Indian land claims of British Columbia."

The formation of the Allied Tribes was a first and most important attempt at native unity. It fell apart as a result of the repressive legislation of 1927, but it taught the Indians something about the administration of a large organization and how to present claims—and a bitter lesson concerning the need for political power.

When the 1929 depression struck Canada, it hit the Indian fishermen badly. They had already had trouble competing with the whites and the Japanese. Technological advances meant that capital was needed. The modern fisherman used a power boat and a power-driven drum to handle the seining nets. Few Indians had money enough to purchase their own boats. This meant that they were obliged to rent boats owned by the canneries.

Thus it was that the Indians felt they needed their own organization to protect their interests. Alfred Adams, a Haida from Masset, knew of the Alaskan Native Brotherhood through relatives in that area. In 1931 he proposed a similar organization to some Tsimshian trolling off the Queen Charlotte Islands. In December of that year a delegation from Masset met with a group of Tsimshian and approved a petition which had been recently drawn up asking for a vocational school for children from the North Coast, moderation of hunting and trapping laws in favor of the Indians, and a conference with the minister, free medicine and free medical care also being on the list.

The delegates adopted a resolution to form the Native Brotherhood of British Columbia. Its stated aims were to unify the Indians, to further their interests, to cooperate with the authorities for the betterment of the natives, and to stimulate education to place them on an equal footing with other inhabitants of Canada. The dues were 50¢ a year, delegates to its conventions were elected, and Alfred Adams served as president until his death in 1944. Most of the officers in the early years were Tsimshian, but there was considerable Haida and Bella Coola participation. The southern Kwakiutl had their own union, but it later was amalgamated. The northern Kwakiutl joined, as did the Salish from the Gulf of Georgia. The Old Metlakatlans did not join for local political reasons, and the Nishga held back because they still had their own land committee. Religion was an obstacle to unity. Although the brotherhood was officially nonsectarian, the official song of the group was *Onward, Christian Soldiers.* The Catholics and some of the Anglicans wanted their own schools and did not support the brotherhood's opposition to residential Indian schools. There were other local unions which weakened the organization's effectiveness. A delegation was finally sent to Ottawa to protest against the federal income tax, which was, for the first time, applied to the Indians. The Indians had enlisted during World War II and were told they would only be taxed during the war, according to James Sewid, an influential Kwakiutl leader of Alert Bay and a vice president of the brotherhood. In his autobiography of 1969, he pointed out that the tax remained—although the Indians were not allowed to vote in federal elections until 1960. He added: "Even to-day we are far apart from being equal with the citizens of the country."

In 1946 the brotherhood founded its newspaper, *The Native Voice.* Paull was suspended as business agent because he, at times, acted without the authorization of the membership. He left the organization, but it seems he had been planning something broader, for in 1943 he called a meeting of Indians from all parts of Canada. In 1944 he founded the North American Indian Brotherhood, of which he became president. Although it was supposed to represent 128,000 Indians, it was not organized on the basis of bands but of individuals. Its aims were to give leadership to the Indians within the sovereignty of the British crown and "to awaken the Indian race." Its democratic base was weak, and it was sometimes considered to be the instrument of Andrew Paull. He spoke out on behalf of grievances and, since he was well known, he was called upon by the special committee of the Senate and House of Commons in 1946 which was reexamining the Indian Act. The new organization did not represent Alberta and Saskatchewan and the Native Brotherhood would have nothing to do with Paull. Eventually the latter group sent two representatives to the committee, Kelly and William Scow, while Guy Williams was accepted as the representative of the unaffiliated Indians. At this point, the interior tribes set up an organization, but they were not asked to participate. In addition to the representatives which met with the committee, various groups and bands submitted briefs. Some did not want the Indian Act revised. One bill was drafted and dropped; the final one, which was passed, was discussed by Peter Kelly, Andrew Paull, and William Scow. The revised Indian Act of 1951 was a landmark in that it dropped the prohibitions against potlatching and against pressing land claims and the ban on selling liquor to Indians, which made them feel like second-class citizens. The Indians obtained the vote in provincial elections. If the revisions were not major, some were strategic, particularly the lifting of the ban on Indian customs.

The revised Indian Act helped, but it did not put an end to contradictions in the situation, nor did it solve the major disputes between the Indians and the whites. There was a sense of guilt on the part of the latter, for it could not be denied that the Indians had been in possession of the land when the Europeans arrived. The whites found it convenient to ignore native rights and to hope the Northwest Coast people would disappear through integration. From the long-range point of view integration and complete racial equality may seem only proper and just; but many Indians do not wish to cease being Indians. On the one hand, segregation on a reserve tends to produce a ghetto, as is certainly the case in the United States; on the other, tribal life has its own kind of coherence and psychic and social unity. Many Northwest Coast Indians do not wish to lose those privileges that have been granted them as wards of the state, and now that the white man has ceased to attack their customs by legal sanctions they are able to see more clearly the significance of what they are in danger of losing forever.

Before bringing the story of Northwest Coast Indian history up to date, it is therefore important to elaborate the salient features of the traditional culture, as it has been recorded and interpreted by those scholars who have devoted their lives to it.

ABOVE: Andy Schooner displays his hereditary mask, representing Echo. *(Photo by the author.)*

BELOW LEFT: Sisiutl grave marker in Bella Coola, said to be a hundred years old. *(Photo by the author.)*

BELOW RIGHT: Bella Coola in 1899. *(National Museums of Canada, Ottawa.)*

ABOVE: Main Street Bella Coola showing cultural center, a reconstructed traditional dwelling. Note that the portal pole of 1899 has been imitated by the modern carver. *(Photo by the author.)*

CENTER: Nimkisch Kwakiutl cemetery at Alert Bay. *(Photo by the author.)*

BELOW: Part of the Bella Bella fishing fleet. *(Photo by the author.)*

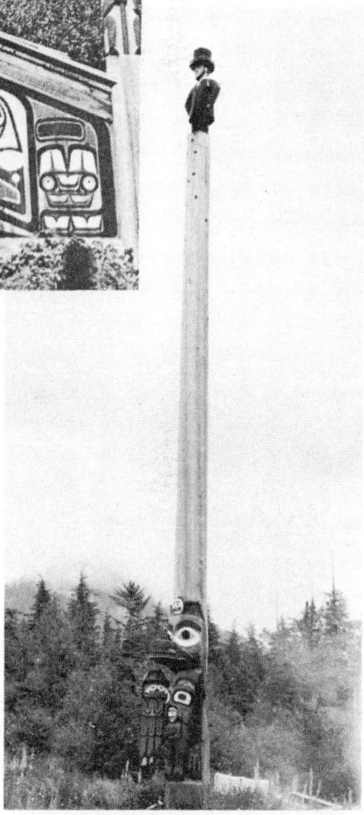

TOP: Replica of clan house, discussed in Chapter 29, built at Mud Bight 13 miles from Ketchikan in 1938 by the Tlingit, a precursor of the cultural revival. *(Photo by the author.)*

LEFT: Chief Johnson's totem pole, 1901, Ketchikan, Alaska, depicting Tlingit legend of the Salmon Woman. *(Photo by the author.)*

RIGHT: Replica of Abraham Lincoln totem pole at the Saxman Park, Ketchikan, Alaska. *(Photo by the author.)*

ABOVE: Main Street, New Metlakatla, Annette Island, Alaska. *(Photo by the author.)*

CENTER: Museum at Old Metlakatla today. *(Photo by the author.)*

BELOW: Old Metlakatla's one street. Nothing but the poplars remains of Duncan's settlement. *(Photo by the author.)*

ABOVE: Bella Bella, home of one of the most progressive Kwakiutl bands. *(Photo by the author.)*

CENTER: The grimy backyard of an Indian village, Bella Coola. *(Photo by the author.)*

BELOW: Part of the fishing fleet at Alert Bay. The majority of the boats are owned by Kwakiutl. *(Photo by the author.)*

ABOVE: Contemporary masks from the collection of the author. Left, Coast Salish Kekwe greeting mask carved by John Jones; center, Kwakiutl seagull mask carved by Peter Moon, Kingcome Inlet; right, Kwakiutl Dzoonoka (Giant Woman of the Woods) mask carved by Jimmy Dick, Alert Bay. *(Philippe Montant photo.)*

BELOW RIGHT: Raven's head, rattle in the form of an owl copper and sisiutl, carved by Kwakiutl artist W. L. Johnson of Kingcome Inlet, from the collection of the author. *(Philippe Montant photo.)*

BELOW LEFT: Contemporary argillite pendant, eagle design, carved by Claude Davidson, Masset, from the collection of the author. *(Philippe Montant photo.)*

ABOVE: 'Ksan cultural center: flying frog pattern for Chilkat blanket. Note traditional type of loom being used to weave a blanket, pattern by Earl Muldoe. *(National Museums of Canada, Ottawa.)*

BELOW RIGHT: 'Ksan cultural center: box drum with design of Raven stealing the sun, by Earl Muldoe. Man with drum wears button blanket and traditional headdress with sea lion's whiskers. *(National Museums of Canada, Ottawa.)*

BELOW LEFT: 'Ksan cultural center: eagle mask by Art Sterrit. *(National Museums of Canada.)*

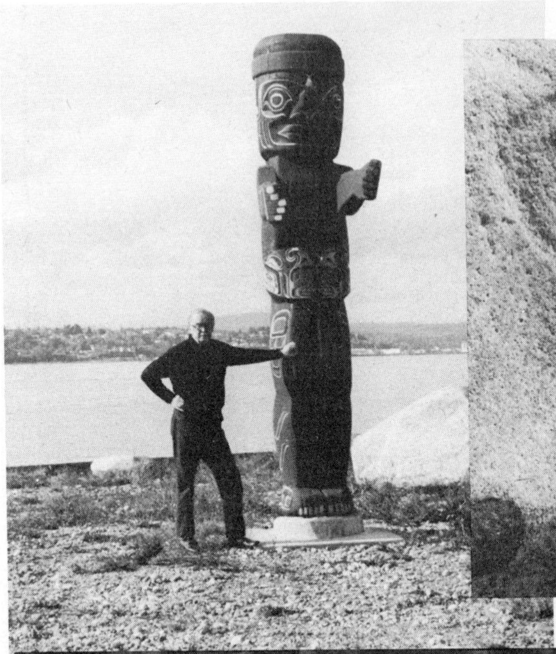

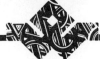

ABOVE LEFT: Author standing beside totemic carving at Cape Mudge. *(Mrs. H. R. Hays photo.)*

ABOVE RIGHT: Petroglyph at Cape Mudge. *(Photo by author.)*

BELOW: Button dance costumes made for the children of the Tlingit by Joe Williams, mayor of Saxman. *(Photo by the author.)*

ABOVE LEFT: 'Ksan cultural center: eagle–human transformation mask by Ken Mowatt. *(National Museums of Canada, Ottawa.)*

ABOVE RIGHT: The five traditional buildings at 'Ksan, Gitksan cultural center at Hazelton. *(Department of Travel Industry, British Columbia Government photo, Victoria.)*

BELOW: Raising a totem pole at 'Ksan, Gitksan Tsimshian cultural center. *(Department of Travel Industry, British Columbia Government Photo, Victoria.)*

ABOVE: Two Nootka carved welcome figures in situ 1911. Figures now in museum. *(British Columbia Provincial Museum.)*

BELOW LEFT: Kwakiutl interior house post. *(E. S. Curtis photo, 1914 Provincial Archives, Victoria.)*

CENTER: Bella Coola dance figure, 1893. *(British Columbia Provincial Museum.)*

BELOW RIGHT: Coast Salish (Cowichan) carved exterior house post. *(Provincial Archives, Victoria.)*

II
THE CULTURE

THE SHARED CULTURE

14

The culture we are here describing was produced by people who differed somewhat in physical characteristics and language but whose way of life was basically similar. There are seven of these groups, from north to south: the Tlingit, the Haida, the Tsimshian, the Bella Coola, the Kwakiutl, the Nootka, and the Coast Salish. Since they comprise a series of tribes generally identified by locality, the seven large groups can be called nations—not in the European sense, for there was no formal political structure, but because of linguistic demarcations and the fact that some of them, like the Tlingit and Nootka, were loosely confederated.

The Tlingit, originally fourteen tribes, spoke a language related to the Athabascan Indians of the interior and occupied the coast of Alaska from Yakutat Bay down to the Prince of Wales Island. They were pushing the Eskimo off Kayak Island in the beginning of European contacts and had begun to enter the Copper River. The Haida, who spoke a similar language, yet one which differed somewhat from that of the Tlingit, lived on the coastal areas of the Queen Charlotte Island and the southern part of the Prince of Wales Island in Alaska. The Tsimshian lived on the mainland from the Nass to the Skeena River and down to the area which is the modern city of Prince Rupert. There were three major divisions involving about 20 tribes. Their language is related to that of the Indians of Washington and Oregon. The Kwakiutl were originally divided into three major groups encompassing a number of tribes. Their area extended from the Bella Coola River Valley down to Rivers Inlet and Cape Cook. The Bella Coola, who lived in the general area of the Bella Coola River, spoke a language fairly close to that of the Coast Salish, but in other ways they were culturally closer to the Kwakiutl.

On the southwest coast of Vancouver Island down to Cape Flattery lived the Nootka, whose language is related to that of the Kwakiutl. The Coast Salish included the territory around the Gulf of Georgia down to the Columbia River. There was a large interior division distinct from the coastal group. Although the Coast Salish can be considered a part of the general culture with which we are concerned, they display certain differences. A few scanty archeological investigations suggest that some of the groups pushed down from the interior to the coast. The northern groups may have arrived with a marine-oriented culture somewhat like that of the Eskimo.

Most Indians of this area are fairly tall, but under 6 feet, light-skinned, often so much so as to be able to pass for Europeans. Their faces and heads are broad but the noses more often hawklike than flat. Some show the "Mongolian" (epicanthic) eyefold.

Some of the cultural traits shared by the seven nations occurred in the areas of practical living. The ability to construct large houses made of boards, skill in the making of canoes, some of these very large and seaworthy, and the ability to navigate long distances along a difficult and stormy coast were shared by them all. Well-developed techniques of fishing produced the staple foods and hence the drying and storing of seafood predominated over hunting of land animals, which was secondary.

Woodworking was always a major art, from the making of houses and canoes to the shaping of household articles such as storage boxes, wooden eating trays and other culinary utensils, wooden cooking boxes, even all-wooden drums.

None of these Indians had graduated into the agricultural stage, although the women gathered berries, roots, greens, and other available vegetable foods.

All shared, to some degree, a stratified social organization where rank was of continual absorbing interest. Many of the groups captured and exploited slaves. Oddly enough, however, unlike European social arrangements in which the aristocrats are a small group at the top of the pyramid, a majority of the Northwest Coast people manage to attain rank, leaving few commoners. It was an army of officers, privates being scarce. The explanation lies in the fact that nature was prodigal and these were a naturally industrious people. Since rank was attained by amassing wealth and giving it away, the commoners consisted of the lazy, the improvident, and the unlucky. While a man might be a commoner because of the failure of his father to achieve, there was no reason why he could not by his own efforts provide for his son and grandson. Thus Northwest aristocracy was both inherited and attained.

The Northwest Coast people could be said to be moderately

warlike. Like the Plains Indians of the United States, where the formality of counting coup was the purpose of martial raids and the ceremonies involving the capture of scalps were just as important as the raid itself, ritualistic head taking by the coast Indians did not result in major casualties—except when they were given firearms by the whites, which ushered in a short period when they decimated each other, until the power of the Europeans outlawed their warfare.

Like most preliterate groups, political organization was weak and the authority of chiefs depended upon their achievement of rank through their own potlatching and that of their forefathers plus, apparently, an element of personal charisma. Decisions were apparently made by consensus. If we can believe Jewitt, several meetings of leading chiefs were held to decide what to do with him. In the beginning there was apparently a kind of consensus of the people who besieged Macquinna's house calling for Jewitt's death. The chief became so angry that he chased them out with a club. Macquinna emerges as a strong personality who could apparently get his way through his personal prestige.

Another aspect of the chief's role appears in Jewitt's account in which he says that the people attributed public calamities to the conduct of their chief. When the fishing was bad, they were inclined to blame him for the *Boston* affair. This suggests that a certain magical aspect was attributed to the chief, that he symbolized the welfare of the group. Macquinna was, of course, a village chief; there were also house chiefs, heads of family groups. Larger political units were developing at the time of contact.

Inheritance in the northern nations among the Tlingit, Haida, and the Haisla-Kwakiutl was matrilineal, that is, inheritance came down through the mother's side of the family. The southern groups, however, were, like Europeans, patrilineal. In most cases the natives married out of the clan or moiety group (moiety, as among the Tlingit and Haida, meant that the tribes were divided into two parts—in the case of the Tlingit and Haida, Eagles and Ravens). The southern groups did not have moieties or clans but rather were organized into extended families.

It should be pointed out that slavery, in this culture of rank, was a terrible disgrace when persons of importance were captured. Kinsmen often ransomed them and cleansed them of the shame by the correct ceremonies. Hence, those who were carried far away were less likely to obtain their freedom. The

Flatheads, to the south, often became the prey of more violent Northwest Coast people, such as the Haida.

Without exception the seven groups were talented artists. The totem poles are the production best known to the general public, but these nations developed distinctive styles in carving, painting, and weaving which can immediately be identified and have never been rivaled by indigenous groups in North America. Aside from the totem poles there were other types of carving, such as house posts, grave figures, shamans' power figures, and beautifully decorated small objects such as gambling sticks, rattles, even fish hooks. War clubs, clubs to kill fish, paddles, headdresses, masks, food dishes—every type of material object might be skillfully decorated in the prevailing style.

Painting always accompanied the sculpture, whether it emphasized the planes of the totem poles or added to the imposing effect of the masks. Even the woven hats and helmets were turned into objects of beauty, and the Chilkat woven patterns of the north were extended from mantles to shirts and leggings.

The decorative style in painting was also used in murals which proudly adorned house fronts, on room dividers, and on screens, and was skillfully adapted to the sides of boxes, the prows of canoes, and finally to the bodies of the Indians themselves—not only on the face but on the breast, back, legs, and arms.

Music we know least about, but we do know that the choral singing, which has been completely lost and nothing of which has been recorded, was, by the testimony of any number of hard-headed ships' captains, extraordinarily impressive. The Nootka were said to practice part singing. Singing went on continually in ceremonies in combination with dancing and dancing was, of course, a major expression of Northwest Coast spiritual life.

Dancing blended into theater, an art in which all of the groups practiced with ingenuity and one which included types of audience participation which used to be considered innovation in the Western drama. The Northwest Coast Indians involved whole villages in their theater; they carried out parts of their presentations in the open air and involved the indoor audiences in the emotional displays and pantomimes of the actors. Since in winter stormy weather precluded fishing and stock of dried food kept the natives satisfactorily nourished, there was time to devote much patient, technical effort, all sorts of artistic embellishments, and a wealth of fantastic imagination to a ceremonial life as rich as that of any known society.

Needless to say, the content of this art and these ceremonies was of a magico-religious nature in that it was an expression of the Indian's relation to the natural world, his sense of unity with the live things on which his sustenance depended and which gave shape to his feelings and thoughts.

Sustaining this elaboration of ceremony was a copious shared mythology involving tricksters and culture heroes, supernatural helpers and beings with dangerous attributes, a mythology which both relates to world mythology and at the same time possesses its specific Northwest Coast color. Along with the cycles of tales involving characters known to most of the groups, there were also individual mythological episodes which were supposed to explain the special attributes, powers, and prestige which belonged to individual families.

Through all of this shared culture—whose leading motivations, as we have already noted, were shame and prestige—there was an interweaving of concepts which unified the life of area and gave it its distinctive and vivid personality. Potlatch, as we have indicated, was built into extended ceremonies and at the same time served to perpetuate titles, family history, and social relationships. Mythology justified rank and at the same time related the Indian to the forces of nature and dramatized his world view. Mythology was externalized in art, costume, dance, and drama and these also served as emblems of nobility; dances, masks, songs, and crests were the specific property of certain lineages.

It was this network of cultural concepts and activities which made the Indian an Indian, which integrated him satisfactorily into his environment, which provided him with variety, entertainment, and enthusiasm for living. The anthropocentric white man persistently refused to see the value of this pattern of living and, enmeshed an idea of "higher" and "lower" peoples, blindly insisted on depriving the native of what he already had, supposedly in order to raise him to a higher level.

In the chapters which follow we shall sketch various attributes of the Northwest Indian culture, whenever possible using early evidence and endeavoring to create a picture of the Northwest culture before it was substantially diluted by acculturation.

TOOLS AND THEIR USES

15

The kind of house a people builds characterizes their culture. The Mayans, for all their impressive stone pyramidal temples, lived in thatched huts—as do their descendants today. The Northwest Coast people were notable for their large, rather sophisticated wooden houses. That they sheltered a number of related family groups and were presided over by a house chief illustrates the importance of lineage ties. They were even big enough to be used as gathering places for ceremonials as well as residences. In the north the roofs were gabled; a heavy ridge pole was supported on great, often carved, posts front and back. Slots in the horizontal members held the side planking. In the north the center of the house was often cut down several feet into the ground—possibly a reminiscence of Northwest Asia, where some houses were entered from the roof. In the south (Southern Kwakiutl, Bella Coola, Nootka, and Coast Salish) the floor was level, but the roof inclined so slightly as to be almost level. The cubicles for sleeping were partitioned off and sometimes roofed like the large structure. The southern houses were walled by adding posts outside the supporting members and tying on the sidings. This was a convenience because of the habit of all these peoples of moving the siding and the roof planking (the roof was always left loose so apertures could be arranged for a smoke hole). The boards were removed from the frame and carried along when the dwellers journeyed inland to their fishing stations where other frames were waiting. Judging from Vancouver's illustration of the Kwakiutl, however, these Indians also built light temporary dwellings. There were variations: Alexander Mackensie, for instance, described how the Bella Coola, in narrow valley with scanty beach, built out on piles over the water. Vancouver also describes Bella Coola houses built on a rocky cliff and cantilevered out on the front and sides on poles 16 to 18 feet high. These apparently were constructed for defense and could only be entered by a notched log ladder.

The size of the houses, with their enormous carved posts and broad well-worked cedar boards, impressed the Europeans from the first. Haswell describes the Nootka dwellings as about 30 feet wide and 100 feet long. Until they obtained sufficient iron in the eighteenth century, the woodworking tools were bone-bladed chisels, or those of stone; various types of adzes with stone blades; stone hammers, bone drills; and wooden wedges. There are indications that some iron was here and there in use before the coming of the traders, but it was rare and may have been obtained through trade with the Eskimo, who obtained it from Asia.

Among the Haida, the building of a house was one of the most important reasons for a potlatch, there being five altogether, including: erection of a totem pole, funeral rites, vengeance, and face saving. When a house was to be built a man and wife collected all the products of their work, trading, warfare, and the wife's dowry—and sometimes secretly borrowed. The wife sent 10 or so blankets (in earlier times, furs) to members of the clan and moiety. Invitations were then extended to both sexes of the host's moiety. Including the children, several hundred might be invited. In one case a whole population of four islands came and stayed a good part of the winter. On the first day the visitors lashed their canoes together and performed special dances. That evening the members of the whole village assembled in the ceremonial house, and there were songs and dancing with special arrangements for the placing of each group or moiety according to rank and protocol. On the following day the host appointed five prominent male guests (of his moiety) to act as foremen to obtain the timber for the house. They selected crews from the same moiety. Next day these left in canoes, taking some women to cook, for the logging camp. They returned towing the logs behind the canoes, singing the appropriate songs to be welcomed with a feast. The host assigned various guests to various tasks, hewing, smoothing with the hand adze, preparing a totem pole. The work was done along with continual festivity, dances, spirit performances, and shaman dances. Since the Haida did not have dance societies, much of what went on paralleled the activities in winter festivals among other tribes. The raising of the totem pole in front of the house was the final act of the festival. At first, pieces of wood were shoved under it until one end was high enough to be propped up on two X's of timber under the end and the middle, and it was raised high enough to slide into the hole prepared for it. In earlier times, in some areas, a slave was put into the hold to be crushed by the pole. The next day everyone, including small children, danced around the outside of the new house. On the last day a final potlatch took place to which the host's moiety were invited by his wife's moiety. (All Haida being Eagle or Raven, if the host was Eagle, his wife was a Raven.) The potlatch in the nineteenth century involved large gifts of blankets, the bestowing of crests and dances upon the host's heirs, property displays, boasting, all the elaborations which came to be part of activity.

It is significant of the culture that even so fundamental a daily activity as building a house could become the occasion for all the elaborate festivity and ceremony in which this people delighted, including all the protocol and stress upon lineage so fundamental to Northwest Indian psychology.

Tlingit houses had sweat baths attached to them, and the Haida, in particular, made use of the portal pole carved with the lineage crest animals, a large round hole in the bottom serving as a doorway, curtained with a hide. The Tsimshian do not seem to have had totem poles early in their history, but they did paint murals of their crests on the house fronts.

The houses, in most cases, were drawn up in a single or multiple line facing the sea, close to the beach. Here, too, the canoes were beached and covered with mats or filled with water, because the great hollowed out logs were in danger of splitting if left in the sun. The largest, meant for cargo or for large war parties, were over 50 feet long and 7 to 8 feet in the beam, the finest being made of the enormous Queen Charlotte's Islands red cedar. Smaller ones were made for fishing. The great ceremonial canoes were made with high bows and sterns; some of the northern types were built up in the bow with a wooden shield for protection in war. Handsome designs were painted on the bow and sometimes crest images were mounted fore and aft. Sails were not used until after contact with Europeans, and then woven cedar bark mats were employed. Since the crafts were without keels they could only sail before the wind. By the time of the missionaries, however, the Indians seem to have obtained white canvas. Paddles often had a crutch handle and the blades were variously shaped for sea or river traffic or for hunting when silent travel was an asset.

Indian dress included furs, woven cedar bark, and woven woolen textiles. The men went naked much of the time and often wore nothing under the ceremonial sea otter cloak fastened over one shoulder or the cloak woven of mountain goat hair interspersed with strips of sea otter fur. Women often wore caftanlike garments or cedar bark shirts and capes of the same material, which came to the waist. In the south the Coast Salish bred wooly dogs for their hair, which was woven into blankets and sometimes mixed with goat hair. The dogs were shorn like sheep. Although the women sometimes dressed in ankle-length woven cedar bark capes, these could be tucked up with a girdle at the waist when they were working.

We have already described the painting of the body with red ocher, black, and other colors. In later times classical designs were painted on the body consisting of formalized animals and there was considerable tattooing. The use of copper in ornaments, which predates European contacts, was widespread, especially in bracelets. Indeed, from mythology in which houses of supernaturals are described as all of copper and likewise sometimes their canoes, we can understand that copper was for these Indians what gold had been in European and Spanish-American ornamental tradition.

Household goods consisted of articles carved from wood or made of wood and objects of woven cedar bark, and there was some use of mountain goat horn in such utensils as spoons. The hats were characterized by their pyramidal form, which reminds us of the Orient. In the south they were woven of split cedar bark and often decorated with a woven onionlike bulb at the top. By dying certain strands a design was created in black or brown. Whaling scenes were particularly elegant; sometimes small hats were in the shape of, for example, ducks. In the north hats were woven of split spruce roots.

Cedar bark could be split and cut into splints about a quarter-inch wide and thus woven into storage baskets and wallets. When shredded and steeped, it was beaten with paddles. Then it was combed and rolled on the woman's thigh to make a tight thread. It was woven into a textile that hung from a cross-stick supported on two uprights. The weaver knotted the cross-threads to the warps. In this way the wrap-around skirt and cape used by women and the cloak used by men were made.

Since the Indians were expert woodworkers but did not produce pottery, wooden boxes served for storage and even for holding liquids and cooking, as ceramic or iron might have been used elsewhere. The carpenters used measuring sticks and cut a long thin cedar plank and then gouged three deep channels at the proper spots for three corners of the box. By steaming, the board was softened so it could be bent at right angles so that the edge of the fourth side could be either pegged or sewn together with spruce root fibers. A rabbet was cut along one edge of the whole board so that the bottom could be fitted into the finished box and pegged from the sides, the bottom being made so tight that it was liquid-proof. The cover often fitted over the top, telescope-fashion. Tapered boxes were made to fit into the bow or stern of a canoe. Since the Northwest Indians did not often employ stretched hide, the most common type of drum was simply a box with a tightly pegged cover which was highly resonant when beaten with a stick.

The interior living cubicles of the house, therefore, were furnished with all manners of storage boxes and baskets and such boxes often functioned as seats. In addition, wide shelves ran along the walls; these were used for sleeping and also for storage. The cubicles in the rear of the house also served as dressing rooms when a screen or curtain was placed across the back during theatrical productions.

The most famous textiles were the so-called Chilkat blankets, made by both the Tlingit and Tsimshian but probably originated by the latter. They were semicircular capes or robes with long fringes made on the same primitive type of loom already described, the warp only attached at the top, the bark cloth and the thread was also rolled on the woman's thigh. The pattern boards were made by male artists and followed by women weavers in yellow, blue, and black, plus the off-white of the natural wool. What with the dying and preparation of the thread such a blanket could take a year to make. The Tlingit wove dance leggings and poncholike dance shirts in this style.

The interior of a Northwest Coast house, best depicted by Cook's artist, Webber, shows the fireplace in the middle of the room and the various storage boxes and bags. Racks, used for drying fish, were gradually moved back as the process was completed. Similar racks were used to broil fish over the fire. A watertight wooden cooking box is shown. Into this the red hot stones were placed with long wooden tongs, a widespread preliterate method of boiling. A fire was kept going continually.

The early accounts of family life vary. The women are sometimes described as modest, but some traders felt they had much to do with bargaining and were deferred to in this by their men. Children were indulgently treated. Both sexes cooked. The women, aside from making clothes, gathered berries, which were stored and eaten with olachen oil, much as we would put cream on them. The Indians had a number of vegetable foods; they are described as gathering wild onions, roots, and skunk cabbage. Shellfish and other marine items obtainable at the water's edge—such as crabs and kelp—were also generally collected by women. Jewitt speaks of a mealy root the size of an onion traded for with tribes south of Nootka.

In general there was the usual division of labor, in that the men occupied themselves with some hunting, using bows and arrows which they quickly abandoned as soon as the traders arrived with muskets, but mainly exhibiting skillful fishing techniques. They, too, of course, dominated ceremonial life—from which, however, women were not excluded—and cultivated the ethos of the warrior.

The feeling for nature and the Northwest Indian connection with it is interestingly exemplified in the Tlingit names for the months. August was the month in which all the birds came down from the mountains. September, the moon child, was the time when fish and berries began to fail. In October, month of the big moon, the first snow appeared on the mountains and the bears began to get fat. In November people had to shovel snow away from their doors. In December every animal on land or water began to have hair in its mother's womb. In January the sun began to start back and people looked for geese. In February the black and brown bears began to have cubs and threw them out in the snow. March was when sea flowers and all things under the sea began to grow. April, the real flower month, was when buds and twigs began to show life. In May people knew that everything was going to grow. June was the time of the salmon. July when everything was born.

We have already described the armor worn by the Tlingit. The Haida and Tsimshian also used armor made of thin saplings or flat rods sewn together with rawhide or heavy multiple layers of rawhide in cuirasses. The same bows employed in hunting also served in warfare. In addition there were basketry slings of spruce root. Clubs with decorated handles and striking areas were made from whalebone and, earlier, of stone. A strange weapon, which has come to be called a "slave killer" because of its ceremonial use for sacrificing slaves, made of hard wood, antler, or stone, looked something like a pick with the blade protruding from either side of the end of the grip. One of these is described as the weapon of the Fool Dancer. Iron daggers with elaborate handles, some with double blades, were the most conspicuous iron utensils in use before the traders arrived.

When it came to fishing there was a wealth of material equipment. Traps made of poles and saplings, like long baskets, were constructed in rivers where the salmon spawned or, with finer mesh, for herring. Funnel-shaped nets were used for olachen, and the southern groups had seines and gill nets. The harpoon with a single barb was the weapon of the northerners, in the south it was two pronged. These could be thrown with a line attached. Hooks for angling in the north were V-shaped, with one side of the V armed with a backward pointing barb, the other often decorated with an animal figure of magical significance. These were adapted for halibut fishing, a fundamental activity of West Coast economy. Other simpler hooks, U-shaped, barbed or unbarbed, were used for other types of bottom fishing. Herring rakes were dragged through the surfacing shoal of herring; at the end of the stroke, the impaled herring was shaken into the canoe.

Hair seal, sea lion, porpoise, and, most difficult, dangerous, and highly prized, whale were all harpooned with detachable multiple-barbed bone point. This carried a line when it came off the shaft. The latter was sometimes propelled with a butt piece or throwing device. The hunter paid out the line and gradually tired out his prey. Strangely enough, it was only the Nootka and their nearest neighbors who challenged the whale. The harpoon head was made of three pieces and the line furnished with three sealskin floats. The line made of sinew was carefully coiled in a cedar bark basket; the harpoon itself was so heavy that the whaler had to be paddled up close enough to thrust it home just behind the left flipper. There was, of course, always danger at the crucial moment should the whale charge the canoe.

Whaling was the privilege of a chief of high rank; he alone possessed the proper magic, knowledge of ritual, and the wealth to man a canoe. Sometimes he was accompanied by a relative in a second canoe who had the privilege of planting a second harpoon.

Jewitt described how Macquinna passed a day alone on the mountain, going early in the morning and returning late at night, having spent his time singing and making magic to insure successful whaling. For the next two days he appeared serious and solemn, scarcely speaking to anyone and observing a strict fast. He wore a broad red fillet around his head in token of humiliation, a large branch of green spruce on top, and his great rattle in his hand. For a week before beginning whaling, both he and his crew fasted, bathing several times a day, rubbing their bodies, limbs, and faces with shells and bushes until they were lacerated. They also abstained from sex with their women.

Goat hunting and deer hunting were also, of course, a prerogative of men. Unlike more nomadic peoples, the Northwest Coast Indians had a strong sense of territory. Among the Kwakiutl, if a goat hunter from one area trespassed on the territory of another, they immediately fought until one was killed. This sense of territory also applied to berry patches, including the nine types of berries which were harvested to be made into cakes for the winter, among these elderberries, salmonberries, huckleberries, currants, and crabapples. Even more serious was any attempt to appropriate salmon fishing groups. According to Boas's informant, such thieves generally paid with their lives for breaking the unwritten property law.

FROM BIRTH TO DEATH

16

A Kwakiutl woman who desired to have a child went with her husband to a place where twins were born and then squatted on her hands and feet in that place. She ate four of the first olachen of the season roasted. She and her husband searched for a bird's nest and took home the nest with the eggs. She ate the eggs and spread the material of the nest under her bedding. As soon as pregnancy was established she was forbidden to do any hard work. It was also useful if the man could locate a frog which had been sitting for a long time on one place. His wife would then squat on the same place. There were many other magical precautions which would supposedly aid in an easy delivery. Nobody was supposed to walk between her and the fire, for this would mean the child assumed a crosswise position in the womb. There were food taboos: no salmon eggs, because they were sticky and would cause the child to stick; no squid, lest the child cling like a squid. Whale meat was forbidden because there was a folk belief that whales did not have young. Of course, there were numerous remedies which could be used if these prohibitions were not carried out.

Above all, a pregnant woman was not allowed to make basketry nor her husband make kelp lines, twist cedar twigs for ropes, or stitch boards together for boxes; all such activities were prohibited lest the navel string be twisted around the child. All of this indicates how much analogy enters into medical thinking. Having obeyed all of the taboos, which seem to have been endless, at the time of birth, she was either taken outside the house or all the other residents left. All during labor the husband was obliged to walk slowly from house to house, enter his own slowly from the rear, and leave quickly from the front.

In actual delivery the woman sat in the midwife's lap, her legs hanging down into a specially dug pit, lined with soft undyed cedar bark, into which the child was allowed to drop. After the birth the mother was put to bed. Until mother's milk was available, the baby was given seal blubber or the foot of a large clam to suck.

The number of taboos and precautions which would influence the future of the child was endless, running from placing the right paw of a bear in his hand to make him industrious to tying the navel string of a daughter around the mother's right wrist while doing basketry, which would make the girl skillful at doing the same kind of work. Many of the Northwest Coast tribes flattened the heads of their children by compressing them early in life.

Twins, as among most preliterate peoples, were considered a magical event. In most cases they were believed to be related in some special way to the Salmon Spirits. The Kwakiutl felt they must be kept away from the water or they might turn back into salmon. They were given special treatment and obliged to conform to many taboos in order to preserve their power. When grown, they were believed to be able to dispel fog, call certain winds, and, if the salmon did not run when expected, a twin went to the river and invited his relatives to come up it.

Among the Kwakiutl, a newborn boy was given the name of the place at which he was born. Children were placed in bark wallets and carried on the mother's back or hung up in them. Ten months after birth a new name was given to the child at a festival in which the parents distributed red ocher and handkerchiefs to tie around their heads.

The upbringing of a boy involved games to toughen him and to display his bravery. Charles Nowell chronicles a number of such games, which seem to be typical of this shame–prestige culture which put much emphasis upon the warrior ethos. The boys would try to pick up wooden pegs driven in close to the fire without shrinking if his hair got burned or his face scorched. Another test of endurance was placing a hot coal on the forearm and keeping it there until it burned the flesh. A brave boy would have scars all along his arm.

Sex play, either between boys or between prepuberty boys and girls, seems to have been tolerated. The boys played at war, according to Charley. They wrestled, and those who won counted their conquered adversaries as slaves. Sometimes they fought with nettles, striking their bare bodies with the stinging plants. When they grew older, they used, in their wars, bows and arrows with very small points which nevertheless drew blood. The transition from this type of training (and it must be remembered that babies were, from the beginning, bathed in cold water to toughen them) to the more rigorous ideal of the warrior is easy. Warriors were supposed to walk with stiff, jerky movements to show how touchy they were. They were not supposed to laugh. The right shoulder was always supposed to be kept free, ready for fighting. They even carried stones in their hands which they threw at anyone who displeased them. To make themselves courageous they boiled and ate the heart of a grizzly bear; or the father of a male child hung a package containing a snake's, toad's, and lizard's tongue wrapped in a piece of grizzly bear's heart around the child's neck when he was ten months old. It was to be worn all through life. Warriors also scarified themselves with sharp bone points before a raid or beat themselves with rough twigs or nettles.

It will be remembered that a boy received a second name when he was about a year old. Whether the Kwakiutl boy was destined for high rank depended upon his being lucky in having parents and grandparents who had given potlatches and acquired wealth and privileges. At the age of ten or twelve he was supposed to borrow blankets from other members of his tribe. (After a year or so he was obliged to repay them with 100 percent interest.) The boy distributed his blankets to other members of the tribe, in proportion to rank, more being given to the chief. This would be repaid with interest inside of a month.

When he had repaid his original debt, he could distribute property in order to obtain a potlatch name. Also, at this time his father could give up his position in favor of his son. This was done formally, with more distribution of gifts, a feast, and the assumption of the father's seat in the council. From then on he could continue a career of giving potlatches, amassing wealth, and competing with rivals. As we shall see, both his marriage and the death of his father or grandfather could also be the occasion for the acquisition of more property and prestige.

If amassing of property, stoicism, and the warrior's ethic were ideals of young males, the important goals of a young woman's life were obedience to taboos. As we shall have occasion to elaborate in connection with religion, her female sexuality was laden with magical potency. Not only could it endanger the game supply, but it was her duty to see to it that it did not infect the activities of males in general.

In consequence, at her first menstruation the girl was secluded, for varying lengths of time; most extreme, in this case, were the Tlingit, who ostracized the girl for one year in a special hut. Care had to be taken that she never approach a river in which salmon ran or eat fresh fish or meat, because this might offend the game. The Kwakiutl had an interminable list of taboos and precautions for the girl's period of segregation and purification. There was much washing by an elderly relative. There was a rite in which heated stones were placed in water with which the girl's head was sprinkled four times. As she sat in a small room erected for the purpose, in the right hand rear of the house, she wore a special costume. Indeed, a list of the frustrating and time-consuming restrictions with which female sexuality were hedged should thoroughly discourage the nostalgia of modern young rebels against the Establishment—those who would like to hark back to tribal society in the belief that it could offer freedom and simplicity, at any rate. The well-brought-up young girl had to sit on a mat, leaning against a backboard facing the door of the house. Only her mother was allowed to enter her room. No fire was allowed. She must always look in front of her. She ate only cold dried salmon, halibut, or boiled clams—and only at high tide, because if she ate at low tide she would be greedy for food all her life. She was allowed only four pieces of food and four mouthfuls of water at each meal. The rest of the time she kept tallow in her mouth so as not to be thirsty. She was not allowed to leave the room during her weeks of purification except to answer physical needs. She wore a hat on her head to protect her eyes against the light, lest she become blind in later life or have red eyes. The restrictions on her drinking water were to make sure she would not have a stout belly. A belt of cedar bark around her waist insured a slender waist, while a wide belt of mountain goat wool, furnished with holes for the nipples, was worn over her breasts to prevent them from being too full. She was obliged to scratch her head with a copper scratcher, for if she touched her hair with her fingers the skin would be always rough. She spoke but little and slowly, lest she become too talkative and prone to laughter. She must not go near the fire when she did go out, and she must keep the hat on so that she would not see the sun. She must never during this period speak to a man. For four months she must not go near the sea or she would have boils on her legs; and, of course, if she went near the river, the salmon would cease to run. Anything touched by menstrual fluid was gathered up and placed under some stones. At the end of the purification her hair was cut and her eyebrows trimmed with tweezers and her fingernails were cut.

After patiently enduring all of this, at the end of the purification a potlatch was given by the girl's father and she received one of the names from her mother's family that were due her as a part of the dowry her mother had brought with her at marriage. A description of the festival which Macquinna gave for his daughter follows, as recorded by Espinosa y Tello, one of the Spanish voyagers:

At one corner of Copti they had set a platform supported by 4 thick pillars, painted white, yellow, scarlet, black and blue with various badly drawn figures on it and 2 busts at the corners with open arms and hands stretched out as if to signify the munificence of the monarch. In the interior of the house on some freshly strewn rushes was a couch, where the princess lay, dressed in the finest cypress threads and loaded with innumerable ornaments. As soon as the appointed hour arrived, Macquinna took his daughter by the hand and led her to the platform, placing her on his right and Quatlaza-pe his brother on his left. The large crowd of natives who thronged the hall and beach remained in the most profound silence. The chief, addressing them all, said, "my daughter, Apenas, is now no longer a girl but a woman; from this time on she will be known by the name, Istocoti-Clemoc," that is, "the great princess of Yucuatli." To this all replied with loud shouts of "Huacas, Macuina!" "Huacas Istocoti-Clemoc," cries equivalent to our "Viva," the greatest praise among these people is to express friendship which is signified by the word "Huacas." The taises and other nobles then began to sing and dance, everyone receiving some gift of importance, which Quatlaza-pe scattered from the platform in the name of Macuina and the princess.

In contrast to the observances connected with birth and sexual maturity, marriage was less involved with magic and more a matter of lineage, social position, and the acquisition of wealth. It was customary to marry out of the group. Boas records a fiction of marriage by capture and warmaking upon another tribe. He also mentions an actual sham battle between the wooing party and the relatives of the bride. Most important, however, was the potlatch aspect of marriage in which various types of reciprocal payments occurred. This involved not only the families concerned but also a whole village group. Among the Kwakiutl the party of the bride were supposed to arrive in a canoe and, at times, did, with dancing and ceremony. In the case of the Tlingit, the father of the bride gave a bridal feast with distribution of gifts which was later returned by the groom. In general, the principle of the transaction was a substantial gift from the groom's family to the bride's family. Later there were return gifts to the man's family.

The Tlingit marriage began with an offer of blankets to the prospective mother-in-law by a group of the boy's friends. She took time to think it over; if she accepted, the gifts were left. The father distributed gifts to all of the daughter-in-law's relatives and also to his son's friends. The Kwakiutl procedure involved an agreement on the number of blankets to be paid for the girl which had to be worked out between the two sets of parents. A binder could be put down until the total number had been accumulated by the groom's relatives. At the festival in which the bride was handed over, her relatives gave her husband presents to represent the household goods needed by the young couple. This often equaled the payment by the groom's family. Further prestige payments of names and privileges or a copper to the groom by his father-in-law were deferred until the birth of a child, which then became the occasion for another potlatch. This payment did not consist of blankets but rather of objects as well as privileges. If the father-in-law delayed in making this return payment, it could cause trouble. In one case a Kwakiutl son-in-law had a sculpture carved to represent his wife. At a feast he put a stone around its neck and sank it in the sea. Thus the delinquent father-in-law was shamed.

One of the problems of patrilineal descent (among the southern groups) was the matter of inherited privileges when the eldest child was a girl. This was sometimes solved by giving the girl a man's ceremonial name—thus she became socially a man.

It can be seen that, on account of the nature of Northwest Coast marriage, the young people often had little voice in the matter (hence the indignation of missionaries, who were influenced by nineteenth-century romantic concepts).

The following is the Polonius-like advice handed out by the father and mother of the prospective Kwakiutl groom after the father had made the arrangements for the marriage:

> O my son, see how I and your mother love you: Look at the labor we bestowed on getting the blankets we have to pay for your bride. Now be careful! Do not talk ill of your parents-in-law and your wife's aunts and uncles. Do not talk haughtily to your wife for that results in quarrels. Work like a slave for your parents-in-law.

To which the mother added:

> Keep in mind the advice given by your father. Do not forget any of it. Do not talk about your mother-in-law and the female relatives of your wife, for that often disrupts a marriage. We should be ashamed of you, if you stay with your wife for a short time only.

The father went on:

O son, learn to have a strong mind and not to answer your wife, if she should talk angrily; else you will quarrel and, if people hear it, they will take everything out of our house, even the roof boards. Do not tease your wife, else you might quarrel, and do not be unwilling to accompany your wife if she asks you to go out with her. If you follow this advice you will lead a happy life with your wife.

According to Boas the son made the proper reply: "O Father and Mother, why should I become indifferent in my ways now when I take a wife? I am no fool and I always think how to behave properly. I wish to live in happiness with my wife." Meanwhile the parents of the girl sat her down between them and initiated a similar dialogue. The father said: "Now, my daughter, listen to what I am going to say to you. You will be married to-night. . . ." "Oh, to whom?" cried the daughter, perhaps more surprised than pleased. She was told the name of her future husband, whereupon the father continued his wise words.

Be careful! Do not hate your husband's parents, his uncles, his aunts and sisters. Answer kindly when they talk with you. If your husband's younger brothers should flirt with you, tell your husband at once. Be willing to work when your sisters-in-law and your mother-in-law ask for your help. That will give you a good reputation. Rise early in the morning and prepare breakfast for your husband and his parents. Do not talk angrily with your husband. When he goes away do not walk about with other women.

The mother had more concrete worries.

Now you will take a husband, my daughter. I feel troubled in my mind that you might not be a virgin. For if your husband lies down with you and finds you are not a virgin, he will get up and tell his father and he will send you home. If that should happen, you would never get another husband. Your father would beat you and drive you out of his house. This troubles me.

Apparently the marriage was made in heaven (we do not know if this was a generalized, fictionalized dialogue invented by Boas or an actual report), but at any rate the girl replied as correctly as the boy: "Father and Mother, do not speak that way. Do not feel troubled about me, for I am a good girl. I have always followed your advice, and I shall never bring shame upon you."

Death, the final event which gives rise to ceremony, was also important in the Northwest Coast life cycle, both from the point of view of inheritance and also psychologically. Apparently there was some fear of the dead. The Tlingit said that sometimes a dead relative would come to them in a dream and announce that he was hungry. This meant that the dreamer had to give a feast. The Tlingit potlatch for the dead, which was an important ceremony, involved offering spirit food and clothing to the deceased. Krause describes a Tlingit chief's corpse placed in a sitting position at the center back wall of the house, wearing a wooden hat with a carved raven on it and a blanket decorated with figures done in white buttons. When the body was carried out, the back wall was removed; in other cases a hole was made in the wall. The Tlingit followed the body with a live dog which either removed the illness or, according to Swanton, a dead dog was thrown through the opening into which the ghost of the dead would be absorbed. At any rate, the actual doorway was avoided in all cases because of some fear of hostility of the dead. The Tlingit widow was not spoken to for eight days. At the potlatch gifts were given, and a little food was put into the fire as the name of the dead man was spoken. In the north the funeral was carried out by the other moiety (Eagle or Raven), for the Tlingit were divided like the Haida. The corpse was cremated (the Tsimshian and northern Kwakiutl also practiced cremation), and the ashes were put in a painted grave box placed on top of a grave pole or in a cavity in the pole. The Haida placed the body in a wooden grave house. Sometimes the remains were, however, put in a box or a niche like those of the Tlingit.

We have a description of a Nootka funeral ceremony from Jewitt who was a witness of the death of the demented chief, Tootoosch:

> Early in June Tootoosch, the crazy chief, died. On being acquainted with his death the whole village, men, women and children, set up a loud cry, with every testimony of the greatest grief, which they continued for more than three hours. As soon as he was dead, the body, according to their custom, was laid out on a plank, having the head bound round with a red bark fillet, which is with them an emblem of mourning and sorrow. After laying some time in this manner, he was wrapped up in an otter skin robe, and three fathoms of I-whaw [tubular shell beads] being put around his neck, he was placed in a large coffin or box about three feet deep, which was ornamented on the outside with two rows of small white shells. In this the most valuable articles of his property were placed with him, among which

were no less than twenty-four prime sea-otter skins. At night, which is their time for interring the dead, the coffin was borne by eight men with two poles, thrust through ropes passed around it, to the place of burial, accompanied by his wife and family with their hair cut short, in token of grief, all the inhabitants joining in the procession. The place of burial was a large cavern on the side of a hill, at a little distance from the village, in which, after depositing the coffin carefully, all the attendants repaired to Maquina's house, where a number of articles belonging to the deceased, consisting of blankets, pieces of cloth, etc., were burned by a person appointed by Maquina for that purpose, dressed and painted in the highest style, with his head covered with white down, who, as he put in the several pieces, one by one, poured upon them a quantity of oil to increase the flame, in the intervals between, making a speech and playing off a variety of buffoon tricks, and the whole closed with a feast and a dance from Sat-sat-sak-is, the king's son.

According to Charles Nowell, the Kwakiutl believed the soul stayed with the body when a man was alive and when he died his soul became a ghost:

The ghost lives until he dies and then goes to another world or returns to his relatives and comes to be born again. If he don't return to his relatives he goes to another world. We call this the second death. They say this second death is long after the first and is when he has rotted and decayed.

According to Boas the Kwakiutl believed that the spirits of the dead are always poor and hungry. When a shaman dreamed that the soul of a deceased person was hungry, he requested the survivors to burn food and clothing for them. The soul could only use objects that had been burned. This explains the burning of property, recorded by Jewitt. As for the soul itself, it "has no bone and no blood for it is like smoke or a shadow."

OF MAGIC AND GHOSTS

17

The religious concepts of the Northwest Indians, involving magic and a host of supernatural beings of all sorts, were never organized into a generally accepted scheme with hierarchies of importance and firmly established attributes and relationships. One of the circumstances which militated against this was the matter of a privately owned mythology which, as we have indicated before, was a part of the intangible but valuable property belonging to specific families and lineages. Hence, informants often differed in their notions of the supernatural realm. There was, however, a certain amount of shared belief. There was, in several areas, a remoter creator, a more or less supreme being who was sometimes said to have created the cosmos and withdrawn or who was sometimes said to be a transformer who merely rearranged things. Sometimes he seems to have been identical with the Atlas-like character who supported the earth. In the case of the Haida, the latter was the Sacred-One-Standing-and-Moving who stood on a copper box. He had a pole on his chest which held up the sky and when he moved there were earthquakes, before which a marten used to run up and down the post causing a great noise. The Tsimshian said it was an old woman who held up the pole. On the other hand, the Bella Coola felt that the earth was flat, resting upon water, and was prevented from capsizing by a being who lived in the far north and held a rope fastened to the earth kept very taut so that it pulled the world against his feet. The same people felt that east was up, south was down, north was the very bottom and west merely opposite to south. Supports—posts—had been built in early times to hold up the sky.

Most groups were generally agreed that there were several realms. The sky was a bowl and several supernatural beings lived above it, according to the Haida. The upper world below the dome was the home of the sun, moon, and stars and the Thunderbird, according to the Kwakiutl. This could be reached by a chain of arrows, according to one Tsimshian myth in which an Indian did so in Jack-in-the-Beanstalk style to rescue his child. Or one could fly up in the form of a bird or perhaps reach it by a ladder. The Bella Coola said no one had been there, and all that was known came from the accounts of the first people, who had come down from it in the beginning.

The Haida believed that Power-of-the-Shining-Heavens, another type of supreme deity, lived there who gave power to all things. They sometimes prayed to him for health.

On the other hand, it was Sacred-One-Standing-and-Moving who, when he was traveling around (before he assumed his stationary task), had killed the first mallard duck and put the grease in a large clam shell. He then put hot stones in it so that the grease ran over. The inhabitants of the forest cried out, "Don't! The grease might spill!" Now, all Haida being divided into Raven and Eagle moieties, the supernaturals followed the same division, and Sacred was a Raven. Hence all Ravens cry out this phrase when there is an earthquake. There is a string from the pole holding up the sky, and if anyone throws a stone at a buffle-headed duck, the duck pulls the string and the mallard feathers come down from on top of the pole—they are the snow. The clouds, however, are the Thunderbird's festive garments. According to the Haida, in this upper realm, which is just below the sky dome, there is a house suspended in the air in which lives Raven, who is a shaman and pulls a stick from a bundle every time a child is born.

Raven is credited by both the Haida and the Tlingit with creating the earth; in fact he was the Tlingit supreme being, remaining, at the same time, partly a trickster. He is called Laxha by the Tsimshian.

The earth, which consisted of the Queen Charlotte Islands and the mainland, which was also an island to the Haida, was, in one version, created when Raven threw stones into the water. He also created trees and, according to both Haida and Tlingit, he created the various bodies of water by spitting. How he brought light to the earth will be recounted in a later chapter.

Both the Kwakiutl and the Bella Coola agreed that there is a land under the earth where ghosts live and where everything is backward—people walk on their heads and the sun rises in the west. They have a village like that of human beings, according to the Kwakiutl, with a chief called Wealth-Coming-Up. He keeps a naked harem on the left side of his house. If a man arrives from the world above and succumbs to them, he can never return to earth, nor can he if he eats the food of the ghosts (recall the myth of Proserpina); but if he controls himself they will lead him along a trail behind the house and send him home.

Whatever is burned in a potlatch—canoes, food, blankets—goes to the realm of the ghosts. However, the Bella Coola felt that the ghosts, with their weird green faces, could rise up and visit earth. They communicated by the whistle language. They were considered to be the patrons and power givers for certain winter dancers.

The Kwakiutl had a good deal to say about the upper world. There is a strong wind blowing there and, strangely enough, there is also an entrance door from under the sea which is near the zenith and can be reached by a diver as he holds his breath and traverses the sea under a mountain. The inhabitants of the upper world come through the door as infants to be reborn. The chief of the sky has the sun and moon as his children. The sun wears ear ornaments of abalone shell and impregnates mortal women with his rays. Ancestors of the Kwakiutl live in the sky in the form of the Thunderbird or his younger daughters. They can fly down from heaven and assume human form. The house of the Thunderbird, where the ancestors live, has murals of the sun and moon to the left and right and the Thunderbird over the doorway.

Since the Northwest Indians have always been fishermen, much is made in their mythology of the undersea realm. The Nootka believed that the undersea world was not far from Vancouver Island and in it the Salmon and Herring people lived, taking off their fish guise when they gave potlatches. Here, too, lived the Whales and Hair Seals, their houses being entered through caves on a certain island. Curiously enough, Wolves were a tribe connected with Killer Whales. (The Haida mention a grizzly bear with fins.) The Haida thought the Killer Whale People were very dangerous. They had many towns in the undersea realm and the other fish peoples served them. They tell the following story:

> Once a man and his canoe passed a Killer Whale and struck its fin with a stone. The following morning smoke was seen from a nearby point and he and his companions went to see who it was. When they got near, they saw a man mending his canoe, which had a break in the side. The man called out to him, saying "why did you break my canoe?" From this they know that the Killer Whales are the canoes of the ocean people.

This, of course, is not consistent with the importance of the Killer Whales, but, from what has gone before, it can already be seen that there is no consistency in Northwest belief. In fact, the lack of coherent conceptions of the supernatural world is fairly typical of preliterate peoples, who do not have an organized guild of priests who have developed the literary talent to coordinate disparate myths into epics. Like the White Queen, such people can accept many contradictory things at the same time, and this also accounts for the ability to accept some version of Christianity and at the same time to retain a good many ideas of the traditional culture.

To return to the sea, the Kwakiutl seemed to divide the realm of the water into two parts. The Salmon Chief lived beyond the ocean in the west. To reach it by canoe, it was necessary to travel to the place where all the driftwood, charcoal, toilet sticks (the Indians used sticks for toilet paper), feathers, and sand go. Here the sand appeared like land—but if the unwary person stepped on it he sank and was drowned. One myth tells of an Indian who passed the house of the Sea Lion and Killer Whale successfully, thus obtaining them as crests. This traveler passed the post holding up the sky, at the foot of which there were seals, whales, and a cannibal dancer. Reaching the house of the Salmon Chief, the lucky man was regaled with cups of fish oil and more special powers.

The other realm described by the Kwakiutl is under the ocean. The ruler of the undersea kingdom—the Master-of-the-Sea—is like a great halibut. People are standing along its edges and on its back. It is so big that it is hard to find its head, which is like that of a seal. When it moves upward, the water begins to grow shallow and dangerous tides flow toward shore. (In several myths, by tricking an old woman, Raven establishes the regular rise and fall of the tides.) The Master-of-the-Sea was also conceived as having a house with posts and crossbeams of sea lions. Or, it is said, his house was all of copper. To visitors he gave valuable property, food, and prestigious dances. He was sometimes considered to be the owner or master of the herrings.

When it came to the creation of man, the task was generally credited to Raven. According to the Tlingit, not only did he make the warm and beneficent south wind but also the cold killing north wind. The Tlingit went so far as to say that he made the post which holds up the earth from the bone of a beaver's foreleg. They have no doubt that he made men. He also made a dog, which started out as a human being. At first this human did whatever Raven told him; but then he became a little too quick to understand. The gods have always been jealous of too much human intelligence—which is, of course, why human beings have made such a muddle of their history. At any rate, Raven was not planning to have any trouble with the creature he had created, so he pushed him down and said, "You are nothing but a dog. You shall have four legs."

The Haida say that Raven made figures like men out of old rotten wood. He then told them to get up. When they did so they walked about like men. He made the leg of one shorter, and when he told the figure to get up it rose and walked lame. When Raven saw the man walked lame he laughed at him and said that he had made a mistake in making one leg short. That is why even today some people have one leg shorter than the other. But when Raven made the sexes he sometimes made a mistake. When he saw the result he said, "This will be half woman and half man." The Northwest Indians do not seem to have had the concept of the transvestite, which the Plains Indians called *"berdache"* and accepted socially.

Raven said people shall live like stones and never die, but a small wren objected. He said, "Where shall I call if men live forever?" He was accustomed to call under a burial box. (The Haida, after cremation, were generally accustomed to place the ashes in a box in the niche in the back of the memorial pole or in a box placed on top.) Raven heeded this rather frivolous objection and withdrew human immortality. The Tsimshian have a more serious explanation for the loss of immortality. There was once a cliff on the shore of the Nass River and at the same time an elderberry bush in bloom. The cliff was apparently pregnant, but the elderberry bush bore its children first. If the cliff had reproduced first, men would have been immortal and their skin would have been hard as stone. Since the bush bore first, they are mortal and their skins are soft. Only the nails on their hands and feet show what their skin would have been like if the cliff had given birth first.

The Bella Coola, however, associate Raven with the cause of death. Raven's son was carried by supernatural means to the Story Man's house, but Raven went about so grief stricken that the supernaturals had pity on him and the boy was returned—unfortunately without his long flowing hair. It had been blown off by the gale which roars through the upper world. Raven did not recognize his son and threw him out of his house. Only too late did he recognize the tattooing on his legs. But the boy was gone forever. If Raven had known him, all men would have risen from the other world four days after their death.

It was also the Bella Coola who had a version of the myth

dealing with the proper technique of sex, often a comic theme in the lore of other preliterates. In the beginning of time the sex organs of women were on their foreheads, those of men on the palm of the hand. Sexual intercourse came about by a man rubbing his hand across a woman's forehead. Raven studied this process and came to the conclusion that from it children would not be produced. He saw to it that the sex organs of both men and women were moved to their present position. Then he picked out a woman and (as precursor of all the sex manuals) carefully showed the men how to do it. He told his cooperating partner that, if this enjoyable process were repeated often, a child would be born. Sure enough: in nine months she had a child. Raven told the Bella Coola to repeat this process energetically and often so as to populate the valley of their river.

The Northwest Indians recounted a flood, as we shall see when we deal with the saga of Raven; but the Tsimshian sound suspiciously as if they had been influenced by Christianity. According to them, in the beginning the earth was almost smooth, with only gentle hills. In those days there was a village on the Upper Skeena, whose inhabitants were very bad people. They were wiped out in a flood, after which the face of the earth was changed and great mountains were formed. A Kwakiutl story tells us what happened after the flood. The earlier men and animals were turned into animals and stones. After the water subsided the Dreadful-Only-One (evidently the same as the Master-of-the-Sea) emerged from the depths of the ocean. He looked like an immense halibut and he carried a man on his narrow side to the shore at the mouth of the Nimkisch River and disappeared again into the deep.

The man looked around at the earth and saw no one. Therefore he called himself "He-Who-Comes-Alone-upon-the-Earth." He had a son named Little Chief. They started a fire on the shore and sat beside it. Then one day Kanigyilak, a warlike spirit who seems to have been an aspect of the Cannibal at the North End of the World, arrived in his canoe and landed on the same shore.

He sat by the fire on one side, He-Who-Comes-Alone-upon-the-Earth and Little Chief on the other. He wanted to show his power to them, so he laid some fish he had with him on the fire and roasted them. Little Chief wanted to eat the fish. His father held his hand below and caught the dripping fat, which he gave to his son. Then Kanigyilak broke the fish and gave it to the two to eat. He thought they would die because the fish were *sisiutl* ("two-headed snakes"), but they were unharmed. He-Who-Comes-Alone-upon-the-Earth also had *sisiutl.* He roasted them and gave them to Kanigyilak, who was much astonished and turned the two men into ducks. But it so happened that they soon turned back into people. Again they sat by the fire—whereupon Kanigyilak turned them into two great mountains. These, too, soon regained human form. Then He-Who-Came-Alone-upon-the-Earth transformed Kanigyilak three times but could not stop him from regaining his normal shape. When Kanigyilak saw that neither could win they became friends and he resumed his travels.

The *sisiutl* was an imaginary creature which we shall encounter in Northwest ceremonial. Supernaturals were generally believed to have preceded men in peopling the cosmos. The Bella Coola said in the past they had more contact with human beings, less so in recent times because they dislike the sound of firearms. This group believed they could be controlled by shamans. The Haida had a specific recipe for control: They could be killed by cutting them in two and throwing a whetstone between the halves which resulted in the two parts' grinding themselves to pieces.

In the supernatural area animals, of course, play a tremendously important role. What I have elsewhere called the "double image," a concept of the interchangeability of men and animals, combined with what in earlier anthropology was called totemism—that is, belief in descent from an animal ancestor—is fairly universal in the Northwest. It was not only the animal ancestor, who was a supernatural, who gave special privileges to a lineage; individuals too could have experiences with spirit animals which also resulted in the granting of power. This has sometimes been described in other areas as a guardian spirit and like the Plains Indians, for instance, the power given was sometimes obtained by asceticism, ordeals, and specific rigorous disciplines, such as washing or rubbing the body with hellebore.

According to the Bella Coola, the supernatural animals had a chief called the Light Giver or the Story Man, who created myths and used the sun as a canoe. He made the four carpenters who cut the posts which held up the sky. On the walls of his house of myth hung the bird and animal cloaks of the first double-image supernaturals. The Bella Coola had first choice of these shapes. When they came down to earth they took them off. Thus knowledge of these first double-image ancestors was important lineage data embodied in privately owned myths. When a Bella Coola died his spirit traveled back to the spot where the ancestor had come down. There he put on his appropriate cloak and floated up to the sky to dwell in the house of myth.

The Story Man was far from a supreme creator, for he was sometimes outwitted by Raven or even human beings with strong magic, and he had a weakness for mortal women, with whom he sometimes had affairs. Impeded by a supernatural Grizzly Bear, who interrupted his activities, Story Man was accustomed to lead the winter ceremonial dances in the house of myths.

The Nootka had a charming version of supernatural animals, who were really shamans. Squirrels, mink, and sometimes Raven could be seen in the woods, singing, dancing, and shaking tiny rattles. They could make old rotten logs writhe and groan. The Bella Coola believed that animals were immortal; it was only their clothing—worthless blankets of flesh—which was killed and eaten. On the other hand, curiously enough, unusual behavior on the part of dogs was a bad omen. If a man's dog spoke to him, it had to be killed immediately to prevent some catastrophe from occurring. It was also generally known that animals could converse together. They had their own houses, ceremonies, and dances; the grizzly bear and the wolverine being particularly gifted as shamans.

The Bella Coola also had considerable lore concerning the supernaturals who lived under the sea, who wore long hair and whose faces were stained black. The Lord-of-the-Sea-Spirits lived in an underwater house with walls decorated with murals of sea animals and seaweed. Wearing a huge hat, he was served by blackfish. He was able to suck down canoes in whirlpools, and he often ate those who drowned. There was a story of four fishermen who were annoyed by a lardfish, which they killed. Suddenly they found themselves in the undersea house. Here an old woman told them that only false hellebore could save them because the Lord-of-the-Sea-Spirits was calling his chiefs to a cannibal feast. The chiefs arrived, causing whirlpools. The four Indians luckily had false hellebore, which they tossed out, preventing their canoe from being capsized. Thus they defeated their host, who gave them shamanistic powers.

The Bella Coola believed in a number of Hieronymous Bosch grotesques which could be either helpful or harmful. The Hermaphrodite served as a guardian of the children of supernaturals and was mimed in the winter dance festival. There was the Death Bringer with a black face whose function was to seduce women, causing them to hemorrhage and die. Another lethal being caused death from falling trees or rock slides.

Then there was the Boqs, which had a penis so long that it had to be carried coiled up. It once took a fancy to a mortal woman and passed its penis under a stream (curiously enough, also one of Coyote's feats) and while it enjoyed her she was unable to move. Then there was the Haohao, a huge bird with a long flexible beak (its also appeared masked in dances). This being was quite dangerous, for it would insert its beak into the anus of an unwary sleeper and pull out his entrails. This could be prevented, however, by leaving a staff upright in the ground before going to sleep.

The Nootka also contributed their share of grotesque conceptions. A mysterious right hand, rising from the earth and shaking a rattle, gave shamanistic power. A left hand, in contrast, brought death to anyone who saw it. There were dangerous dwarfs who lived in houses inside mountains and enticed mortals to dance with them around a wooden drum. Sooner or later they would stumble against it and become infected with a disease called "earthquake foot." With every step these people took, the earth shook. They did not live long. Most curious was the belief that there were huge quartz crystals in high mountain caves. These swayed back and forth with a humming sound. A myth told of a man who plucked one such crystal from the center of a cave and it became night all over the world.

The concept of a detachable spirit in human beings was fairly general. It was the task of shamans to recover it when it went astray. The Bella Coola localized it in the back of the neck, resembling a thin bone, shaped like a maple leaf.

All the myths which we have been sketching, though varied and often conflicting, do have a certain character. If the lore of the supernatural does not deal with the concept of rewards or punishments and is seldom moralizing, it does stress respect for animals, which should not be wantonly destroyed, nor should the food they bestow wasted. Similarly propitiation—magical precautions which might be called worship—dealt mainly with animals. Although, as we have indicated, there was some praying to a remote creator deity, more important and immediate concern was the proper attitude toward, for instance, the salmon. We have recorded how, even in the narrative of Mackensie, the explorer related how the Bella Coola took away his iron kettle because the salmon were running and the Indians believed these fish did not like the smell of iron. The phenomenon of the salmon which ran up the rivers to spawn every year in enormous numbers and thus provided a staple food was naturally impressive and cause for much mythology.

Since the Salmon were supposed to be immortal and a race of supernatural beings who lived much as the Indians did and put on their garments of salmon to sacrifice themselves for the good of mankind, it is easy to see why the Northwest Indians were careful never to offend them. They had to be treated with respect, and any behavior that might anger or "shame" them—for they were touchy, like the Indians themselves—was to be avoided. This was not exactly worship, but rather magical precaution, and it is characteristic of the behavior of most hunting and fishing tribes toward their benefactors. As Malinowski pointed out, preliterates are not without their scientific preoccupations, in that they are careful observers of nature, both animal and vegetable, and make use of their knowledge in their daily lives. All of them, however, feel there is an unpredictable element in the world which can only be controlled or manipulated by the formulas of magic; hence the innumerable rites and taboos which must be respected in connection with practically any human activity. Nevertheless, the attitude toward their animal benefactors works out to an instinctive ecological good sense, in dramatic contrast to the heedless destructiveness of the so-called civilized man. In many cases it was believed that all the salmon bones must be returned to the water or the eternal double-image creature might miss some of them and be unable to return up the stream the following year. The Kwakiutl not only prayed that the salmon and olachen would accept their gratitude on arriving in the spring but that they would come again the following year. On the whole they felt that all of nature was imbued with magic power; they prayed to a tree before felling it, to dangerous rocky islands and points, to tools before using them, to plants used as medicine. In short, the magical essence which has been called mana, which can be either helpful or harmful, was in everything and to be propitiated or controlled.

A Kwakiutl prayer to a beaver after killing it went as follows:

> Welcome, friend Throwing-down-in-One-Day, for you have agreed to come to me. I want to catch you because I wish you to give me your ability to work, that I may be like you; for there is no work you cannot do, you Throwing-down-in-One-Day, you Tree-Feller, you Owner-of-Weather, and also that no evil befall me in what I am doing, friend.

The Kwakiutl prayer to the salmon is also sincere and dignified. After catching nine sockeye salmon a Kwakiutl strung them on a ring of cedar withes and said:

O Swimmers, this is the dream given by you, to follow the example of my late grandfathers when they first caught you at your play. I do not club you twice, for I do not wish to club your spirits to death so that you may go home to the place where you come from, Supernatural Ones, you, givers of heavy weight. I mean this, Swimmers, why should I not go to the end of the dream given by you? Now I shall wear you as a neckring, going to my house, Supernatural Ones, you, Swimmers.

He took them into his house, placed them on a mat and continued:

O, Swimmers, now I come and take you into my house. Now I will go and lay you on this mat which is spread on the floor for you, Swimmers. This is [according to] your own saying when you came and gave a dream to my late grandfathers. Now you will go.

The attitude in various magical acts varied from merely symbolic—such as a pregnant woman dropping pebbles down inside her dress in order to have an easy birth—to the prayers cited above, which are definitely tinged with supernatural awe. Magical avoidance was also practiced in the Northwest. The Tlingit avoided direct address by a man to his mother-in-law. And when digging soft-shell clams, which can easily disappear into the sand, the clammer would cry out, "Don't go down so fast—you'll hit your mother-in-law in the face."

Though taboos were sometimes thought of as bringing down the anger of supernaturals, many simply brought their own punishment. Magical recipes, like so many other elements of the culture, were often privately owned and could be practiced with success only by members of a family. If they were used for the benefit of others, payment was expected. For instance a Bella Coola recipe for training a dog to be a successful hunter of mountain goats consisted of breaking the head of a wolf or wolverine and, after smoking it for four days, letting the blood drip on the head of the puppy. The wolf or wolverine head was then to be buried beneath a spot where mountain goats had been sleeping. It was dug up four days later and concealed in the ground under a shelving rock by which it would be protected from rain. The dog would not only grow up to be an expert on mountain goats but would also absorb the bravery of the wolf or wolverine.

In the training of warriors, it was apparently customary to burn a nest of wasps and sprinkle the ashes on an infant's face. So strong was the effect that an old Bella Coola who beat his wife explained that this had been done to him and, since he was no longer able to be a warrior, he had no other outlet. His wife accepted this explanation tranquilly.

Crying children need to be controlled because such weeping could cause the death of a relative, thus justifying tears. The Bella Coola formula was for a man of even temper to place the child in a large basket which would swing with its every movement. When the child cried the man would say, "Cry as much as you like. If you become hoarse like a heron, you will turn into one."

Love potions and charms to attract the affection of the other sex, which seem to be universal among mankind, were certainly not lacking in the Northwest area. The Kwakiutl man proceeded as follows: he first got hold of some combing of the woman's hair, which he deposited in a dry place, on top of a post. Then he got four pebbles over which she had urinated. Then he gave her fair warning that if she did not give in he would use witchcraft. If she refused, he got a snake, put it in a box, and placed the hair and stones in the snake's mouth. The pebbles, when swallowed by the snake, would cause the woman to urinate blood; the hairs would give her a headache. His incantation to the snake went as follows: "I pray you, friend, take pity on me, on account of my prayer to you and please help me. Now you will turn the mind of the one I try to bewitch, friend!" If the woman did not give in, she would die.

A woman used the hair of the man she wanted to attract, snake skin, and the skin of a toad. These were tied in a bundle and worn in the waistband.

Sex, of course, has always been considered by preliterates to be deeply imbued with mana. As we have mentioned before, the taboos against women which seem to derive from fear of their sexual processes are in full force among the Northwest Coast Indians, who avoided contact with females before embarking on important hunting activities or going to war and segregated girls for long periods at puberty and during menstruation. The Bella Coola, however, had a specific technique for manipulating sexual power, which they seemed to believe could be controlled. Sometimes they merely practiced continence before hunting or war, but they also believed in the value of intense sex activity after continence. For instance a man might be continent for four nights then indulge in sex until exhausted. Then came eight nights of continence—and then more intense sex activity. This formula could go up to 12 and 14 nights, four of course being the sacred number, after which the man would be sure to have enormous success in hunting.

On the whole it can be seen that religious activity in the Northwest was diffused over the whole culture, in the very lineage theories of the social structure, in the dances and ceremonials and also in the small rituals of daily life. In fact, no hard and fast line can be drawn between religion and magic; one shades off into the other, and both are evidence of a firm belief in an unseen power over and above daily reality.

We have so far been dealing with magic, religion, and the supernatural in a general way. We have still to discuss the specific cycle of Raven stories which—among all of the groups except the Coast Salish, where he is a minor figure and his place is partly taken by Bluejay—almost amounts to a saga. In a sense the Raven cycle might be called the Bible of the Northwest Indians.

THE EPIC OF RAVEN

18

We have already had occasion to mention the ubiquitous character Raven several times. He is a personage with counterparts all over the nonindustrial world. He is basically the trickster, but he also shades into culture hero and magician—with episodes in which he is pure schlemiel. It has been suggested that he is the oldest god, and in sophisticated mythologies he lurks on the edge of the pantheon, not quite part of it. He is always an animal in preliterate stories, yet part of the time not an animal—indeed he is an outstanding example of what I have called the double image, the man-beast or beast-man, an interplay of characterization which is found in all oral literature. It will no doubt always be a psychological mystery why in different areas certain animals crystallize in popular story telling as the trickster—why in Africa Anansi, the spider, plays the role; why Kaggan, the mantis, in Australia; in Malaya the mouse deer; among the Plains Indian the coyote; in the United States Brer Rabbit; and on the Northwest Coast the raven. The main qualification such an animal must have is that of being not too big and not too strong or powerful, because the trickster is an underdog who, when he succeeds, generally triumphs over a larger and stupider beast.

When he operates as a pure unadulterated trickster, he clearly fits into Freud's formulation of the id in conflict with the superego, which is the Establishment. The situation borders on Lévi-Strauss's notions of the cooked and uncooked, the various mediations and conflicts between nature and civilization. But the cooked-uncooked imagery is oversimplified. When the trickster is found in conjunction with another character, they are generally brothers. The two-brothers mythology occurs all over the world with the trickster, who is disreputable and even evil, linked to the good citizen, who symbolizes the virtues of society and has to endure all sorts of indignities and injuries from the wicked twin. Sometimes the latter seduces his brother's wife; sometimes, when he plays the role of Cain, he kills him.

Raven, as we have said, plays several roles. In the north, especially among the Tlingit and the Haida, he is creative and a culture bringer. We remember that, when the Tlingit first saw La Perouse's ship, they were awestruck and thought it was Raven. Likewise, when the Reverend Green incautiously asked the Haida who made the world, they were happy to tell him it was Raven. Many of the stories are found in all sorts of variants in all the areas, except that of the Salish.

One universal tale is the deluge. What follows is the Tlingit version:

Once a brother and a sister were the only people living in a certain place. The brother wanted no one but his sister and himself but she was very lonely. [In some versions the characters are a husband and a pretty wife of whom he is jealous.] One day the girl walked along the shore and climbed up on a rocky point above a small clear pool. As she sat there crying and thinking how lonely she was she noticed a small white pebble, in the pool below, which was shaped like an egg. Still crying she walked down and got the pebble and swallowed it, thinking it would kill her. After a while she realized she was to have a child, but she did not want her brother to learn about it for fear he would try to kill the baby. After the child, who was Raven, was born, he grew so rapidly that she had difficulty in hiding him. She walked along the beach calling for help from the animals of the forest and the birds of the sky. She got every sort of answer from each of them when she asked, "What can you do?" She wanted her child to be trained to be strong and brave so that her brother could not harm him. Finally the Crane answered her pleas, saying "I'll raise your child." She asked again, "What can you do?" The Crane answered, "I stand in the water winter and summer alike. I will raise your boy that way." She was glad and gave the boy to the Crane, who took him down to the beach and out into the cold water every day. The boy rapidly grew into a strong and hardy young man, for that was the way, in olden times, people treated their brave men. When Raven grew up Crane sent him back to his mother. His uncle was very angry and tried to kill him. First he sent him for wood and caused a tree to fall on him. Since he was born from a pebble, the tree broke over his head and did not harm him. Then his uncle tried other ways, but each time he was outwitted. Finally the uncle told Raven that he was going to cause a flood. The water began rising and Raven went out and commanded the tides to stop. Then the uncle commanded them to rise and Raven could not stop them. Realizing that he was beaten by his uncle's stronger magic, Raven went out and shot a bird similar to a sandpiper. He put the birdskin on and flew up into the sky. There he was entertained by the sun. [In one version he married Sun's daughter and stayed there a long time before venturing to earth again.] He put the birdskin on again and flew until he was tired. Finally he saw a thick cloud and stuck his bill into it. How long he hung there no one knows but the waters finally receded. Raven prayed for a good grassy spot on which to light and then let go of the cloud. He landed safely and removed the birdskin.

This universal deluge story portrays Raven as an invincible magician and almost a culture hero. The creation or discovery of the salmon makes him a benefactor. The beginning of the Tlingit version is interesting because of the concept of the Fog Woman. Fog is associated with rivers in which salmon abound.

Raven was fishing with two slaves and was returning to camp when a heavy fog settled over the bay. Suddenly he saw a woman sitting in their canoe. She asked for a spruce root basket, put it on her left side, and began to collect the fog in it. Soon it was bright and sunny as they reached camp.

The woman becomes his wife and produces salmon—but for the latter part of the tale we turn to the Kwakiutl, who contribute more interesting details.

In the time of the very ancient people they were hungry. Kwakwina, the Raven, leaned against a tree and thought. Then he went to his canoe and paddled along close to a rock and asked of the dead people, "Is there any twin child among you?" One after another the bodies of the dead answered no, but after a while he came to one who said she was a twin child. He laid the coffin on the ground, removed the bones, and laid them in their proper relation. Then he sprinkled the living water four times over them and they came alive. Raven brought this woman to the Narrows and then sent all the people in their canoes to bring round stones, which they piled up at the rapids of the Narrows until the water became shallow. Then Raven said, "Now, young brothers, get split cedar sticks. We will make a salmon trap." In one day they had all the necessary sticks, and when the weir was complete they put their basket traps in place. Deer set his in the middle but being a fool did not have an opening in it by which the salmon could enter. When all was ready Raven commanded his new wife to walk into the water below the weir. As soon as the water reached her waist, the stream was filled with salmon and the traps were quickly filled. These were the first salmon and they came from the woman's body. The woman told the people to throw all the bones and other refuse into the water so that new salmon would spring from them. It is for this reason that the refuse from the first catch of the season is returned to the water. When Raven came home from gathering fuel the house was filled with fish. He entered the house, but some drying salmon hanging low caught in his hair and he muttered, "Oh why do you catch in my hair, you that are from the dead?" The woman answered quickly, "What did you say?" I said, "Why do you catch in my hair, you that are drying?" "No, you said, 'You that are from the dead.' " She looked up at the fish, clapped her hands, and cried "Wee!" And all the salmon fell down and rolled into the water where they at once became alive and began to jump and swim. The woman disappeared at the same time. Then Raven leaned back and thought. He called his fighting men together and said, "We will prepare to fight with some tribe. Get your weapons ready." When they were ready, he told them he was going to make war on the Salmon people in order to recover his wife. On the beach opposite the Salmon village they hauled out their canoes and Raven crossed secretly to a place where he found the young son of the Salmon Chief and kidnapped him. When the Salmon found that the child was missing, they sent messengers to all the fish people from the Smelts to the Killer Whales. Now Raven and his paddlers saw the water behind them boiling with the commotion caused by the canoes of the fish people. Soon the pursuers overhauled them, but Raven's son broke their canoes with his stone club and the fish people finding themselves in the water had to assume their fish forms in order to escape drowning. Raven, standing in his canoe, was seizing this one and that one and throwing them in every direction, exclaiming, "You will be the salmon for this river! You will be the olachen for that river." And so he designated all the places where the salmon and the other fish were destined to be found.

In the Tlingit version the story does not have a successful ending: Raven merely loses both wife and fish and is left hungry and disgusted. Notable in the Kwakiutl version is the connection between the creation of fish and the wife's sexuality. More often, as we have seen, the magical mana of female sexuality is considered dangerous and all sorts of sanctions are used as a defense against it. We have already cited the fact that on the Northwest Coast girls are segregated for long periods at the time of their menarche. Likewise warriors refrain from sex before battle and whalers also before pursuing such important prey as the whale. Yet here female sexuality is regarded as a source of abundance.

Another element in the tale is the reference to Deer as a fool. In a Bella Coola story a deer is again a victim:

Not long after people had reached this earth, Raven met Buck. "Let us go to some quiet spot," he said, "where I shall sing of your ancestors and you of mine, who they were and so forth. I know a good place on that mountain over there." Buck was at first unwilling but at length consented to follow Raven to the brink of the canyon, where the two sat down. Then Raven said, "Go ahead, you sing first." "No," Buck replied, "you first. I have no fit story." So Raven began to sing. "Buck is an ugly fellow. His legs are skinny and he has a long nose." This made Buck very angry. When his turn came, he retaliated by singing of Raven's ugly feet and beak. Then Raven shoved his companion over the edge of the cliff and the fall killed him. Raven flew down croaking happily and began to feast on the grease which he pecked from Buck's entrails, some of which he carried away to a hiding place of his own. In his joy he could not refrain from mocking a nearby stump. "Stump," he said, "has no good food like mine." When next Raven flew away with some of the grease, Stump fell by his own power and covered Buck completely. Raven, much distressed, repeatedly begged Stump to move, but the latter refused to budge and continued to cover Buck's carcass.

This biter–bit type of plot is typical of the trickster tale, in which the character who is all appetite overreaches himself. In nearly all of the episodes of his saga, Raven is drawn as intolerably greedy. Another Tlingit tale deals with this appetite. In this case he was walking along the beach when he saw a whale far out to sea. He planned how he might kill it. He flew out over the monster; when it rose to breathe, he went into its mouth. First, he made a fire in its stomach and cooked the fish it had swallowed. Then he cut pieces of blubber from the whale's insides and ate them but, of course, this ended in the whale's death. Then he sang, "I wish the whale would drift to a fine sandy beach." It soon did, to a beach at the end of a village. When the young people hurried out to cut up the prize they heard a voice singing, "I wish there was a man strong enough to cut open the whale." Frightened, the young people ran back to the village. Finally strong men did come to cut open the whale, whereupon Raven, dripping grease, flew out and away to clean himself. The people of the village, who did not recognize him, made up a song ridiculing the greasy one. Raven was so ashamed he never came back. Meanwhile they ate his whale.

It will be seen, from the examples already cited, how the animal–human characteristics are woven in and out of the episodes. At times Raven is a bird among other birds and beasts; at times he is a bird who mingles with human beings; at times he behaves entirely as a human being. In many animal tales, including Raven's exploits, the man–beast changes by taking off his animal skin. In the story of the woman who had puppies, her lover takes off his dogskin at night and, when the wife destroys the skin, he disappears very much in the manner of Cupid in the classical fable of Cupid and Psyche. Raven sometimes puts on a birdskin; another favorite manner of shape changing is putting on a raven blanket which transforms him. It seems clear that the acculturation which made the blanket such a basic item of barter as well as wearing apparel is responsible for the appearance of this detail in Northwest folklore.

Another tale, also Tlingit, describes Raven in the guise of culture hero, bringing daylight. In the days when the world was very dark, Raven wanted to bring about daylight. He went to the Nass River at whose head lived a chief who owned the sun and moon. On the way Raven encountered some fishermen and begged for a little fish. They not only refused but ridiculed him when he promised to exchange daylight for food. They called him lazy and a trickster and told him to go to work. Raven left them angrily and came to the chief's house. The latter had a daughter whom he guarded closely. Everything she ate or drank was inspected and tested. Slaves were on the alert to keep such characters as Raven out of the house. Raven, however, turned himself into a crumb of dirt and got into her drinking basket. The dirt sank to the bottom and was detected and thrown out. Then Raven turned into a pale green hemlock needle and tried it again. Since this was not noticed, the girl drank the water and swallowed it. Presently she became pregnant. The chief was infuriated; he called in great shamans, but there was nothing they could do. When the baby was born, however, he became the idol of his grandparents. But one day the grandmother said, "There is something very queer about this child. Under its skin it feels almost as if there were feathers." Raven grew very fast and soon began to beg for the moon, which hung on the wall of the house. At first this priceless treasure was denied him, but he begged and cried so that finally it was given to him. He stopped crying and rolled it about on the floor. Then he tossed it up through the smoke hole into the sky. He immediately pretended to cry bitterly because he had lost his plaything. Pretty soon he began to beg for a box which contained the light of the world. After a great deal of begging and crying, he wheedled this most priceless possession out of his doting grandparents. This time the slaves watched him closely. There was a big fire in the fireplace creating an updraft. Raven rose on this toward the smoke hole. The chief commanded him to stop—and Raven found himself halted at the smoke hole. Raven concentrated all of his magic in his wings and got away. He soon came to the fishermen who had refused him food. Once more Raven begged but they refused him. He said, "If you don't give me some, I will open this box and frighten you all to death. You will turn into the animals whose skins you wear." Since they paid no heed, he laughed and lifted the cover and with a thunderous flash the world was light. The people turned into sea and land animals and birds and ran away. Those who were naked remained human.

In a Tsimshian story Raven plays the Prometheus role of fire bringer. In an earlier episode he was born into a human family and developed such an appetite that he endangered the food supply of the village and was sent on his travels by his father. As he journeyed about he saw that people were multiplying on the earth, but they had no fire to cook with or to keep them warm in winter. He remembered there was fire in his home village. He put on his Raven blanket and flew home. His father refused him fire and sent him away again. He tried several strategems, but all failed. Then he sent a seagull to announce to the village that a handsome young chief was coming to dance at the village chief's house. He borrowed a canoe from the Great Shark and filled it with his bird cohorts. They arrived, took their places in the dance house, and waited. Meanwhile Raven had killed and skinned a deer. All of a sudden he appeared in the dance house wrapped in the skin, in the likeness of a deer. As he danced, his bird companions sang and clapped. Raven had smeared pitch on the deer's long tail. Now he waved the tail over the fire until it caught. Then he ran out of the house as his bird companions flew away. When Raven's canoe came ashore, he went up to a fir tree, struck it with the flaming tail, and said "You shall burn as long as the years last." This is why the deer has a short black tail.

This unexpected just-so story ending is very characteristic of many of the episodes and indeed the just-so story runs all through preliterate mythology. The Tsimshian have a number of episodes which show Raven in a culture hero role. At one point he encounters the old woman who holds the tide line. He blinds her by throwing dust in her eyes and gets all the clams he wants. When she demands her sight back, he cures her on condition she agrees to slacken the tide line twice a day. It was Raven who saw to it that the olachen swarmed up the Nass River every spring. Two seagulls taught him how to cook by putting red hot stones in water. Unfortunately they called all the other gulls and ate up his olachen. Raven threw them in the fire—which is why the tips of their wings are black.

The Bella Coola story of Raven and Cormorant combines the just-so format with the brutal selfishness characteristic of the true trickster in every social situation. Since he is the embodiment of appetite he is quite without ethics or human feeling. He can be seen as a literary safety valve for all the frustrations which the individual has to undergo when he gives up part of his autonomy in order to live in harmony with his group. Raven and his parallels are like the cartoon characters who beat and injure each other unmercifully while a civilized audience enjoys seeing its most private and disreputable desires acted out. And, like the same characters, when Raven comes a cropper or even seems to be killed, he comes to life, unperturbably ready for the next adventure.

Once upon a time Raven suggested to Cormorant that they go halibut fishing; the latter agreed and they set out in a single canoe. When they started fishing, Cormorant took his place in the bow while Raven stationed himself in the stern. Cormorant, who was an expert fisherman, soon got a fish, then another, then a third, while Raven did not have so much as a bite. He hated to be outdone by his partner, so whenever the Cormorant landed a fish Raven hauled in his line violently as if he too had one on his line and even went through the motion of clubbing a halibut. Cormorant was so much engrossed that he never even turned round. Thus they continued for some time, Cormorant catching fish after fish, Raven pretending to do the same. At length, disgusted but determined to outdo his partner, Raven drew his line into the boat and stood in the bow behind Cormorant. First he admired the other bird's method of baiting his hook. "I have never known anyone who could equal you," said Raven. "That is how you have such success at halibut catching." The cunning fellow went on to praise Cormorant for his method of dropping his line, admired his sharp eyes, his fine teeth, shapely form, and sweet voice. "There is only one part of your body," Raven said, "that I have not been able to admire, and that is your tongue. Please stick it out so that I will have the pleasure of looking at it." The flattered Cormorant stuck out his tongue, and Raven complimented him upon that too. He asked him to put it out a little farther, and when he did so Raven seized it and cut it off. Cormorant gurgled and croaked but could not speak. When they got back to the village, Raven called out, "My partner has had a serious accident to his mouth; he has become dumb." Everyone came to see what had happened, and Raven continued, "I don't know what can be the trouble. Cormorant did not catch any fish. He must be very ill." Cormorant gurgled, hopped to and fro excitedly, in his anger, pointing from the fish to himself, but Raven said, "What he would like to say is true: I caught them all." Cormorant grew more and more frantic. "Yes, yes," said Raven, "don't be in such a hurry.

I will give you some." Raven continued to interpret Cormorant's desperate signs and gurgles as supporting his own lies. Then he gave him one fish and took the rest home. Since that time Cormorant's tongue has been so short that he cannot speak like other birds but can only grunt and gurgle.

On the same order, reminding us of Brer Rabbit's and Reynard the Fox's exploits, is Raven's fishing expedition with Bear. Raven pretended to cut off part of his belly to use for bait for salmon. Bear did the same but actually destroyed himself.

An example of the type of tale in which Raven is destroyed is the Bella Coola story of Raven and Worm:

Once upon a time Raven decided to get some halibut. The only person who understood how to catch this fish was Worm, an old man who lived in a waterlogged stick at the bottom of the ocean. Raven went to him and said, "I have come to pay my respects to you." "Please sit down," said Worm. He took his line, opened a hole in the bottom of his house through which he dropped the cord, and presently hauled up a large halibut, which he killed. Raven watched him with interest and delight. Worm built a fire, boiled the fish with hot stones, and provided a fine meal. It was the first time that anyone had seen a halibut caught and Raven was delighted to have learned how. When the meal was over, he took the food box containing the leftovers with him, promising to return it later. When he got home he gave the food to his sisters without explaining either what it was or where he had obtained it. Raven was determined to get the better of Worm, so the next day he assumed the form of a merganser duck and set out. Taking the food box he flew to a point under the ocean across a river from Worm's house. In that country the bottom of the fiord was like a river. Here Raven lit a large fire. Then still in the form of a duck he flew across to Worm's house. "Good morning, chief," said Raven. (Worm was not a chief; this was Raven's flattery.) "I have brought you good news. I have just met your father and told him where you are. He had lost sight of you for a long time and is delighted at the thought of seeing his son. He is waiting for you by that big fire you can see across the river." "You must have made a mistake," Worm answered. "I have no father. I just grow by myself." "Not at all," Raven answered. "You have made a mistake. You really must come to see your father. If you don't want to walk so far I will carry you on my back." "I have no father," Worm insisted and refused the invitation for a long time; but finally, when Raven said, "Your father is waiting and he gave me instructions to bring you to him—he will be very angry if I do not obey," Worm unwillingly climbed on his back. Raven flew up in the air; presently he side-slipped. "Oh, don't do that," Worm cried, "I am afraid." But Raven flew on until he was in the center of the straight between Worm's house and the fire. Then he side-slipped so violently that his passenger fell off into the ocean. Raven was delighted, quite forgetting that Worm was at home beneath the water. If he had dropped him on land he would have died. Raven flew back to Worm's house while the owner walked across the bottom of the ocean because he could not swim. At the house Raven stole the halibut line, opened the hole in the floor, and threw down the line. While he was waiting he sang a song about his defeat of Worm. Presently he felt a tug and eagerly hauled up the line hoping for a halibut, but it was a waterlogged stick. Raven swore and angrily threw it in a corner. He did not know that Worm had entered the stick in order to get back into his house. Behind Raven's back Worm quietly plugged all the openings in the house. Then he went out and locked the door from the outside. Raven was not having any luck and began to grumble, "Take my hook, old crooked-face: Your eyes are crooked and your ass is on your shoulder." But Halibut heard and would not take his bait. Worm now called the tide. "Please help," he urged. The tide rose up through the floor, to the confusion of Raven. He tried to open the door; he looked for a chink or crack—there was none. The water continued to rise and the thief, floating and half drowned, was forced up to the roof where he managed to stick his beak through a small hole. Worm was outside and Raven begged for help. "I will never do it again," he begged. "I am a poor man and you tried to rob me," the little fellow answered; "I won't help you." Soon the water rose over Raven, who gurgled and ceased to speak. Then Worm told the tide to recede and as soon as his house was dry went to put it in order, first throwing out Raven's body. But the wretch was not really drowned. As soon as the bright sun shone on him, he came to and, wet and bedraggled, limped home.

We have stressed the fact that Raven's unvarying characteristic is greediness. But an inhibited sexual appetite is characteristic of the trickster as well. In the north, where the character is a good deal of a culture hero, it is often mink who assumes the lecherous role. Indian bawdiness runs to detachable sex organs which performed extravagant tricks. For instance, Mink sees Sawbill Duck Woman take off her vulva and put it in a box. He takes it out of the box and has intercourse with it. Raven, himself, however, is capable of sexual greediness, as in the Bella Coola story of his human son:

Once upon a time Raven invited a woman to his home and built for her a fire of the type of fire which gives off numerous sparks. It was so cold that he told his guest to warm herself by sitting naked near the blaze. As she did so a flaming spark jumped out and burnt her between the legs. Raven pretended to be much distressed, told her that he knew of a remedy, a small plant growing in the woods which could be recognized because it wove to and fro. "If you place yourself so that it enters your organs," Raven said, "you will be cured." As soon as he gave this advice, he went into the forest, lay down on his back, covering himself all over with leaves, except for his eyes and his penis. As the woman drew near he waved it to and fro so that she thought it was the plant she was looking for. She was about to squat upon it when she saw his beady black eyes. She shouted at him and Raven flew away, croaking hoarsely. However, he did not give up, and when he came home he told her, "I have just taken a very strong medicine. If you sleep with me you will be cured." "Perhaps," she said, "but your penis is much too long. I will let you come into me only if you put it a little way into my vagina." She showed her vagina to prove how small she was next to his organ. She let him begin but he kept urging her to let him in a little further and then he asked her to move her body along with his so they ended up copulating, the woman giving as much help as possible. "I am most grateful to you," she said when they had finished. "My burn is entirely cured." The woman became pregnant. Much faster than usual a young raven grew within her. Raven suggested that he should pull the young bird out. First he thrust his arm down her throat and pushed the raven into her stomach; then he inserted his beak into her vagina until he could reach the beak of the fledgling bird, which he drew forth croaking from between her legs.

Boas sees the trickster cycles as on the whole fairly unorganized. Viola Garfield, on the other hand, sees signs of progression in which Raven becomes more responsible. In Paul Radin's view, apropos of the Plains character Coyote, the culture hero aspects of the creature are a sophisticated editing superimposed upon the pure folk image by shamanistic shaping. Garfield instances the last episode of the series as the culmination of his transformation. This is the Tsimshian version:

Raven had been away on a trip to the north, and when he flew back in his raven blanket he gave a great feast to all the monsters on the outer islands. He had built himself a new carved house and this was the first potlatch the monsters had attended. He told them he was glad they had come and added, "I wish you would stay and become rocks." They all became rocks. Then he said, "I, too, will become a rock." He became a stone shaped like a raven. The devilfish, however, seeing what was happening, dived quickly and stayed at the bottom of the sea.

When the devilfish comes out of the water the people cry, "Caw! Caw! Caw!" like a raven and the devilfish dies. All around the island are rocks shaped like monsters—whales, killer whales, sharks.

Thus Raven achieves his apotheosis. It is perhaps valid to see the saga of Raven, the trickster, as an expression of the deeper layers of folk consciousness, a mirror of the slow evolution of the heartless greedy individual who is all appetite into the socialized member of the community—an evolution which, unfortunately, is still far from being wholly achieved.

CARVERS OF MAGIC

19

While he was living in the United States, the celebrated French anthropologist Claude Lévi-Strauss wrote:

> Certainly the time is not far distant when the collections of the Northwest Coast will move from anthropological museums to take their place in the art museums among the arts of Egypt, Persia and the Middle Ages. For this art is not unequal to those great ones and unlike them has displayed, during the century and a half of its known development, a prodigious diversity and had an apparently inexhaustible power of renewal.

Indeed, the sculpture and painting of the Northwest Coast has inspired many handsome art books and resulted in exhibitions which have, in turn, elicited the admiration of present-day art critics. Since the bulk of the work had been created in wood—soft cedar at that—tremendous amounts of it have been lost; yet, since there was an efflorescence of culture in the area in the nineteenth century, a substantial number of examples have been preserved in museums, even though many a beautiful totem pole is rotting away in an abandoned village site or at an untended grave.

The history and development of this work is largely conjectural. We do know, from the testimony of many eighteenth-century voyagers, that the tradition which has been preserved was already substantially the same as that at the time of European contacts. There has been elaboration since, especially in the matter of totem poles; but certainly many decades must have elapsed before the coming of the whites for such a formal style and such authority of execution to have been achieved.

The chances are there was an evolution from the simple to the complex. Wilson Duff has published some photographs of stone clubs from the Skeena and Metlakatla area which he assigns to "late prehistoric times." Many of these are very simplified representations of birds, fish, and other animals; one ends in a human head. They are not, apparently, in a shape or balance suitable for actual warfare, but seem to be magical ceremonial objects. The simplification of form and the skillful shaping of the clubs, with their curiously phallic handles, testifies to considerable artistic sophistication. While there is not much to connect them with classical woodcarving tradition, in which the decoration of clubs tends to occur on the handle, one might see a faint foreshadowing of the later treatment of the animal's muzzle in certain masks—reflected, for example, in one club showing an unidentifiable animal snout with an exaggerated row of teeth. Duff says they might provide a hint as to what preceded the classic style.

In this connection we might mention the petroglyphs which are found from Alaska to Puget Sound, which seem to possess similarities of style and thus are associated with the Northwest Coast culture. There are simplified human figures sometimes masked, sometimes wearing headdresses. There are numerous animals and fish in outline form. The commonest examples are pecked-out eyes, sometimes a dot within a circle, and an oblong mouth. These faces may or may not be enclosed in an outline or joined to a body. Edward Meade conjectures that they were pecked out by shamans for ceremonial purposes. Many of them are found in isolated sites difficult to locate. Modern Indians know nothing about them. Occasionally they suggest an image that bears some connection with the classical style. This brings up the question of dating. Some of the rocks on which the glyphs were executed are submerged at medium or high tides. Since it does not seem likely that the workers in stone waited for low tides to do their chipping, it is reasonable to believe that when they were executed tides were lower than today. There were tidal fluctuations from 2000 to 4000 years ago, which might mean that some of the petroglyphs are quite old. Others show details that suggest they fall within the historic period. Another interesting fact is the large number of pecked images which cover some rocks while others which seem available are left bare. The fact that the rocks selected often seem to have been carved successively suggests that they were thought to possess special powers. The carvings have always been found, with a few exceptions, far from village sites, and this suggests that they were secret shrines.

The fact that there is no tradition concerning the petroglyphs, even though Indian ceremonies continued into the nineteenth and even twentieth century, does suggest that they are old and perhaps have some bearing on early artistic traditions on the Northwest Coast. What does emerge is the fact that the earliest graphic art probably consisted of single figures, animal or human. Single human (and sometimes animal) images continued to be made in shamans' figures, potlatch figures, grave figures, and on carved house posts during the classical period.

Going back to written historical evidence, both Meares and Haswell speak of single images carved on house posts, and Bodega says the figure Macquinna had in his house was in memory of his daughter who had just died. We also know from Meares that portal poles through which one entered a house were used in his time among the Nootka. Marchand in 1791 describes both portal and mortuary poles among the Haida, and Alejandro Malaspina speaks of a bear mortuary pole of Tlingit manufacture in 1793.

Archeological artifacts from the Frazer River are in what is called the Wakashan style, a simple, rugged type of sculpture embodying single images. Something similar is preserved in Coast Salish carving which, in turn, is believed to have been influenced by the earliest art of the northern nations. It has also been pointed out by Drucker that some kind of pole or post, painted, plain or simple, or with attached ornaments, was erected at or near the grave over large areas of eastern Siberia and Alaska.

Assuming that the single images came first, aside from shaman ceremonial images, these might have developed simultaneously in an urge to decorate the memorial at the grave and to adorn the house post. These last were, after all, structural and for this reason could have preceded the external pole. The magical shamans' figures may have persisted unchanged from very early times.

There is no doubt that the elaborate multiple-tiered pole developed along with elaboration of the crest and rank system. Even this, as Drucker points out, must have existed long before European contacts, and Marius Barbeau's thesis that it is a product of trader influence can be dismissed, as Duff has shown, on the basis of the historical evidence.

Moreover, the archeologist of the National Museums of Canada, Dr. George Macdonald, points out that radio-carbon technique gives a date of 4500 B.C. for an excavation near the Skeena at Terrace, the material recovered being similar to that of late prehistoric times. Also, in the harbor area of Prince Rupert the discovery of plank house villages that date back to 5000 B.C. are evidence that the culture has been in existence in an unbroken sequence for this period of time.

If we attempt to characterize Northwest art as a whole, the

most convenient descriptive term is expressionistic. The word has been applied to a movement centering in early twentieth-century Germany, but some of Picasso's work, especially that influenced by African sculpture, could also be included. Essentially, most of preliterate art is what we have come to describe as expressionistic now that the term has been absorbed into modern criticism. It is notable how important the influence of so-called "primitive" art has been on the contemporary movement. Specifically, the American Adolph Gottlieb and the Uruguayan Torres García have both absorbed ideas from the creations of the Northwest Coast.

The characteristics of expressionism are the retention of a basic representational image but with the utmost freedom to simplify, distort, or exaggerate in order to produce an emotional effect. Modern artists sometimes used this technique as a means of social comment; the Northwest Coast wished to stress supernatural awe or terror.

Northwest Coast art is not totally expressionistic. The examples shade off to naturalism in some of the human figures and in a number of masks, but the classical style, with its reductions of humans and animals to grotesque and violently dramatic forms, sets the tone of the work created by this highly emotional shame–prestige culture. It speaks to those of us who have been exposed to modern art, with its rejection of the idealized and almost prettified naturalism of the Greeks, even though we do not have the inherited background of mythology which would allow us to appreciate the full impact this art must have had upon its creators. As Lévi-Strauss remarks, "To appreciate it we had to wait for Picasso."

The classical decorative style, which is common to all the groups except the Coast Salish, has been analyzed by William Holm. It is the most distinctive type of Northwest Coast art. It is so closely linked to painting that the carved and painted elements seem to have developed together. Holm separates the elements into *configurative,* which preserves the animal form quite clearly; *expansive,* in which the image is distorted or split; and *distributive,* in which naturalistic form is ignored and formalized elements, which are sometimes hard to recognize, are used. This decorative style is always adapted to the surface or shape which it adorns. It is used in shallow relief and deeply carved relief. As painting alone it appears on house fronts, interior partitions, screens, canoes, spoons, rattles, dressed skins, and body painting.

Eventually, as acculturation took place, new materials were

absorbed. Copper had been surface mined but silver, as a result of trading, and black slate were used, while beads, buttons, and abalone shell were applied to blankets.

As Boas pointed out, animals are identified by a kind of symbolical treatment which stresses certain characteristic details. The beaver, for instance is clearly marked by the large top incisors, the crosshatched tail, and the clawed feet, although the body may be modified and the head highly formalized. The ears stand up above the head. The sculpin is symbolized by two spines and a jointed dorsal fin. The hawk has a large, backward-curving beak, though the face may be semihuman. The killer whale has a long dorsal fin. The wolf's muzzle is long, set with an even row of teeth, and the nose turned up at the end.

Formal treatments of eyes, different for different species, occur; fins, feathers, tails of animals, birds, and fish—all are stylized, and joints are represented by ovoids or circular elements, sometimes eyes. X-ray treatment also occurs, as the artist easily represents what he knows is beneath the exterior, such as the gullet of the wolf or the backbone of the sculpin. In certain painted decorations these pictorial elements are dismembered and some parts of the animal often left out—Holm's distributive effect. The expansive image is simply split down the back and opened out sideways.

Carving was originally done with stone chisels and round stone hammers, the smoothing accomplished with shark skin. Color, before culture contact, consisted of blue-green from oxidized copper and red from earth ocher. Bright Chinese red was eagerly accepted after contact; black came from charcoal and white from clay. The medium used was chewed salmon eggs, which created a paint as durable as the commercial product of the whites. The brushes were hair, often obtained from the porcupine.

The famous Chilkat blanket—which was originated by the Tsimshian and in which the pattern is almost abstract and is divided up into rounded squares—was woven by the women, but the patterns to be followed were painted on boards by the men. The women's own weaving used only geometrical patterns, which, as Boas has shown, develop naturally from the stitches of weaving.

To return to the style which is found from Yakutat Bay to the Bella Coola, Kwakiutl, and Nootka area: we find it characterized by what Holm calls the "form line," a heavy black linear pattern generally connected except for the ovoids of eyes and joints. The ovoid shape is ever-present—heads, bodies, and portions of limbs are fitted into it. The line often changes from thick to thin, which lightens and varies the design. To fill in certain areas simple hatching, crosshatching, and parallel broken lines are used. The beaver's tail, for instance, is crosshatched. Interestingly enough, both bark and leather templates were used in drawing in the ovoids. The artist did not make a preliminary sketch but worked from a pattern in his head.

In carving, the areas of flat surface generally coincided with the black form line. Red usually forms a secondary network, although it sometimes did duty as the form line. The blue-green areas were generally "negative" space between the calligraphic elements of the line. The Northwest artists made total use of their space, avoiding empty areas and creating an even distribution of weight and detail with bold flow of form line. It was a curvilinear art of closed circuits, sharp curves played against gentle curves with horizontal symmetry, but an avoidance of concentric organization.

Actually, the traditional stylized elements became an alphabet of form which could be adapted endlessly, giving scope to the imagination of the individual artist. Holm's distributive or dismembered effect in which this alphabet was shuffled about disregarding naturalistic arrangement very often closely approached abstraction.

The characteristic ovoid, the rounded corners and flowing lines, remind us slightly of certain characteristics of Mayan design, both hieroglyphs and the way images are fitted into certain stelae. Going farther afield, the flowing curves appear in Maori art and, finally farther to the East, we are reminded of the linear designs on certain Shang bronzes of south China produced in the second millennium B.C. While no concrete evidence of diffusion has ever been established, the similarities are tantalizing and raise the never-settled problem of trans-Pacific contacts.

Although, as we have said, this style extended to all of the nations except the Salish, there were individual differences. The Tsimshian were restrained; in the poles they preserved the sense of the shaft, using little color or distortion. The areas were sharply marked off on or above one another. They contrasted groups of small figures against large ones. The Haida, Kwakiutl, Bella Coola, and Nootka carved more deeply, often interlocked their figures and created a bold, dramatic imagery with much color. Tlingit totem poles at least may have been a late development. They were not observed in the Alaskan area until late in the eighteenth century. This, however, is only negative evidence. La Perouse did not see them, but he is quite capable of not thinking them worth mentioning. At any rate, Tlingit pole sculpture is characterized as somewhat weak—thinner poles with the figures separated, a less effective statement. Viola Garfield characterizes Tsimshian sculpture as classic, Haida baroque, Kwakiutl as eclectic, and Tlingit as rococo.

The poles served several functions. One was, of course, the memorial pole erected by a chief's heir, recording the crests that the descendant had inherited. The southern Tlingit and the Tsimshian erected these along the beach in front of the village. The mortuary pole proper was set up alongside the grave of the deceased chief. The house portals recorded the owners' crests and were built into the house front with a large opening as a doorway at the base. Sometimes they were placed at the corners with a mural between. These crests, representing encounters by clan or lineage ancestors with supernatural animals or beings, were thought of as actual history. What follows is a chief's explanation of a wolf clan totem pole of the Kitwancool-Tsimshian which Wee-kha (Ernest Smith) recorded when the pole was donated to the British Columbia Provincial Museum in 1959:

The bird at the top is the giant woodpecker; the figures around the top are the house carvings; next is a large bird, *skim-sim,* the mountain eagle; fourth is a row of carvings representing children or small people, the ones who fish through holes in the ice; the figure at the bottom of the pole holding the child is the important figure Will-a-daugh. The name of the pole is Skim-sim and Will-a-daugh. On these two depends the history of the pole. . . . The story begins a thousand years ago more or less at Ke-an [the present Prince Rupert] where the clan had its village. The chief had many nephews and nieces. One of the nieces of the chief went out to gather wood. She found a wood grub of the kind that eats pines. She had a child from this grub and she put it in a wooden cradle and stood it up against the wall. She sang the baby a lullaby about its little hands that were moving all the time. The child was, of course, supernatural and the hands moved all the time like those of a human child. Unknown to the mother and the chief, the grub worm child had eaten its way through the wood of the house and reached the underground next to the house where it was eating the walls, boxes—everything of wood. It went underground to house after house, and the people could not understand what was eating everything up. Just a part of this "child" was doing that. The people in the house at the end of the village decided to keep a watch on their wooden boxes. They heard a gnawing noise in one box and found it was a huge wood grub. They stabbed it and dug a trench following its huge body, stabbing each part as they discovered it. They followed it right back to the bay in the cradle leaning against the wall. The trench they dug can be seen near Port Rupert by anyone who knows the story. The mother felt very sad at the loss of her child. She went down to the edge of the water and cried over its loss. She made a wish that the water would rise and flood the village. However, the only person drowned was herself, Will-a-daugh. The people got together and the chief decided they would move. They moved to the Nass River and made a village which they called An-lath-gauth-u, which means "to see in both directions." After the village was established the chief went up to the mountain to hunt ground hogs. On the mountain a ground hog spoke to one of the young hunters saying *"hea-uk, hea-uk."* It was telling him that his wife was being unfaithful to him; the word *"hea-uk"* means "she is at it again." The young hunter left the people on the mountain and secretly went down to the village. He arrived late at night when it was very dark and found his wife asleep in bed with another man. The boards of the wall were only tied with roots and he pushed them aside, entered, and killed the man. He looked at the man he had killed and saw that he was a prince, the son of a great chief. He wore chief's clothes. His blanket and robe were trimmed with ermine skins on one side and marten skins on the other from shoulder to the bottom of the robe, about 8 inches apart. At the bottom between the skins were unborn caribou hoofs. (A likeness has been preserved to this day as the ceremonial robe of the Wolf clan.) The chief took the robe off the dead man, with the intention of keeping it, but as he stood holding it he heard a voice calling to him. It was the mother of the dead prince weeping and asking for her son back. The son was really a wolf, Prince of the Wolves, who was impersonating a human being. His name was "One-Who-Killed-and-Ate-Ten-Deer-at-a-Time." He also had a second name meaning "One-Who-Bit-off-the-Ears-of-Deer-and-Ate-Them." [Walter Derrick now carries the name. It is a very valuable name, worth many hundreds of feasts.] The mother kept crying and asking that her son be given back to her. "If you do not give my son back, something terrible will happen to you." The figure of the large bird on the totem pole is the mother of the dead prince and holds the history of the pole and also the funeral song of the wolf clan. As this bird flew over the village she was crying, "Give my son back" and singing the death song *"lou-see-tee-au, lou-see-tee-au, lou-see-tee-au."* Then the bird spoke, "If you do not give me back my son, something dreadful will happen to the village." The chief spoke: "Give her back the robe of her son, the robe you kept." She would not take it from their hands. They put it on the roof but still she would not take it. She kept flying over the village singing the funeral song. Then she sang a funeral song calling for heavy rain to punish the village. It began to rain very hard until streams ran through the village. The chief decided they would have to move the village. They moved farther up the Nass River and made a new village on the bank of a small river called "Protected River." The chief and the members of his household examined the hills, the valleys, and the mountains to see if it was a suitable area to live in. During this inspection of the country they camped by a beautiful spring of clear water. The chief's name was "Borrowing-a-Shinbone." His nephews were "In-the-Water-Went-the-Frogs" and "Frogs-Sitting-in-a-Spring-of-Water." They saw something strange at the bottom of the spring, like a box with figures carved on it. The chief sent his nephews to bring it to him to examine it. They examined it but they could not understand what it was, except that it was a square-looking box with figures carved on it. After looking at the box they again heard a voice crying, "Give me back my son or something dreadful will befall the village." The dirge was repeated again and again. The chief took the box and examined it more closely. He found that it represented a house which was built as though it had a basement of rock. At each of the four corners was carved a bear. All this time the bird was crying, "Give me back my son. If you don't something dreadful will happen to all of you." He held the box over the fire. She stopped crying and spoke, "Nothing will happen to you, as I have got my child." She did not take the box. The chief kept it and passed it on with its name, *dhak-gam-loab,* to the present day as a coat of arms or crest.

The small figures are said to be "house carvings," of people fishing through the ice; presumably this means on house posts. The rather confused nature of the story suggests that details have been lost or distorted and the story of the wood grub may not have originally belonged to it.

There is another use of totem poles, and that is for the purpose of ridicule. Sometimes when a guest at a potlatch did not repay his debts, the image was put on a totem pole with some shaming figure. In an Alaskan Haida village a pole displayed the image of several nineteenth-century Russian priests to signify that Chief Skowl was proud of the fact that he had successfully resisted their attempts to convert him.

If totem poles are characteristic of Northwest Indian art, something ought to be said about the imprecision of the term. Totemism had been variously defined and discussed by generations of anthropologists. It always involves a relationship between humans and animals. But these relationships vary all over the world, from real ancestor worship, in which the family is thought of as descending from an animal, to a way of identifying tribal groups. Claude Lévi-Strauss's most recent analysis restricts totemism to a way of thinking about lineages and clan or tribal relationships. In any case, the animal–human relationship in the Americas generally involves a supernatural protector or mythical animal with magical power. This is the case of the Northwest Coast, but since the term "totem pole" is so firmly established, it is convenient to continue using it.

Next in importance to totem poles is the mask, generally associated with various types of costume or personal symbolic adornment. Masks are, of course, made by preliterate people all over the world for ceremonial purposes and those of the group we are discussing are particularly impressive and imaginative.

By wearing the mask the performer becomes temporarily identified with his protector. It seems clear, especially in the case of the Kwakiutl masks and those similar to them, that the distortions are intended to produce fear and awe. The great eyes, the flaring nostrils, huge beaks, snouts, and exaggerated teeth are impressively dramatic and certainly tie in with the fact that so many of the dances involve violence and fear. During a Bear dance the audience sang

> How shall we hide from the bear that is moving all around the world? Let us crawl underground! Let us cover our backs with dirt that the terrible great bear from the north end of the world may not find us.

The bear mask, when worn with the fur costume of the bear, is indeed striking. But it is only one among many strangely beautiful and terrible creations by which these people identified themselves with something greater than themselves and induced heightened emotional states.

Lévi-Strauss, impressed, as many observers have been, by the similarities between Northwest Coast, Maori, and ancient Shang art, develops an interesting thesis concerning the split representation which is found in the productions of all three areas. He bases his interpretation upon the mask and, ultimately, facial painting or tattooing. This disguising of the face and body allies the supernatural animal with the human. He instances in particular the Northwest masks, which open out to reveal a human face inside them:

> Their role is to offer a series of intermediate forms from symbolic to meaning—from magic to normal, from supernatural to social. They have the simultaneous role of masking and unmasking—to unmask we have the object which opens out.

As we become more and more aware of the Northwest Coast psyche, it is possible to see considerable justification for this view. The world is full of supernatural forces, symbolized in animal forms, and these are often dangerous if not handled by magical science. The gradual taming of the cannibal dancer is a case in point.

Lévi-Strauss returns to the split figure, which he feels is not simply the result of a technical effort to fill a certain space (as Boas would have it) but rather a representation of the three-dimensional mask which carries with it the mediating or protective powers of the mask. Just tattooing (or, on the Northwest Coast, face painting) gives the face its social dignity and mystical meaning, so the split representation on a storage box, for instance, guards and surrounds the contents and the whole becomes a complex of utensil–ornament–object–animal–box-that-talks. The ease with which objects in Northwest mythology become animated is exemplified in tales such as that of a canoe which refused to perform its duty unless it was fed olachen oil.

Turning to the Maori and Shang cultures, the French anthropologist finds not only split representation and the use of masks but also high estimation of rank and badges of rank. He maintains that this whole complex of mask doubling turning into an art style is only present in cultures in which the supernatural validates a class system. In other social organizations the religious actor represents a god only occasionally; here, "The double representation expresses the strict adherence of the actor to his role, and social rank to myth, to cultures and lineages." And its presence running through all of the material culture as decoration proves it is more than decoration—it is an expression of deeply held emotional concepts and psychic configurations.

We have spoken of the more naturalistic side of Northwest Coast art and this is clearest in certain masks, masks which are clearly portraiture. A Tlingit helmet adorned with the face of an old man, who has evidently had a stroke partly paralyzing the face, is often reproduced and also certain masks used to simulate the face of the victim in a sleight-of-hand decapitation carried out in the female warrior ceremony. The planes of the face, the sense of skin texture, are subtly and skillfully rendered, indicating that if Indian ideology had supported a naturalistic ideal the artists of the region could have easily created such a tradition.

It is when we turn to the houseposts, grave figures, and shaman's images that we find another sculptural tradition both varied impressive. What is particularly evident is a simplification of form; all detail is suppressed in favor of the dominant masses. The Salish house posts, for instance, are great blocks of wood, topped with hats, only enough definition being achieved to give them human form; yet they give off a feeling of power. Other images from the Salish area are strangely reminiscent of the South Seas in their oval faces with their dished planes.

Again, the small figures of Kwakiutl chiefs called "potlatch images" are, in their simplicity, also monumental. The artist Wolfgang Paalen has commented that they are not surpassed by the most powerful works of Byzantine art.

The bears, eagles, frogs, and other animals which were carved as memorial crests to be placed on graves are equally skillful in terms of the selection of expressive form and successful stylization.

The most beautiful examples of the single-figure sculptural tradition adorn the entrance to the Provincial Museum in Victoria. They are a male and a female greeting figure set up on the beach by the Nootka. At least 15 feet high, elegantly attenuated, the weathered wood only lightly touched with a few reddish ceremonial markings on the faces, these grave giants, conceived with enormous authority, express a tranquil at-homeness in the world, the greatness of spirit with which these extraordinary people of the Northwest Coast succeeded in imbuing their creations.

All in all, the remarkable fecundity in producing a variety of artistic form displayed by the Northwest tribes and their sure sense of style has not been equaled by any native group of North America.

NORTHWEST THEATER OF VIOLENCE

20

Most preliterate rituals have theatrical elements and nearly all involve dancing, but the Indians of the Northwest are notable for having developed a real theater; in fact, theater was the key to their ceremonial life and the dominant element in their psycho-emotional culture.

Franz Boas, whose knowledge of the Northwest Coast was encyclopedic, feels that the Northwest theater of violence stems from the Kwakiutl, for it was among them that the secret dancing societies were mostly highly developed; and the complex of performance, potlatch, initiation and tribal festival known as the winter ceremonial seems to have been borrowed from them and to have spread to the other nations. The types of societies, the badges of cedar bark, and even many Kwakiutl words were borrowed by the other groups. The Haida, in Boas's view, did not acquire the complex earlier than a hundred years ago. Since we have no early data, we know nothing about the evolution of their dramatic art, but many mythological elements, some borrowed, were welded together for a basis for the dances, while the theme of warfare runs all through the various societies and produces their predominantly violent character. It is significant for our understanding of the roots of the drama that the Northwest theater illustrates so clearly how ceremonial performance socializes basic unconscious drives, particularly aggression.

The three themes of death and resurrection, kidnapping by supernatural forces, and demonic possession are central to all Northwest drama. They produced intense emotional experience in the community—experience in which all could share and which, by embodying religious notions, tribal ethic, and forms of social organization and rank, were a unifying force which satisfied basic human needs. And as the Winter Ceremonial was elaborated it acquired, as does all theater, elements of entertainment, suspense, and identification. The fact that the activities were not concentrated in a performance area but spilled out into the whole village, that there was continual audience participation, created a total theater that was even more genuinely a community expression than that of the Greeks. And, indeed, the Northwest Indians achieved dramatic values which many avant garde theater directors are groping for today—but which they have little chance of achieving, because there is today no generally accepted body of myth through which the dramatic artist and the community can come together.

Although this communal nature of the theater must be stressed, it is also interesting that a considerable degree of professionalism was involved. For the elaborate illusions and puppetry there were prop men and stagehands. Individual societies had their songmasters (based on talent) who composed songs. There was a baton master who made ceremonial batons and planks on which choruses beat time. There was an eagle down dispenser and cedar bark head ring distributor. There were choral leaders and song prompters. Various societies had their stage managers. When we learn that the Kwakiutl had 50 to 60 societies we realize what a large part of the population, during the slack winter months when fishing was difficult or impossible, was involved in creating the presentations which made their lives colorful and satisfying.

We have already more than once sketched the Cannibal Dancer initiation, and this rite was the core and the most intense activity of the Winter Ceremonial. A member of the Cannibal Dancer Society had the highest rank, and the spirit which possessed him was called The-First-One-to-Eat-Man-at-the-Mouth-of-the-River, or sometimes The-Cannibal-at-the-North-End-of-the-World. There were different series such as shaman dancers, war dancers, female war dancers, and Ghost Dancers. Among the first group, one of the most interesting was the initiation of the Grizzly Bear Dancer novice.

As Drucker describes it among the southern Kwakiutl, horns were used to represent spirit voices instead of whistles. These are heard outside the dance house. The novice began to growl like a bear and disappear (he was spirited away). This meant he had been kidnapped by the supernatural bear and taken up to the sky. Four days later a Grizzly Bear was seen on the shore opposite the village. Certain men prepared to cross in canoes and attack him. When the horns were heard both the Bear and the novice were driven into a canoe. As they approached the beach they sang and the Bear danced in the canoe. He jumped out and chased the assembled audience up and down the beach. It was all done in the spirit of fun, and the people pretended to be terrified. He was prodded with spears until he was driven into the curtained or screened area at the rear of the dance house. This took place in the morning. The women gathered and sang in honor of the novice. Later in the day there was a feast in the dance house. During the dinner the Bear became aroused, growled, and tried to get out from behind the curtain. A terrible struggle seemed to be taking place. The people were frightened and ran to the walls. The people sang:

How shall we hide on the beach before this terrible Bear, the cannibal spirit, moving around the world.
We had better go underground and cover our back with dirt!
That we may not be found by the terrible mouth of this great Bear of our world.

The curtain was dropped or a board smashed out of the screen as an attendant of the Bear was sent sprawling—and suddenly a decrepit old man tottered out from the curtained or screened-off area.

There were four nights during which fun with the Bear continued; on the fourth the spirits were sent away and the Bear vanished. The following morning there was a potlatch and the initiated novice was purified with smoke, signifying the end of the initiation.

The War Dancer was purely destructive. His possession took the form of going through houses in the village and breaking things. His dance was a jerky movement, hopping with knees stiff, feet together. On subsequent nights he broke things with his club, which was carved with his crest, such as a blackfish or a sea lion. On the fourth night he could be accompanied by other masked dancers—among them his club, which had now turned into a masked spirit.

In the dance called "Hearing the Spirits of the Sky," the novice disappeared and was not seen for four nights. The master of ceremonies stood under the smoke hole and called to the spirit. He requested that "The honored one will descend from the sky to show himself to the people."

Suddenly a tremendous thud was heard on the roof, a blare of spirit horns and a commotion at the door. The M.C. sent to learn if the spirit had arrived. It was reported that something strange and terrifying was outside. Attendants assembled at the door, holding their blankets out to form a screen. They backed into the room slowly, prolonging the suspense. They broke away to reveal a naked dancer, painted black and wearing a human mask. He danced and disappeared behind the screen.

A sea spirit was dramatized by the sound of the horns outside and repeated announcements that the tide was rising. When it was nearly at the door of the dance house, the doors were opened and an attendant shouted, "Be kind enough to enter, O Chief!" The same screening with blankets went on until the figure was revealed wearing a robe covered with mollusks, starfish, seaweed, and other marine objects. The mask was human but painted blue and adorned with long loose hair.

The wooden screen covering the end of the room behind which characters disappeared and from which they also appeared was generally painted with figurative murals; among the Bella Coola it was a large image whose mouth covered the entrance to the compartment. In other cases a curtain was used, held up by a rope which was dropped or raised in scenes of revelation or transformation. Sometimes at the beginning of a ceremonial, it was raised to "show the masks" belonging to the particular group or lineage giving the ceremony. The masks were hung on ropes and jiggled about. Edward Curtis speaks of a curtain raised by three ropes.

Objects were sometimes used theatrically in front of the screen. In a rite to call down the spirit of a Making Heavy Dancer, after the horns were blown and the usual suspense worked up, a mask representing the moon appeared in front of the screen (managed by ropes). The chief paying for the ceremony said to the M.C., "Blow the sacred down on it and ask it if it is really the moon." The M.C. blew eagle down toward it and inquired, "Is this really you, great moon of the sky, whom we called?" The mask replied "Hm! Hm! Hm!" and waggled from side to side. The M.C. announced, "Yes, this is the one." The singers shouted *"Wai!"* and the spirit vanished.

After the shamanistic Cannibal Dancer performances, when the novice had become a shaman, among the southern group he customarily performed a feat of magic to show his power. For instance, the M.C. would say, "This great shaman is going to perform a miracle. He is going to cause a stone to float." An attendant got sea water and poured it into a box. Another got a stone. The initiate dropped the stone four times, making a loud noise to show it was real. Then, using the principle of misdirection, the standard method of the magician, one of the cannibals cried out and created a disturbance. Meanwhile the initiate by sleight of hand substituted a piece of wood carefully carved and painted to appear the double of the stone. It was triumphantly made to float.

Describing the theater of the southern Kwakiutl, Philip Drucker says:

> Shamanism provided the plot of the drama, mythology the key figures, the concept of hereditary prerogatives selected the actors and provided the incentives for their participation, warfare the concept of graduated social rank, potlatching and the carver's art were all drawn in to enrich the ceremonials.

The northern Kwakiutl had two or three ceremonial systems—or at least distinctions were made between the major and minor groups, for only in the major rite were the Cannibal Dancers active.

The whole tribe was divided into the secular and uninitiated, who were the audience and who were not supposed to know what went on behind the scenes or how the effects were achieved. Those participating in the acting were Seals and the managers were Sparrows. But the Sparrows were also the comedians and kibitzers and were involved in the lighter forms of theater.

Among the dancers in the major rites there was, of course, the Hamatsa or Cannibal, who sometimes moved in a squatting position, arms extended sidewise, trembling violently. He first extended his arms and legs to the right and then to the left and then in the same way backward. He moved slowly with long steps, his head up, his eyes wide, his lips pushed out as he uttered his cry of *"Hap! Hap!"* (Eat! Eat!). In his moods of excitement and uncontrolled possession, he might faint, run wild, or break loose and rush out of the dance house. An outburst of frenzy could be caused by certain words or a mistake in the rite.

The Raven Dancer, who was also a warrior, crouched low to the floor, his long beak extended, his body covered with the shredded bark costume. He turned his head with sudden jerks to the right and left. Both hands were hidden under his costume (in later times a blanket), and he could thus, unseen, pull the strings which opened and shut the beak, producing a loud clattering. Sometimes this mask wore a necklace of skulls, hung in the feathers and cedar bark, which meant that the property had been obtained in war or that (in early times) a number of slaves had been killed in honor of the novice.

Boas, in his early work *The Social Organization and the Secret Societies of the Kwakiutl Indians,* describes the Fool Dancer as carrying a knife which he drew along his neck as he danced and finally threatened to stab himself—and did so, causing blood to flow from a bladder hidden in his neck ring. In the Winter Ceremonial of 1895 at Fort Rupert the Fool Dancers seemed to function as buffoons. Their masks terminated in long noses, about which they were supposed to be sensitive. One of these dancers, who intended to give up his dance and become a Sparrow, was teased by the head Sparrow, who pulled his nose and threw snowballs at it. Later other Sparrows spat on it and rubbed it with grease. Finally they tied him to a house post and continued to maltreat his nose.

In the ghost dance, which involved a visit to the underworld, the performer wore a neck ring set with skulls. (In the south he had long human bones tied to his arms and legs and a skull on top of his head.) In preparation a ditch had secretly been dug and in it long hollow tubes of kelp had been hidden. The dancer appeared led by one attendant at a rope's end and danced around the fire four times. Then slowly he vanished into the unseen ditch behind the fire. Various attendants tried to cling to the rope in vain—the underworld had claimed him. Then many voices appeared to come from the fire (through the kelp tubes, the speakers being hidden in bedrooms). They announced that the ghosts had taken him away, that he would reappear after four days. On the night of his return a carved effigy of a ghost arose from the ditch carrying the dancer who sang:

I went to the underworld with the Chief of the Ghosts,
Therefore I have magic power.
The Chief of the Ghosts made me dance,
Therefore I have magic power.
He put a beautiful ornament on my head,
Therefore I have magic power.

The *sisiutl* is one of many imagined beings which entered into the Northwest Coast art and theater. It was a double-headed snake with a human face in the middle, a horn on each snake head, and two on the face in the middle. It appears in many paintings and carvings, as well as being prominent in the theater. The War Dancer who conjured it up carried a painted image of the creature which could be lengthened or shortened telescopically. Then he seemed to throw it from him into the air so that it flew up above the people's heads. (It was, of course, a double manipulated by ropes.) As it disappeared, he seemed to catch it again. Then he staggered, almost collapsed, and tried to vomit out the disease-bringing object. Blood flowed from his mouth (he had a small bladder in it). Then he vomited up the snake. As a final gesture he threw it among the spectators. A number of them jumped up, rushed to the fire and fell lifeless, blood pouring from their mouths. The performer danced around them, blew on them. As attendants came to carry them out, he succeeded in bringing them to life. He sang:

Behold this great magic power, carefully swing the sacred implements.
Truly it kills people, no time to escape.
Truly the magic ends their lives.

Here is a description of a warrior's dance involving an ordeal from the personal experience of Charles Nowell, a high-ranking Kwakiutl:

I had spruce twigs thrust through the flesh on my thighs by one of the men. He first put a sharp iron through. Then when they took the iron out, he put the twig through and put a knot in the twig to hold it together, and the same way in two places in my back. That hurted a little bit, and then they tied a rope onto the twigs and tied it to the frame of a double-headed snake mask. And they have three poles and lift me up by lifting the mask and the ropes lifted me and take me all along the beach toward the Kweka chief's house. All the time I say, "Hi-i-i-i-i-i-i-i-i, Hi-hi-hi-hi," and all those that has the same dance comes close around watching and make the same noise with me. They were the only ones supposed to come close. They all have their knives with them, cutting their foreheads. When we got to the front of the house, they put up a rope on the house and pulled me up the the roof, and all the singers under me, holding up their hands while I was pulled up toward the roof of the house. When I got up to the roof, they pulled me to the back end, and put me through a hole in the roof and I was there hanging up until all the peoples came in. When they all came in they lowered me down. But when I was hanging up there, they all sing my song, and at the words, "Cut with your knife," I cut my forehead and the blood came down all over me. I showed the knife to the people smiling to show the people how brave I am. When I am lowered down, they take off the frame and the rope is holded by several men and they begin to pull while I am dancing while they sing my song. Then they begin to say, after the song is ended, shouting, "Go to war." And then they begin to pull the ropes and try to break the twigs out of my leg and back. Two strong men come on my both sides to hold me so that when my skin breaks I don't fall. When they couldn't break my skin, they took my knife away from me and cut my skin, and when they pull the rope away, the Grizzly Bears, they say, "Wo-o-o-o-o-o-o-o-o." Everybody was standing in the house at the time, and I go around the house after all the ropes is off and go back of the screen and stay there, and in the night when they begin to dance again, they have small paddles painted red—that is the blood of the people I am supposed to have killed. Hanging around tied with white thread and a needle stuck in me all over, holding each one of these little paddles, holding a double-headed snake made out of cedar wood in my hands all carved, and I come out and dance. That's all I have on when I dance. Hemlock branches is around my head. I go back again and I am finished with my dance. All the time before this I was staying in the house for I was supposed to be out in the woods. I was just sitting down there, sometimes go to sleep. I eat because they bring me something all the time when they eat. I had to wait till nighttime to go to the beach to the toilet so nobody see me. I had to go through the back door and then go where there is no houses. While I was doing the dance, I didn't hardly feel any pain at all.

The myth rationalizing this rite was that of a superhuman warlike being so possessed with martial fury that the people, in this way, attempted to restrain him and to ceremonialize his dangerous ecstasy. He did not mind the ordeal but rather enjoyed it. After they took him down, he went to war and performed great deeds.

Nowell's last comment is significant, for it seems to indicate that some type of unusual psychic state was produced during the dance and, while much of the Cannibal frenzy was doubtless skillful playacting, some of it was undoubtedly a genuine sense of possession. Indeed, during the many days on which the ceremonies were taking place the whole community was in a state of heightened tension. Boas describes how day after day the dramatic excitement was maintained. The Fool Dancers and the Bears were sent out every now and then from the dance house to get food. At other times they ran out of the house with their lances, struck and scratched people, and threw stones. In the afternoon all the members of the Seal Society appeared on the roof of the house. Every secret society howled its peculiar cries, such as "The food of the Killer Whales is sweet!" or "The great Sea Lions throw their heads downward!" or "The great Seals keep on chewing!"

The convention was that people were forbidden to pass in front of the house. The duty of the Seals was to frighten them away. While they were assembled on the front edge of the roof, Boas says a man approached. Immediately the Hamatsas and the Bears jumped down and ran after him. Meanwhile the Fools climbed down the sides of the house and they all pursued him until he escaped into a neighboring house. Spirit whistles resounded in the dance house all day.

Aside from the dances owned by the various societies, there were also those belonging to specific lineage groups, for each of these was supposed to be descended from a single ancestor, represented by the ranking member of the family.

An example of a myth follows to show the type of tradition behind such family property:

Yakayahlnuhl saw a very large bird covered with down of dazzling whiteness sitting on a rock. The tip of its beak could just be seen in the midst of the thick down. He cried out, "Whatever you are, I demand special powers from you." The bird threw back the feathers and skin from its head, revealing the head of a man, and spoke. "I am Kolus, yet I am a man. My name is Born-to-Be-Admired." His face was steaming with the heat because of the thick covering of feathers. Soon the entire coat fell away and he stood forth the full figure of a man. The bird accompanied Yakayahlnuhl to his home and told him that he must give a Winter Ceremonial and receive these dances from the Kolus: Thunderbird, the Weather Hamaa [an imaginary bird], the Holnluq [another imaginary bird], the Wasp, and the Kolus.

Yakayahlnuhl founded the Kolus clan. Its members are supposed to perspire easily since the bird did so because of its feather garment.

Boas describes one of these lineage dances in which the squid was the power giver. The floor opened and a huge rock (made of wood and bark) covered with kelp appeared. Under the rock was a cave out of which came a large Squid, its arms set with hooks which caught the blankets of the audience and tore them. The song of the Squid was sung by women sitting on three platforms in the rear of the house.

It shakes the sky, *hayai!*
Now for the first time comes the great magical being
Who lives inside the water
To look at the people.

After this the rock and the Squid disappeared; a dancer in a sun mask began to sing his song and a movable sun began to turn in front of the screen. The performance was staged by the chief's son to commemorate a distant ancestor of the chief of the lineage, who had just died. Afterward a totem pole was erected as a memorial to the deceased.

The most impressively theatrical series of dances were those performed by women. These were called Tohuits and the dances were those of warriors. The performer in most cases called for violence—either to have her head cut off, her throat cut, or to be burned. In some cases a dummy was thrown into the water and she was supposed to be drowned. Edward Curtis gives us an excellent description of one of these productions. The performer wore only a kirtle, a headband, wristlets, and armlets of hemlock twigs. She walked about crying *"Op! op! op!"* The speaker or M.C. said, "I will ask her what she wants." He went and whispered to her then turned and announced: "I know what she wants. She says she wants to be burned in the fire."

The Sparrows, in the role of comics, cried that they would do it. The dancer moved about throwing magic from the palms of her hand while the Sparrows continued to shout, "Build up the fire! Push her in!" They continue to shout remarks, asking what kind of a dance it was and offering to burn themselves.

The M.C. consulted her again and announced, "She wants a box." One was brought. The speaker announced it would not do. Another was brought—"It is too small." Still another was brought: "It is too large."

At last a box the right size with a cover was brought. She danced four times around the fire and got into the box. The cover was lashed down securely. A tunnel had been dug secretly from the rear of the house to behind the fire and covered with grass mats; at the fire, the tunnel hidden with an earth-covered board which could be slid aside. The box was placed upside down over this; two men in the tunnel opened it and helped the woman into the tunnel, replacing her with a prepared dummy. The box was then placed on the fire while her secret song was heard. She was lying in the tunnel singing through a long kelp tube as the box burned.

Then her father came forward and complained that he gave the dance as an entertainment and they had burned his daughter. He took a pair of tongs and picked certain bones from the fire, saying he would bury them.

The older Hamatsas said she whispered, "I will come to life again." It was her own fault she was burned, they insisted, and they must put the bones in a box as she told them to. "I hope it is true," said her father. The bones were picked up and dropped into a coffin. The other Tohuits sang their songs as they carried the coffin around the fire. The woman could now be heard singing faintly from behind the curtain where she was hidden. For three nights she was heard singing, ever more distinctly, and on the fourth night her voice was loud.

Her parents said, "Is that our daughter singing?" Then the eldest Tohuit came out and announced, "We have brought her to life." The members of the society came dancing out from behind the curtain in single file, the resurrected girl in the middle.

Nowell describes the women's decapitation dance, in which the performer asked for a knife. At the fourth request a man entered with a knife, went around the fire with it, took some charcoal, crushed it and put it on his face, then announced, "Take hold of [the woman] and lay her on a board." He then aimed at her neck four times and on the fourth seemed to take her by the hair and cut her head off:

> And he went away from her and walked away from the head while the head was still standing on the ground, and the mouth kept opening and the face twitching as if there was still life in that head, and the man came around and picked it up and put it under his blanket again, and he goes to another side of the house, and puts the head on a box, showing the people it is the same face as this woman has, and he went to the rear of the house and put it down on the ground again so the people on the front end will see it.

This production was worked by a sleight of hand and by a mask which was a perfect portrait of the dancer who was spirited away and into a tunnel with several branches so that, when the mask was apparently set on the ground, the actual head of the dancer was put up from the tunnel.

One other Tohuit production involved a complicated set of props. The dancer made the gesture of calling something from above and then pretended to catch something in her hands. She then threw this toward the back of the fire (always hidden from the audience). First the horns of the *sisiutl* came into view; then the whole image, rising from the ground; then a white bird flew down from the roof and lit on its horns. In still another dance a wooden kingfisher swooped down from the roof, followed the dancer, and seemed to thrust its long bill through her wrist. Suddenly a huge hand arose from the ground behind the fire and a great rattle descended from the roof. The hand grasped the rattle, shook it, and both disappeared.

In contrast to the Kwakiutl, who developed a considerable variety of theatrical images, the Nootka organized their winter drama festival around an involvement with wolves, which was rationalized by a myth in which an ancestral chief's son was kidnapped by wolves. This festival involved the entire village, even slaves and children being initiated. Various chiefs had their own sets of wolf whistles of different pitches. They also had the right (also hereditary with them) to involve certain commoners to play wolves. The faces, arms, and legs of the wolves were painted black, and in modern times they wore black blankets with a corner draped over the head to represent the snout. We have in Jewitt's narrative an interesting reference to the ceremony in his time:

> On the morning of the 13th of December, commenced what appeared to be a most singular farce. Apparently without any previous notice, Macquinna discharged a pistol close to his son's ear, who immediately fell down as if killed, upon which all the women of the house set up a most lamentable cry, tearing handfuls of hair from their heads and exclaiming that the prince was dead, at the same time a great number of inhabitants rushed into the house armed with their daggers, muskets, etc., enquiring the cause of their outcry; these were immediately followed by two others dressed in wolf skins, with masks over their faces representing the head of that animal; the latter came in on their hands and feet in the manner of a beast, and taking up the prince carried him off on their backs, retiring in the same manner as they entered. We saw nothing of the ceremony, as Macquinna came to us and, giving us a quantity of dried provisions, ordered us to quit the house and not return to the village before the expiration of seven days, for that if we appeared within that period, he should kill us.

Modern Nootka interpret this as the usual disappearance into the woods of novices, indicating that Jewitt and his co-prisoner Johnson were actually being initiated, something they never understood. The kidnapping by wolf spirits is clearly indicated, and we learn that in those days a full wolf costume was used. Interestingly enough, Boas reproduces an illustration of a wolf mask collected by Captain Cook from the Kwakiutl which is identical in style to those used in Boas's time at the turn of the nineteenth century.

Essentially, in modern times, the ceremony's basic drama was a beleaguerment by the Wolves. These ran through the village howling, blowing their spirit whistles and whirling bullroarers, which were called wolves' tails. Sometimes they struck the wall boards of a house with clubs, whereupon a child, who had been coached, blew a tiny shrill whistle and collapsed on the floor as though dead and was taken to the sponsor's house. This, of course, reminds us of the episode with Macquinna's son. In the actual ceremony the novices were spirited away. When they were abducted they were pursued at a distance by armed men who shot at the Wolves and boasted that they had almost killed the enemy. If a novice merely disappeared, his or her clothes, ripped to shreds, were strewn on the beach. The armed men in their war paint scolded the parents of the kidnapped novices for being careless about their children. At times they broke into houses searching for the lost ones, broke things, dragged people out of bed, and poured water over them. Whenever the Wolves appeared the spectators pretended great fear. In the ceremonies at a dance house, along with whistles outside building up the sense of approaching spirits, there was a whole network of taboos which must not be violated—the word "wolf" must not be used, for instance, and "crawler" was to be substituted. In modern times the punishment for a mistake was to be stripped. An informant told Drucker that some women actually sang ditties using the forbidden words in order to achieve this striptease. The ordeal element in the ceremony was rationalized as the penalty for a mistake, but actually it was a hereditary privilege of certain war chiefs to be spared. Again we have Jewitt's evidence of 100 years before. When he and Johnson returned at the end of seven days, the festival—

> . . . terminated on the 21st, the day after our return with a most extraordinary exhibition. Three men, each of whom had two bayonetts run through his sides, traversed the room backwards and forwards, singing war songs and exulting in this display of firmness.

If George Clutesi's testimony is to be accepted, the emotional participation in the drama of all actors and spectators in the wolf ceremony was as intense as that of any Stanislavski student. Clutesi, a Nootka writer, in *Potlatch* has reconstructed the Winter Ceremony in fictional form. Here is his description of the official announcement of the kidnapping of the children by the Wolves:

> A young man staggered into the great lodge. He was disheveled, panting and gasping for breath as he stood not far from the entrance, unwilling to go further in; great beads of sweat stood out on his fore-

head and trickled down his tired, tired face. He stood panting, his shoulders hunching more and more in his dejection. . . . No one moved. No one spoke. There was no help.

The young man whispered to the master of ceremonies, who called out the names of the 10 children.

The old man with the black cane put his head down once again, his thin shoulders slumped down with it. He was staring at the earthen floor and his weak voice came again. "The children of these names are gone. They are not with us. They have been abducted by the Wolf People." His voice trembled, the last words rasped out in dismay and utter defeat. "Not here. Not here."

WHOOOOOOOOOOOOOOooooooooooooo . . .

It was the call of the wolf again.

The ceremonies were often enriched by mimetic dances. Squirrels would climb the house posts and crawl along the beams. A Cormorant flapped heavily and threw handfuls of flour behind it to simulate the bird's profuse dung. A Woodpecker climbed and pecked the house posts. The Kelp Dancer wore long yellow silk streamers, floating down her back, while the Frogs, with whitened faces, large black circles around their eyes, wide mouths, and great padded bellies, hopped and croaked.

Clown acts were put on by professionals who had demonstrated their talent. Drucker describes a team of these whose humor often consisted of burlesquing the serious ceremonies. The two had a battered old box on one side of which a fish was painted and on the other a frog. It contained their paraphernalia over which they fussed and fiddled exaggeratedly. One of their routines involved a piece of a cast iron face they had found washed up on the beach. They brought it out covered with cedar bark and announced they had encountered a new supernatural being alive and did not know what it was. Various women were called up to open the bundle and identify it. The clowns would jiggle it—the women pretended great fright and refused to open it. The clown made long speeches, thanking them, and gave them each five cents, in burlesque of the potlatch procedure. They then unwrapped the face and said it was the white man's deity.

At the end of the main portion of the festival, there was a rite to resuscitate the kidnapped novices. The people of the house sat in a row behind the curtain in front of the novices wearing cedar bark headbands with two upright feathers; in front of them were two women dancers. Two men entered the house, one with a harpoon line and the other with a paddle. Supposedly spirits, they moved like whalers in a canoe, approaching the curtain four times, each time the unseen chorus singing and drumming. At the fourth time the chief gave a ritual cry and struck the curtain of mats with the harpoon. The line holding it was cut so that it fell. The two dancers rose and danced in front of the chorus, which drummed while the novices whistled. The giver of the wolf dance thanked the chief, who had revived the novices. The novices came forward and sang a song given him or her by the Wolves. Some described their kidnapping and how they were given the names of their ancestors. This paralleled the legend in which the chief's son was taken to the place of origin of his lineage and given masks and magic power. Thus the whole festival was quite well unified, and it strengthened the ties between members of the group at the same time that it entertained them and served as a socializing outlet for various emotional drives.

One other group with an interesting theater is the Bella Coola, whose territory is situated between the northern and southern Kwakiutl and who have been involved in reciprocal influences between them and these groups. If the theater impulse stems from the Kwakiutl, certain types of masks with a kind of aureole around the face are characteristically Bella Coola and have been borrowed by the Kwakiutl.

The Bella Coola possessed Cannibal Dancers and they also performed five dances involving mutilation, death, and resurrection. These Kukusiut performances involved beheading, drowning, burning, the swallowing of hot stones, and stomach cutting and were done supposedly at a "call" from a supernatural patron.

The stomach cutting illusion took place after an elaborate buildup in which the dancer entered every house of the village and called out, "Please say what you want; I will do it." He appeared with a knife in his hand which showed that he had received power from above. He strengthened himself by calling down other powers in the form of puppets, worked by ropes, the most effective of these being a giant toad. The actual preparation consisted of covering his stomach and chest with a dog or deerskin which was fastened to his breechclout and around his chest, the blanket he wore disguising this arrangement between the skin and his body in which the entrails of dogs were concealed. Morning songs were sung by the women bewailing the danger to which he would be exposed. A boy was chosen who agreed to do the deed. There were cries of pain from the victim, growls from the Cannibals; the boy disemboweled him. He dropped back as if dead. He appeared to be sitting on the floor with his legs in a hole while a confederate, with his legs in the hole, stretched his legs out in front. After the disemboweling of the dancer, the women wept and wailed, the whistles sounded, and there was a great commotion. One of the uninitiated said to the Kukusiut, "You have gone too far, you powerful people. We know that you are powerful and are in league with the supernatural ones but now you have killed a man. Your power is too great, it is dangerous. Unless he is restored to life before dawn we will kill you." As the disemboweled one lay exposed, a singer in the rear of the house sang:

Perhaps you perceived correctly,
Hence you did what you were empowered to do
But too much power has been given you.

She was answered by a singer in the opposite rear corner:

Let the voice of Snitsman-a
Come to earth to revive
The one who has so mortally injured himself.

The whistling went on and various puppet patrons departed and went to the region above. After a time they returned with thuds on the roof and spirit whistling. Now it was pointed out to the uninitiated that the wound was slowly closing. (It should be noted also that all the illusions described were aided by the dimness of the dance house, which was lit by only the central fire.) There was more singing and whistling—which was the signal for the entry of the Giant Toad. This was a cunningly contrived wooden figure which by concealed string could be made to hop toward the dancer and bend four times over him. The wound came together; the excitement built. Those near him announced his little toes were moving. Gradually more toes moved; the M.C. called out that he was alive again. He grew stronger, he began to shake his hands as though he were trying to dance, and in a weak voice began to sing a song in which the name of Snitsman-a, the supernatural who had saved him, occurred. There was joy and dancing; the patron puppets lent to the dancer were recalled, and the evening ended with a feast. There were two other nights of ritual but they were dramatically anticlimactic. The relation in theme between the Bella Coola Kukusiut dances and the Tohuit performances is clear, however: once more death and resurrection are related to dangerous supernatural power which must be controlled by ritualization.

The Bella Coola made a practice of burning the masks after a production, which tended to blur the firm outlines of tradition in all cases except those of the best-known mythological images. Informants told Thomas McIlwraith that they had thus forgotten many beings known to their ancestors and that they were in the habit of creating new designs and naming them for natural phenomena which they assigned to supernatural causes. Thus, in the case of this group, the dramatic tradition had probably been in the process of continual development and evolution. Thunder, for instance, sounds like a rather abstract concept. He was announced by a speaker, sticks were beaten on the floor and the curtain was drawn back to reveal Thunder standing on a raised box. He wore a huge mask with a hooked nose and a bulbous forehead, so heavy that the dancer must have soft pads of felt to ease the weight. The upper parts of his body were entirely covered with dyed and undyed cedar bark and he had wristlets and anklets of the same material; around his middle was a dance apron, and in each hand he carried a stick tufted with more bark. He stood still for some time, moving his arms toward the corners of the house where a number of prop men were rattling heavy stones in boxes to manifest his power in sound. When he had created an impression he leaped down, the drums beat, the stone thunder was shaken, and Thunder shrieked as he danced around the fire and the women created a droning accompaniment. Since the mask had only one opening, the performer could not see and had to be guided by three other Kukusiut. He drew power from the smoke of the fire, went back to his box, and was given a rattle full of coals which gave off burning sparks as he danced around the fire a second time to the accompaniment of the tremendous din; he then drew more power from the fire and returned behind the curtain, which was then drawn. The M.C. called out, "The fire Kukusiut of the supernatural ones has been with us; his fire is too wonderful for us."

A masked figure with a bowl of water then danced around the fire, silently drenching the audience; this was the rain which accompanied the storm. The whole performance was repeated twice.

Even more untypical and perhaps recent is the dance of Nunuoska, which McIlwraith labels "Mother Nature." Much carpentry was necessary in order to create a large masked figure which represented this character. The number of other masks to be made were mostly constructed from flowers and trees. Two old women were given masks of great age and ugliness. These went to every house in the village and announced, "We are in great trouble. Our daughter's child is long overdue. If you know of any good medicines, won't you give them to us for her?" Some of the Kukusiut gave these supernatural medicines. At night when the audience assembled they saw the large wooden figure behind the fire apparently in the pangs of labor with an enormously distended belly. The uninitiated did not yet know who she was. She lay on some raised planking and below her were the two old women with sponges of dyed and undyed cedar bark which would be used to wash a newborn infant. Two mat-enclosed structures had been built, one in each rear corner of the house, and in these were hidden the rest of the characters. One of these came forth from beneath Mother Nature's belly, as if just born, wearing a mask surmounted by a carved stick representing willow leaves. The old nurses treated him as if they were washing a newborn child and announced, "It is a boy, Willow Leaves." He danced around the fire saying at intervals, "I am Willow Leaves." He disappeared into one of the mat-covered enclosures. The same routine was followed with Gooseberry, Nettle, various kinds of grass, and Skunk Cabbage. Black Cottonwood and American Aspen continue to dance on each side of the fire until the South Wind was announced. He came in by the front door, wearing the mask of a handsome young man. He went up to Nunuoska as if he were a doctor and at the same time a joyful mask was substituted for the one indicating the pains of labor. South Wind joined the two trees as North Wind rushed in—too late to succeed in destroying Mother Nature in the act of delivery. He joined the other dancers. There followed a whole series of plants and shrubs, more or less chronologically according to their appearance in spring. Actually, by changing masks or using the same mask with different leaf representations about fifteen actors accomplished the whole performance, North Wind always being repulsed by South Wind. The last figure of all was a late-growing moss, the afterbirth.

At the end, one of the Kukusiut explained that the population would have no food if the South Wind had not been able to save Mother Nature from North Wind before she gave birth to plants. The whole concept sounds rather Western literary, especially since the Indians were, it appears, so much more oriented toward animals than plants. It may well be an example of the Bella Coola ability to absorb new influences into their dramatic productions.

There is also a dance of what McIlwraith calls "The Supernatural Charmer," a beautiful and promiscuous young woman, which allowed for bawdy humor which the anthropologist is too inhibited to describe. She was followed by men of all nations—not only Indian but also sometimes a white man and a Chinese. They all pursued her, complaining that she had left them, that they had only had her once, etc. The speaker called upon a good-looking woman present and demanded to know the number of her lovers. She numbered them in the hundreds and took part in bawdy repartee. The supernatural woman was followed by an old man, her father, who urged her to give up her promiscuous life. The last lover of all was an old man tottering on a stick who was captivated in his youth and had followed her ever since. The whole assemblage visited all the houses in the village. Since all of the lovers could not get inside, some remained outside, holding a live mountain goat—who was also numbered among the lovers. Toward evening almost all of the group had entered the house of the giver of the dance. The woman stood on a low box encouraging all her followers indiscriminately. They scuffled among themselves. Sometimes a cradle was brought in, and while the woman crooned over it she was described as the mother of many creatures of whom the fathers were animals. (There was also a dance, paralleling this one, in which the supernatural figure was an irresistable male pursued by women.)

If the Bella Coola dramatic literature was somewhat atypical, the basic Salish ceremony does not relate to the body of Northwestern theater at all. We have already indicated that the sculpture of those people does stem from the general early tradition. The Coast Salish had only a couple of masks, however, which are believed to have been borrowed from the Kwakiutl. The spirit canoe ceremony is suggestive of northeast Asia—more concerned with shamanism than the theater—but it does express the death and resurrection theme.

The theater of violence which we have been describing fits remarkably into the theories of the poet, madman, and prophet of the theater Antonin Artaud. It was he who, in rejecting the drama of rhetoric, social criticism, or polite comedy, called for a theater of cruelty, a theater inspired by myth and magic. He preferred movement, gesture, pantomime—all sorts of visual violence—because he felt that by creating symbols of this sort it would be possible to give free rein to man's basic drives and repressed conflicts, his repressed savagery. This was to be a participatory as well as a therapeutic experience. It would situate the drama once more in the midst of communal life and regain the primal emotional experience which is so rapidly being lost in the alienation created by our technological civilization.

Artaud involved himself in the peyote ceremonies of the Tarahumara Indians of Mexico, but had he been aware of the Northwest Indian theater he would have seen—in the death and resurrection theme, in the deliberate exploitation of the horror of cannibalism, in the beliefs in the possibility of harnessing the supernatural, in the spectacle of the ordeal of torture, in the monstrous and violent visual symbols—precisely that theater of cruelty which he envisioned. Sophisticated Indians today speak of their ceremonies as purging the savage drive of appetite. The whole process relates to Lévi-Strauss's theory of myth as the taming of uncivilized id. There is no doubt that the Indians of the Northwest were socializing their unconscious drives in art, dealt in with the deepest ambivalences in the human animal: possession, cannibalism, violent self-destruction. In the crude but vivid achievements of their drama, in their resourcefulness in creating wild and exciting pageantry, they were doing something, on a much simpler plane, parallel to the dramatic aims of the Greeks, who were able to socialize similar violent themes but, thanks to the sophistication of their urban culture, finally clothed them in dignified rhetoric and intellectualized them with philosophy.

The Northwest Indians achieved brilliant and fragmentary flashes of intense power, and their total drama deserves particular respect, for from it we have much to learn about the roots of drama and the theatrical impulse. The most fitting comment is Artaud's pronouncement: "True theater has always seemed to me the exercise of a dangerous and terrible act."

INDIANS AS POETS

21

We have continually referred to the songs which accompany the rituals of the Northwest Coast Indians and are an integral part of their culture. When this poetry is examined, to the extent to which it has been collected by anthropologists, it is less accessible to a contemporary Western reader than the other arts of the area. There are two reasons why this is the case.

Many of these songs are entirely functional in terms of the rituals with which they are connected. Thus they express traditional sentiments, and there is no great premium upon individuality of expression. The contrast with Eskimo culture, for instance, is significant. The Eskimo are individualists; their prolific output of songs is subjective, expressing personal feeling about the hunt, the hazards of life, their relation to nature. Since all this is quite in the Western tradition, their poetry possesses a spontaneity to which a literate audience can easily respond. Northwest poetic art, being a part of a highly formalized social system, is much more difficult to respond to, for its aims are not those of the individualist aesthetic.

The second difficulty is the reliance upon reference to myth. For the literate Western reader this means that line after line must be interpreted or footnoted. Still, with the death of the classical tradition, we are even beginning to encounter this sort of difficulty in understanding the literature of the Greeks and Latins.

Granted that Northwest songs exhibit an alien quality, they are nevertheless revealing of the wellsprings of motivation and do dramatize the manner in which the shame–prestige culture expressed itself. It must be remembered, however, that the available versions of Northwest poetry are recorded by ethnologists generally with word-for-word translations, which are therefore wholly foreign to poetic English in structure and word order; plus a free rendering of the meaning. The result is generally that both versions are wholly without style and lose the original rhythm. The writer has compared the two versions and tried to edit the result into something slightly less crude. He has also tried to choose the most accessible poems. In any case, on the printed page we have only a few hints of the effectiveness of these compositions when they were sung in their proper settings. We do know, however, that song makers were chosen for their talent, which means that the Indians were not without critical standards.

To start with basics, John Swanton has recorded some Haida cradle songs:

Be careful of this child, be careful—
He is a noble man.
His face will change, wherever he may be,
When he sees his powerful grandfather coming.
Be careful, this is going to be a great man.

This is of course an expression of pride of lineage; the reference to the grandfather suggests that he will see to it that the child will inherit family power and distinction at the proper time. Most of these Haida songs express the same sentiments:

You only are going to be a rich man.
You only are going to be a rich man.
You will fill up the seaside of your grandfather's town with property.
Born of high lineages, your chiefs' houses
Will have enormous carvings on the side to the sea.
You will be a rich man.

More indirect and even more poetically boastful is the following:

All things that grow,
All things that grow,
Dog salmon he will not need to kill.
All things that grow,
All things that grow,
Cedar bark he will not need to chop.
All that grows!
All that grows!

The implication is that the child will become so rich and powerful and the owner of so many slaves that everything that grows will be his. He will not have to lift a finger! Then we have a song which is more imagistic:

In your father's house seagulls cry out as they eat.
You are going to bear yourself proudly
In the midst of all this.

The seagull image refers to the guests invited to a potlatch and indicates the proper amount of boastful arrogance. Another cradle song expresses the pride of the mother who sings it:

You came to me, ye, he, he!
You came to me, ye, he, he!
You came walking to me, calling me mother.
To me my child, a chief's child, came walking,
Calling me mother.
Mother of noble family!
Mother of noble family!
Mother of noble family!
Mother of noble family!

Yet strangely, in the midst of the pride of lineage songs, one simple expression of emotion stands out:

Even dogs love their puppies,
So I love mine.

A song of derision always a part of the potlatching:

Laugh at the chief!
Though he is a chief,
He has no rattle in his hand.

Most effective of these Haida songs is one of mourning for a brother:

What medicine shall I use in my grief?
What medicine shall I use?
There is nothing I can use.
I long for your dear face.
If I could see the trail of the dead,
I would follow it.
Elder Brother, I long to see all of you.

Turning to Kwakiutl poetry we find, as might be expected, that they excelled in songs meant to shame their guests in potlatch rivalry. Some of these were quite elaborate.

I thought someone else was
Causing this smoky weather,
But I am the only one on earth,
The only one in the world
Who makes thick smoke arise
From one end of the year to another,
For the tribes, for my guests.
What will my rival say now?
He is a Spider Woman.
What will he do next?
His words don't travel far.
Will he brag about giving away canoes?
Break coppers or give a grease feast?

These will be like the words of the Spider Woman.
For your face is dry and moldy,
You, standing in front of
The bellies of the chiefs.
Sometimes I treated you roughly
So that you begged for mercy.
Like an old dog
You'll spread your legs before me
When I grow angry. . . .
This I throw in your face.
You, whom I always vanquish,
Whom I treat roughly. . . .
You, who dare not stand up
When I am eating,
You, whom every weakling can triumph over!

In its proper setting, with goods being thrown upon the fire, which is built up to such a point that the guests are almost scorched, this is indeed an expression of barbaric arrogance. As an example of rather obscure mythological reference we have the following song of a clan ancestor:

A bear is standing at the river of the Wanderer who traveled all over the world.
Wild is the bear at the River of the Wanderer who traveled all over the world.
A dangerous fish is going up the river;
It will put an end to the lives of the people.
Ya! The *sisiutl* is going up the river;
It will put an end to the lives of the people.
Great things are going up the river,
With them the copper of the eldest brother of our tribes.

The salmon song, which follows, was danced with stiff legs, feet in the same spot, the body turning to the right and left, the palms stretched forward.

Many salmon are coming ashore with me;
They are coming close to you, post of our sky.
They are dancing from the salmon country to the shore.
I come to dance for you at the right-hand side of the world,
Towering above, outshining, surpassing all, I, the salmon.

In the light of the importance of the salmon as a means of sustenance, and its resulting religious significance, this glorification of the fish can easily be appreciated. A Tlingit dance song has some interesting imagery.

Slowly we walk a race through the world.
Slowly we walk a race through the world.
Ha! I am the one who made sky cloudy, when I came from the north end of the world.
Ha! I am the one who brought the fog, when I came from the north end of the world.
Ha! I am the one who brought the dawn when I came from the great copper bringer.
Ha! I am the one who brought the warmth when I came from the great one who brightens the world.
He! And he will dance like a Tongass, your successor, whom we praise.

Before the songs of the more violent ceremonies, it is worth citing some of the Bella Coola poems in a different vein. Here are a couple of love songs:

They say I love her dearly.
No!
The dimple in my left cheek merely smiled.

A somewhat more passionate avowal:

If you went up to the sky, I would become a star.
I would capture you.
If you went into the ocean, I would become a bullhead.
I would capture you.

And most basic of all:

If you went into the domain of the bullhead,
I would change into a kingfisher.
I would eat you.

There were songs appropriate to occupations, for instance, fishing songs. The Bella Coola addressed the trout:

Come along trout,
I want to triumph,
I want to triumph,
Over you, biggest of all.
I fish for trout, I fish for trout.
Swallow the bait down to your tail,
To your tail,
To your tail!
I dare you to break our lines.

While the Nootka had a very simple whaling song:

Hi! Hi! Hi!
Go straight to my wife,
She's a magic treasure.

The Bella Coola had a simple mourning song for a child, which refers to a myth we have already cited:

The luck of my family shortens my days
Like a dog's.
Alas, give me back my child!
I am like Raven when the great bird's talons
Seized his son, his joy and delight.
Alas, give me back my child!

In the realm of shaming and ridicule, the Bella Coola have a song to an unmarried mother:

Don't boast so much, Som;
You're in trouble,
You unmarried mother.
You women are cunts
Who pretend to be virgins.
Alas, I am ashamed.
I am Som.
My little boy's nose is just like
Round-headed Golosti's.

And the following is a fairly elaborate Kwakiutl mourning song:

Where has my son gone?
Come all you people from foreign lands,

Hear my mourning song.
He is gone.
The chief, his power-giving spirit,
Has taken him away.
He has gone to where our ancestor singlehanded
Made the river at Rivers Inlet.
Hail to Raven who made the river.
My son will soon be turned to stone there
Where Raven carried off his mother years ago.
Oh Chief, my son,
You will sustain the guardians of the sun and moon.
He will help to carry them
When he ascends the river.
That is where Waakis, his ancestor,
Turned the whale to stone.

And from the same group is the song of an initiate who has become a shaman.

They all gave me
The power of a shaman.
They gave strength to my mind.
They opened the sky.
They saw me as they peered down.

Just as the Winter Ceremonial was notable for its theater of violence, so the songs which accompanied it were intended to inspire terror and were functional—mainly descriptions of what the dancer was dramatizing. To start with a Bella Coola song sung by the chorus to the dancer we have:

No one spoke at the council of spirits
When his sponsor counted how many he should eat.
Two men, one after another, kept giving him food in his house.
There was a continual growling.
His footsteps shook the wooden floorplanks.
Hail to the giving of gifts,
Hail to the power spirit,
Sehsehkalaih!

The Kwakiutl songs of violence are most intense. The chorus sings to a Cannibal Dancer:

You are looking for food, you Great Magician.
You are looking for men you wish to eat.
You tear men's skin, Great Magician.

Everyone trembles before you, Great Magician,
You who have been to the end of the world.

The dancer himself sings:

Now I am going to eat.
My face is ghastly pale.
I shall eat what is given me
By the great cannibal spirit.

The Fool Dancer, as described by Boas in his early work, is one of the warriors and appropriately savage. The chorus sang:

Ha! the great madness came down
And is disturbing our friend.

The Dancer sang:

The weapon flew into my hand.
With this I kill,
With this I cut off heads.

The chorus added:

The great madness has entered our friend;
He kills old and young.

The song associated with the Raven Dancer whom we have described and who also was associated with cannibalism is similar in tone:

Wa! everyone is frightened by his winter mask!
Wa! everyone is frightened by his cannibal mask!
His hooked beak makes us tremble,
His Hohok mask makes us tremble.

And one more Fool Dancer's song in which the chorus sang:

Go on, go on, you are great, *haya, hai!*
Do not look at the curdled blood on the water! *Hai!*
Hai!

With the reply:

I cut them!
I am the Fool Dancer's comrade!

Boas commented on the fact that literary technique varied. For instance, he explained that sometimes the words were somewhat distorted—as in literate societies' singing—to adjust to the rhythm of the tune. Thus "I saw the great spirit traveling about" might be sung as the Indian-language equivalent of, "I sawhaw the greaheat Sp'it tra'ling 'bout, *Ham! Ham!*" The particles which occur at the beginning and the ends of lines were both used for emphasis and to punctuate a rhythmic unit, and sometimes are associated with a certain character as the *"ham, ham"* or *"hap, hap"* of the Cannibal Dancer, which means "eat, eat."

Rhymic patterns repeated with certain variations were characteristic of lyric oratory, which also seems to have been sung. For instance the following lines would have been chanted by the speaker or M.C. on introducing a dance at a winter festival:

Now you will witness, Northerners, the dance of
Many-on-Fire, daughter of Giver-of-Presents.
Now you will witness, Great Kwakiutl, the dance of
Many-on-Fire, daughter of Giver-of-Presents.
Now you will witness, Rich People, the dance of
Many-on-Fire, daughter of Giver-of-Presents.

It is probable that it was this kind of lyric chanting with which the chiefs greeted the whaling captains when they circled their ships in the late eighteenth century. Apropos of metaphor, Boas maintained that its scarcity in recorded Indian literature was more likely due to imperfect records than to its absence, which behooves us to be all the more wary of the form in which the anthropologists have recorded Northwest poetry. Among the Kwakiutl, in particular, it was used a great deal in eulogizing the potlatch chief, who was compared to a mountain, a precipice, a great tree, a loaded canoe at anchor—He Who Covers the Whole World with Smoke. His people follow him as the young sawbills follow the mother duck. His rival is the one who loses his tail (like a salmon), he with ruffled feathers, old dog, broken piece of copper. In one song he says of his rivals:

I am too great to be bitten by those little mosquitos
That are flying about.

Wilson Duff has also commented that the name crests which were the private property of the Tsimshian lineages are in themselves images almost amounting to an art form, close to haiku. There was:

Sunshine glinting on the emerging dorsal fin
Of the rising killer whale.

Or:

Misty spout of the killer whale.

And:

Raven cawing as he flies out to sea in the morning.

And most charming of all:

Grouse, making itself a robe
Out of its tailfeathers.

As a final example of Northwest poetry there is a song recorded by Boas which accompanied the presence of a mask which opened to reveal a human face (whose ceremonial he did not identify). The deer, however, is generally identified as a fire bringer. Of all the Kwakiutl poetry available, this has the most mysteriously lyrical quality.

We will drive away the great deer, who comes standing on his forelegs, towering over all the people, covering the tribes, the great deer, said by all to be foolish.

We will all be thin-faced, dry in our mouths. We will go and cause him bad luck, staring at him, staring at him until he grows sleepy, the great deer, said by all to be foolish.

He was the first to make things beautiful again, lighting the world by his radiance, by the copper of his body. His antlers are pure, unbroken solid copper. The speakers of all the tribes take off his antlers. Let him jump over the greatest chief, the one who is famous among all the tribes, the great deer, said by all to be foolish.

THE UNSEEN POWERS

22

Inextricably a part of preliterate man's philosophy and involved with the activities of his daily life as well as his complex rituals is the concept of the shaman. His role combines the functions of physician, instinctive psychoanalyst, and, in more complex urban societies, he will develop into the priest. He was, of course, the immediate target of the missionary, who recognized him as a rival and a defender of tradition. Many anthropologists have concentrated upon his clever use of deception, but beyond the sleight of hand and the showmanship there was always an area of belief in supranormal powers and the conviction that certain formulas, traditional procedures, and a respect for taboos would enable him to control and exploit them.

Boas wrote that, although both the practitioners of shamanism and the patient were aware of trickery used, yet the power was still believed in:

> The initiation of the shaman who takes his task seriously entails a weakened state of health—owing to sickness, to fasting and other forms of castigation of the body or a tendency to fits. It is more than plausible that, as time goes on, imaginary experiences of this period, sometimes due to direct suggestions from older shamans, may take in the mind of the shaman a reality which in the beginning was quite absent.

Actually, certain basic tenets of shamanism are universal in the Americas. One of these is the relationship with a giver of power, sometimes called the guardian spirit, which generally takes the form of an animal. Paul Wingert comments, in the case of the Salish shaman, that once this power is obtained (through supranormal experience) there is no doubt of it and no fear of it. The power is never propitiated but worked with as a partner. It is never worshipped as a god and the symbols used are to express this supernatural cooperation through ceremony.

It is interesting to note that Carlos Castaneda's recent portrait of the Yaki shaman, Don Juan, emphasizes the same mentality although the Yaki made use of mescal. Nevertheless, Don Juan personified the mescal spirit exactly as a Northwest Coast medicine man would refer to his animal spirit. Don Juan was explicit that mescal was not a god but a protector and teacher. For Castaneda, when under its influence, the mescal spirit appeared in the form of a dog.

Boas described an informant, who had been subject to fainting fits, being visited in a dream by a killer whale spirit who said to him, "Tomorrow you will perform your first cure."

Some groups felt that certain animals had special powers. The Tlingit shaman, whose long hair must not be cut because it was a source of power, went off into the woods to obtain his power giver. The land otter was the animal most highly prized. When the candidate saw one he would exclaim "Oh!" in a loud voice. When the animal heard this he would immediately fall on his back and die. Then the shaman-to-be ripped out the tongue, saying, "May I be successful in my new calling, may I conjure and dance well." He put the tongue in a basket and subsequently hid it, because if an uninitiated person saw it he would lose his senses. He buried the meat of the animal in the ground but kept the skin. In the past no Tlingit would kill a land otter. One story recorded by the Russian priest, Veniaminov, recounts that a shaman (apparently voluntarily) was wrapped in a mat tied with an otterskin strap and thrown into the sea, where he went to the bottom, anchored to a line held up with a land otter's bladder. For four days nothing happened; then the people of the village heard sounds like a drum. They followed the sound and found the shaman hanging head downward from a cliff, his head streaming blood, small birds swarming around it. He was gotten into a boat, came to, and recovered. As a result of this strenuous ordeal he acquired a new power spirit.

The Tlingit shaman had to fast and use emetics to purify himself before his activities, and in death he was embalmed, not cremated. Krause describes a shamanistic festival.

In the deeper level of the house hundreds of naked men were standing about a fire. Along one wall on the upper level a row of men and women sat, wearing clothes. Most of the men around the fire had a dagger in the right hand. Singing started slowly, then increased in tempo and volume. After several drumbeats a curtain rose in the back of the house. The shaman appeared with flying hair and many decorations hanging from a cape. As he rushed toward the fire, the singers waved their daggers and made as if to pursue him. He eluded them, leaping and twisting. Pulling a burning log from the fire, he threw it toward the roof. Some of the naked men followed him; others menaced the spectators with their daggers. Finally the shaman was caught in a net and tied down. They then covered him with a mat and dragged him behind the curtain. There he could be heard groaning while the chorus sang more slowly and softly.

The parallels with the Cannibal Dancer described elsewhere are evident, for Krause is clearly describing possession and a ceremony used to control the temporary madness of the one possessed.

Krause speaks of sanctions against destructive witchcraft. In the Northwest (as in all preliterate areas of the world) the shaman was believed to be able to use his power to cause sickness or death. On the basis of sympathetic magic, or analogical thinking, the method always consisted of procuring something from the victim's body, such as hair or nail cuttings, something touched by it, such as clothing, or even something urinated upon. As a result of the spells and ceremonies used upon the object the person would be affected and sicken or die. McIlwraith, in discussing the Bella Coola, stressed the matter of suggestibility which resulted in the victim's succumbing through lack of will to live. Krause maintained that the Tlingit carried on active sanctions against those accused of harmful witchcraft. They were dragged off and kept in an empty hut, sometimes tortured by being forced to drink sea water until they confessed or died. This, he maintained, was still going on in 1882.

In a typical shamanistic initiation, as recorded among the Kwakiutl, an Indian went out hunting and saw a wolf which had a deer bone wedged in its mouth so that it could not shut it. The Indian got it out with a rope, and the wolf disappeared into the woods. That night the wolf appeared in a dream. He gave his name as Harpooner-Body and said that he would reward the Indian by making him a successful hunter. After this he had great success in killing seals. Two years later, the same Indian was ill with smallpox, and while unconscious he dreamed that many wolves were near him and two were licking his body. They vomited a white foam on him, then licked it off. Among the wolves was Harpooner-Body, who vomited power into the pit of his stomach. It was explained to the man that he was now a shaman and able to bring about cures.

The theory of disease, which, as Boas pointed out, is widespread, takes two forms; one is the belief that some harmful object has entered the body. Universally, throughout the preliterate world, the cure is to suck the dangerous intrusion from the body. Even Don Juan, whom Castaneda quotes in 1968 speaks of the *maiz pinto* or dark grain of corn, which can kill a man by being projected into his body by a shaman. Don Juan describes the process:

> It immerses itself in the body; it settles on the chest or the intestines. The man becomes ill, and unless the brujo who is tending him is stronger than the bewitcher, he will die within three months from the time the kernel entered into his body.
>
> Is there any way of curing him?
>
> The only way is to suck the kernel out. . . .

Some psychiatrists have seen this curious dependence on sucking in psychoanalytical terms, a deep-seated breast fixation giving rise to this practice. At any rate, among the Kwakiutl the foreign object was thought either to have entered the body accidentally or to have been thrown by a shaman—by holding the disease in his hands and tossing it in the right direction. The cure went as follows:

> Four shamans were standing, two on each side of the one who was to cure the patient. The leader of the four old shamans asked the patient's mother for a new dish with fresh water for wetting the mouth of the shaman. It was placed by the leading shaman on the right hand side of the practitioner, who dipped up the water with his right hand, putting it into his mouth, while with his left he continued pressing the chest of the patient. He squirted the water on the place he was pressing and began to suck. Finally he lifted his head, took a bloody substance out of his mouth and squeezed it so that the blood dripped into the dish. Then he resumed his sacred songs, going around the fire. He stretched out his left hand, on which the sickness was seen appearing something like a worm; threw it up and it disappeared. Finally he blew once more upon the patient.

A bit of down was often secreted in the mouth before the ceremony and blood was produced from the mouth by biting the cheek. Although the cures of the shaman did not always work, psychologists have pointed out that their activities served a social function, the relatives' anxiety being appeased because something was being done; and the failure of the cure could be rationalized in various ways.

The other theory of illness involved the detachability of the soul or spirit, often conceived as a maple-leaf-shaped bone in the back of the neck. It was, however, also immaterial, for it could be lost from sudden fright or taken away by a supernatural being. The Kwakiutl process of recovery could be managed by a single shaman. He went around the fire carrying his rattle and singing his sacred song. The patient sat in the rear of the house, his hands upon his knees. The shaman felt the crown of his head and announced that the soul was absent. He told the father of the man to throw some of his clothing, food, and oil into the fire and to ask for the help of the spirit of the fire. Thus the unattached souls which were apparently hovering about were induced to come into the house. They quarreled among themselves over the burned clothes and food. Meanwhile, the shaman ran about looking for the missing one. He caught it in his hand and swallowed it. After circling the fire, he went up to the patient, pressed the top of his head, blew upon it—blowing in the soul which went back into its proper body.

It is the Coast Salish, however, who developed the procedure of recapturing the lost soul into a complicated ceremony which combined theater and shamanistic practice. Since they did not possess the Winter Ceremonial of the northern peoples, the Spirit Canoe Journey became their most important psychic event.

The Duwanish (of Puget Sound) version of the canoe ceremony has been described by T. T. Waterman, who compares it to the sun dance of the plain in that it was a sort of welfare ceremony and not a matter of initiation or dramatization of lineage myth, as in the case of the northern groups. A much closer parallel seems to exist in northeast Asia where shamans of the Yakut, Koryak, and Chuckchi tribes, all carried out the journey to another world in order to bring back the soul of a sick person.

The Duwanish affair had a communal aspect, for the shamans, while they were at it, often brought back a number of souls. The ceremony, which took place in winter, was staged when an individual who was ill or generally unfortunate in his life's activities put up the money to pay for the feast which accompanied the event. It generally involved four shamans and could last five days. If less money was forthcoming it went on for two. The shamans met for 12 days beforehand to paint and prepare the paraphernalia. The important objects were six canoe boards, oblong-shaped pieces of wood, sometimes with a hooked top or a small round knob for a head. On these boards, which were several feet high and pointed at the bottom so they could be stuck in the ground, were painted figures of simplified mythical animals, schematic human figures, or formalized representations of whales, salmon, or mud puppies. The figures were power givers who helped the shamans in their journey. Around the figures were painted dots called their songs. The six canoe boards were set in the ground in the middle of the dance house in a rough rectangle of 10 by 20 feet, thus creating the magical or spirit canoe. In addition to the powerful boards, the shamans also set up sculptured images 3 to 4 feet high. These were also painted with dots, and had crude heads on which features were painted, the bottom being merely pointed to be stuck in the ground, each being placed in the shaman's own compartment of the magical craft. They were described as small spirits the size of children who danced in wild and lonely places. When seen by a Salish they became his power giver.

After a performance the canoe boards were not used again; the images were washed and stored to be repainted. One other piece of equipment of importance was the shaman's staff, which could be a simple rod 4 to 5 feet long or might be shaped, sometimes suggesting an animal form.

The patient was placed in the center of the house with a circle marked out on the ground during the ceremony. The rest of the community formed the audience which took some part in the drama.

During the journey, which was based on the theory that the ghosts in the world of the dead had captured the missing soul, the spirit portion of the shamans and their power givers actually performed the journey which their material counterparts mimed in the dance house. Shamans had the power to go into a trance and locate the lost soul. The immaterial canoe in which they were to be transported to the other world had the power of turning land into water.

The actual journey involved a number of obstacles or difficult areas to be passed through. The shamans sang continually as they mimed and worked up excitement among the members of the audience. The first place visited was the land of ceremonial objects. Here each thing sang its own song—the little basket sang of gathering, the arrow point of hunting, a part of a canoe sang of fishing, even a pack strap could sing. The shamans were able to collect some of these songs and bring them back for future use. The second stop was the land of berries; these hopped around on their bushes like birds. They could only be gathered by experts. The shamans might bring back some to make the berry crop plentiful. At this point in the trip a ghost might be met, walking with his head thrown back and his eyes closed, weaving from side to side as he walked. The shamans would surround him, and with the aid of their various powers force him to tell his name and whose soul he was on his way to steal. He could also be made to give valuable information concerning what souls would be found at the end of the trip.

The next obstacle was a wide lake. Here, ignoring the fact that they were already in a canoe, the magicians arranged their staffs to make another boat. They then called upon an animal helper. When they cried "Otter! Otter!" for example, they would whiz across the lake as fast as an otter could swim. The journeying group then reached hunting grounds at which they halted and engaged in a hunting pantomime, using their staffs as weapons. The fifth stop was highly dangerous because it was the place of mosquitoes as large as birds. If a shaman were to be bitten by one, his body would swell up and he would die. There was a pantomime fight in which the mosquitoes were killed. Stop number six was the beaver place. Here a pantomime of breaking into a beaver lodge and spearing beaver took place. They then reached an open place and since, as we know, everything is reversed in the underworld, it was now dawn. This meant that the light was "bearing down on them." To overcome this hazard they had to "lift the daylight." They pointed their staffs toward it, hooked them under the daylight, and lifted it over their heads. It was explained to Waterman that the light was fivefold, "like five people," so this remarkable operation had to be repeated five times. This customarily ended the first night's performance. Apparently when larger sums of money were forthcoming to pay for the feasting which accompanied the festival, the tendency was to prolong the affair.

On the second night, the occasion of the eighth difficulty, the path taken by the magic canoe went along the bank of the river of the dead. Here there were continual caverns, and large rocks were being carried past by the current. It was customary to hold a consultation to discuss how to get across. The suggestion would be made that they go upstream. This they would do and come to the brink of a canyon called "the Jumping Place." Two posts surmounted by a crosspiece had been set up in the dance house. A plank was raised with one end on the ground, the other leaning on the crosspiece. Each shaman must walk up the plank and, with his pole, vault down into a circle marking on the ground. This meant that with the aid of the various power givers his spirit part vaulted from the cliff through the air and landed on the other bank where the village of the ghosts was situated. If he should fail and his spirit should fall in the water, he would die. (Once again the presence of the spirit canoe seems to have been temporarily ignored.) This was a dangerous point in the journey because sometimes one shaman, jealous of one of the others, had been known to try underhanded tricks to destroy him.

It was now night in the village of the ghosts. The head shaman, who always occupied the bow of the canoe, the post of danger, reconnoitered the village and finally located the lost soul or souls. The canoe was then reversed, the bow and stern boards being exchanged, the soul thrown into the canoe—but instead of making a quiet getaway (no doubt out of a dramatic feeling for climax) the head shaman hurled his power into the village wakening the slumbering ghosts. At this point there was apparently a certain amount of audience participation. The spectators had mimed the sleeping ghosts; and now, as the furious dead attacked the shamans, in some cases boys from the audience took part in the mimic warfare during which the shamans used their staffs as bows and spears and their assailants supposedly also shot arrows and hurled burning splints. Sometimes the shamans held a mat over the stern of the boat to protect themselves. Shouting, singing, the whole group reached a high point of excitement. In theory, if a shaman was hit by an arrow of the dead he would die. But in the end the soul was brought triumphantly back to the patient, into whom it would be inserted with difficulty—it might keep slipping, in which case the patient might go into a fit of trembling or the shaman would tremble professionally in a crouch position.

If it was a question of bringing back the patient's "power" or luck, once that was given to him, he would jump up and all would sing his special song as he joined in and took part in the dance. The end of the show was a general outburst of joy and excitement. Small children, who did not know what was happening, were generally terrified.

The parallels with northeast Asia are striking in that, among the Tungus, for instance, the shaman sang and drummed himself into ecstasy until he fell motionless after describing the journey he was going to make—which also involved obstacles, crossing a mountain range, passing through a small hole where his soul was in danger, crossing three rivers, and fighting with the spirits of the lower world for the soul of the sick person. He was aided by an assistant who sang, talked to the spirits, and drummed when the shaman was unconscious.

Through all of these shamanistic activities the concept of supranormal states exists. The death and resurrection theme is closely connected with it and the achievement of varying degrees of ecstatic intensity. The spirit canoe embodies it in another form. In his study of Kwakiutl religion, Werner Muller, disagreeing to some extent with Boas, sees the beginning of a pantheon emerging from the ritual of the Winter Ceremonial. He identifies Bahbakwalanuhsiwe, The-Cannibal-at-the-North-End-of-the-World, as a death god, Kantsoumps as the creator spirit, and Komowogwas as the sea spirit. Initiation of all sorts, and especially possession by the cannibal god, implies the death of the initiates and their eventual rebirth into normal life. It is true that most of the rituals, including the Nootka wolf ceremony, do imply the temporary death of the novices. Muller would go further and make a distinction between the violent set of warrior dances as the winter–death series and the lighter ones involving comedy as the spring–resurrection series. Something like this does seem to be the case for the Bella Coola. As we have suggested before, we can see in Northwest Indian culture a stage of development which might be comparable to very early Greek nature worship out of which a theater was to develop. Regardless of whether Northwest Coast Indian spirits should be technically called gods, what runs through all of the related cultures is the high regard for ecstasy, a certain Dionysian potential which achieved its most intense outlet among the Kwakiutl.

The search for supranormal experience is, of course, one of the preoccupations of our time, generally accompanied by the use of drugs—hence the popularity of Castaneda's reports on the techniques and philosophy of Don Juan. Man, it seems, has always been dissatisfied with the ordinary tenor of his daily life and even more so now that he is imprisoned in mass society and technology. He does not cease to seek for heightened forms of emotional experience. In consequence, the way of life of preliterates who do not question the existence of other types of reality and who firmly believe in unseen powers acquires a new interest and earns a new kind of respect from Western scientific civilization.

It can be seen from the foregoing account of Northwest Indian culture that this group of hunters and fishermen had developed the pre-urban way of life to extraordinary complexity.

Aside from their material achievements, especially in the area of art, theirs was an imaginatively rich society. For their adjustment to nature and their ability to shape it and absorb it into their imaginative world we can only feel admiration and nostalgia. There is no doubt this remarkable people made one of the most important contributions to early culture on the northern continent, a contribution which we can only preserve in retrospect but which deserves an honored place in our heritage.

ABOVE: Nootka whale harpoon, 20½ feet of sinew line. *(British Columbia Provincial Museum.)*

CENTER LEFT: Haida goat horn spoon. *(Provincial Museum, Victoria.)*

CENTER RIGHT: Nootka spruce root basket from the author's collection, with design of Thunderbird carrying off a whale, about 100 years old. *(Philippe Montant photo.)*

BELOW LEFT: Tsimshian painted wooden box. *(British Columbia Provincial Museum.)*

BELOW RIGHT: Kwakiutl skin drum, deer hide over red cedar. *(British Columbia Provincial Museum.)*

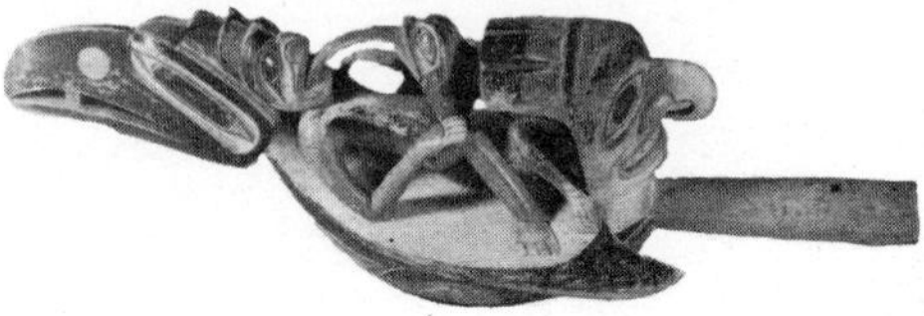

ABOVE LEFT: Haida chief's dance rattle, raven design. *(British Columbia Provincial Museum.)*

ABOVE RIGHT: Tsimshian carved bone shaman's charm. *(Provincial Museum.)*

BELOW: Haida village at Skidegate, Queen Charlotte Islands, 1878, showing style of totem pole. *(Provincial Archives, Victoria.)*

ABOVE: Kwakiutl painting of Raven on screen used as curtain in winter ceremonial. It is believed that Raven can transform himself into the chief who stands behind the *sisiutl. (E. S. Curtis photo, 1914, Provincial Archives, Victoria.)*

CENTER LEFT: Kwakiutl Wolf Dancer. *(E. S. Curtis photo, 1914, Provincial Archives, Victoria.)*

CENTER RIGHT: Kwakiutl deer mask used in dance of the animals, carved 1936. *(British Columbia Provincial Museum.)*

BELOW: Nootka wolf mask, red, blue, and white. *(British Columbia Provincial Museum.)*

TOP: Nimkisch Kwakiutl village at Alert Bay, 1914. *(E. S. Curtis photo, Provincial Archives, Victoria.)*

LEFT: Classic ancient Haida pole at Skidegate. Note semi-anthropomorphic figure of a beaver. *(Provincial Archives, Victoria.)*

RIGHT: Tsimshian totem pole from the village of Kitwancool discussed in Chapter 19. *(Pole is now in Provincial Museum totem pole park. Photo by author.)*

ABOVE: Photo of a group of Bella Coola Hamatsa dancers, taken in Germany in 1885. Captain F. Jacobsen brought a group of these Indians to Berlin, a group which captured the interest of Franz Boas, who subsequently came to the United States and became an expert on the Northwest Coast Indians. *(National Museum of Canada, Ottawa.)*

CENTER LEFT: Bella Coola ghost mask from the author's collection. Hair originally cedar bark, twine added later. *(Philippe Montant photo.)*

CENTER RIGHT: Kwakiutl Hamatsa Dancer emerging from the woods in a state of possession. *(E. S. Curtis photo, 1914, Provincial Archives, Victoria.)*

BELOW: Thunderbird mask, painted red and black, dyed cedar bark hair. *(British Columbia Provincial Museum, Victoria.)*

Kwakiutl Bear Dancer discussed in Chapter 20. *(E. S. Curtis photo, 1907, Provincial Archives, Victoria.)*

ABOVE: Kwakiutl fleet under full sail. *(E. S. Curtis photo, 1914, Provincial Archives, Victoria.)*

BELOW: A Coast Salish (Snoqalmee) spirit canoe ceremony showing use of canoe boards and spirit images. *(Museum of the American Indian, Heye Foundation.)*

ABOVE: A Gitksan Tsimshian shaman treating a sick boy. *(National Museums of Canada, Ottawa.)*

BELOW: Coast Salish masked dancer. *(E. S. Curtis photo, 1912, Provincial Archives, Victoria.)*

III
THE NORTHWEST COAST TODAY

RAVEN'S COUNTRY

23

When Raven was busy creating the Northwest Coast he turned out some of the most awe-inspiring scenery on the northern continent. Flying so much of the time, as we have done, we were continually aware of the deep network of fjords and rivers which lend endless variety to this part of North America and at the same time precluded anything like a system of roads. Roads there are on Vancouver Island and here and there inland from the coast, but from the north to the south unbroken expanses of evergreen forest cover the shoreline, while 8000- to 10,000-foot mountains rise just behind it, some of them topped with snow, some even supporting a glacier like a giant octopus.

Looking down at the handfuls of islands everywhere strewn along this coast, from a plane it is easy to see the cruel hidden rocks just below the surface, and it is also easy to see how tentative the old voyagers must have felt, especially during the frequent fogs and rains—and why they often feared to put in to shore and often did not succeed in making a landing.

By and large, the evidences of human habitation aside from the cities are a tiny scurf of settlements on the shores of inlets, islands, and rivers absolutely lost in the expanses of unbroken forest which separate them for miles and miles. No longer are scores and scores of great dugout canoes drawn up on the stony beaches, but instead there can be seen, from the air, all along the waterline, a collection of driftwood, most of the time large logs that have been lost in the process of lumbering, seemingly a thoroughly wasteful operation.

To the Easterner a very definite flavor of the frontier lingers in the Northwest. The smaller cities have an impermanent look, as if they had just arrived and were not sure whether they intended to stay. Prince Rupert is the focus of the northern area; from it a road leads to Terrace and Hazelton along the Skeena River, this being the territory of the Tsimshian. Prince Rupert is the self-proclaimed gateway to Alaska, for from here one can take the ferry which traverses Clarence Strait and which then runs up through southern Alaska to Juneau, through the country of the Tlingit. The Nass River, further north than the Skeena, also the haunt of the Tsimshian, can only be reached by plane, and the beautiful valley of the Bella Coola River, the historic home of the people of that name, is also most easily reached by plane.

We were naturally on the lookout for Raven, but at first we only encountered his small relatives, the crows. These did not behave like any crows of the East Coast, which are generally heard in the distance but not seen. Northwest crows are impudently familiar. They sit on rooftops, on pilings, and on fence posts and make critical remarks, sharing the scene with the seagulls. Raven we saw behind our hotel in Masset, disputing the garbage with his smaller relatives. It seemed rather a comedown for the creator of the world.

One is always aware of trees on this fabulous coast. The great cedars loom up in Stanley Park, which girdles the northern projection of the city of Vancouver against a background of snowtopped mountains. Later they are seen fringing every inch of coastline and covering the ever-present islands. Growing down to the edge of the generally stony shore, they look as if they are about to step into the water.

On mentioning to our neighbor at the table next to us in a restaurant at Campbell River that we were going to Port Alberni, in the middle of the island, he said: "What do you want to go there for? There's nothing but trees."

Later when we made the trip (in search of the Nootka), we remembered his remark as we drove through Cathedral Grove of Macmillan Park. It was a winding route, through a forest which is probably surpassed only by the redwoods of California. The spruces and hemlocks are a good 10 feet in diameter and many are a couple of hundred feet tall at least. Bare of branches until near the top, the great columns are crowded together as these giants seek the light—then at the tip a thick tuft of needles obscures the sky. There are always mountains in the background, and, as the road curves, dark vistas open and close only opening out widely where the route follows the edge of Lake Cameron.

Even Vancouver Island itself, the settled area with the longest history, presents only snatches of farmland. Along the east coast up to Campbell River, the focal city at the north end of the island, a number of settlements proclaim themselves summer resorts. But occasional shingle beaches and those covered with large stones are not very inviting. On the whole the coast settles for being a fisherman's dream.

What becomes very clear from actual experience of the Northwest Coast is the difference in population density from most areas in the United States. This has resulted in a different experience for the native inhabitants. By and large they are still living where they have always lived, even though they may be dissatisfied with the amount of land the surveyors have allowed them. Relatively less pressure from the whites has resulted from the fact that the region is not particularly adapted to agriculture. Hence the shifting to undesirable localities, the ruthless attempts to eliminate the Indians, which have gone on in most of the United States, have not taken place. Since the Indians have remained where they were, they have retained access to the sea—the means of their livelihood—and they have in many cases been able to make the transition from the hand-operated nets of the past to modern power boats and power-operated drums. Thus there has been a continuity in their lives. More than once an informant has told the writer, "Fishing is in my blood." Thus this activity involves a connection with nature, and, indeed, Howard Wale, the Tsimshian chief councillor from Hazelton, said he looked forward to fishing as if to a holiday.

Actually the other major activity is lumbering and working in the pulp mills. When it is remembered that the Northwest Indians have always been skilled woodworkers and have been accustomed to handle totem poles and build great wooden houses, we can see that once again the circumstances of the environment have remained constant and, again, that the Indians have been able to make the transition to woodworking with modern technology while retaining some kind of feeling for the material. All this has an effect on morale. Compare the elimination of the bison, often done consciously to destroy the Plains Indians' livelihood. Compare, too, the case of the 137,000 Navajo condemned to a reservation 37 percent of which is semi-arid and only good for subsistence sheep grazing while more than half is desert, good for practically nothing, while the federal government fails to grant money to build a reservation irrigation system with water from the Colorado River. It can be seen, then, that the Northwest Coast Indians have enjoyed certain advantages.

Not that their situation has been a bed of roses. As we shall see, their housing is inadequate. Gone are the old long houses with their handsome painted house fronts and their proud totem poles. In place of a brilliant native architecture, there are now meager little three- or four-room frame houses utterly without style. When you have seen one you have seen them all. In this, except for quality, they do not differ much from the rest of rural British Columbia, which also lives in meager frame houses destitute of style. This is a painful reality which obtrudes upon the traveler. Against the backdrop of magnificent sea and mountains, man lives, except for a handful of more substantial cities, insofar as his dwellings go, in imaginative poverty.

Sometimes the Indian community has its own settlement apart from the white village, as in Haida Village near Masset on Graham Island or the Cowichan Salish band near Duncan. In other cases like Alert Bay, the two settlements are pretty much continuous, and in Bella Coola one of the main streets cuts the village in two—on one side the reserve with two totem poles at the corner, on the other the white settlement with the general store, the cooperative, and the hotel. In other cases the reserve is absorbed into the town, as the Salish in Vancouver City or the Nootka in Port Alberni, and the Indian settlement is only distinguishable as an obviously low-income area.

The average citizen of the United States, who does not live near a reserve, can pass his whole life without ever seeing an Indian. While Indians only represent 5 percent of the British Columbia population, they are more in evidence, perhaps because more evenly distributed in numerous small bands. On the whole, discrimination does not now seem to be a major problem, although instances of it admittedly do exist. We shall have occasion to mention the attitudes of the Bella Coola whites. Joe Daniels of Kitwanga, near Hazelton, complained of the attitude of the whites in his valley who had consistently opposed amalgamating the white and the Indian schools. Howard Wale, the chief councillor of Hazelton, felt the problem did exist but that more whites were moving in to work in the new sawmill and that the attitude would change and a new and integrated secondary school would be built. Allan Hall, a member of the North Shore District Council based in Prince Rupert, said he had encountered discrimination in hotels in Prince George and once when he tried to buy a house. On the other hand, the hereditary Tsimshian chief, Kenneth Harris, remarked that he never knew he was an Indian until he went to Europe.

Actually, it has been said that there is scarcely a pure Indian on the coast. It is true that mixed marriages take place all the time and that many persons whom we met, who were "status" Indians, looked no different from Europeans.

It must be remembered, however, there are various linguistic strains on the Northwest Coast and hence a variation in ethnic stock. We saw many dark-skinned, broad-cheeked, and round-faced people much like the aborigines of Mexico—and yet we also saw many who were light-skinned, with aquiline features. At the same time, it is interesting to remember that several of the eighteenth-century traders remarked that they saw many natives who could pass for Europeans.

We had been told that the Indians were fed up with anthropologists. Although Louis Demerais, acting director of the Union of British Columbian Chiefs, was willing to give us a list of Indian contacts, he warned us that a procession of graduate students had haunted the coast, making studies for their doctorates. Since most of the time nothing of value for the groups studied seemed to emerge from their efforts, the Northwest people were tired of being guinea pigs. We made it our business to explain that we were not doing an anthropological "study" but rather a kind of inquiring reporter job, asking questions concerning the current scene and listening to opinions. In every case we found that Indian contacts were courteous and agreeable, quite willing to answer sensible questions and often happy to express their opinions. There is a tradition of hospitality and openness toward strangers.

There was often criticism of anthropologists. Bill Scow complained that Philip Drucker had referred to the Scow family in *To Make My Name Good* and had not checked with him. Scow told a story of another anthropologist who had written of the group on Guilford Island, thinly disguising individuals by fictitious names. Apparently he had published a number of indiscrete facts. On returning, he visited Scow. The latter asked him if he was going back to the island. He said he had been there and everyone seemed happy. He then proposed a second trip with Scow. Scow was skeptical but finally they went. As they approached, first one boat and then another put out from the island, all loaded with people. When the anthropologist stepped on shore he was greeted by an empty village.

James Sewid also complained of some of Boas's work. There are many local variants of tradition and custom and every lineage possesses a great store of carefully guarded tradition. Hence, when anthropologists generalize from one informant, every Indian with a good knowledge of native history and a rich lineage finds reasons to disagree with him.

On one occasion I ran into an odd misunderstanding. When I was introduced to the Bella Coola Band Council, I happened to mention a book by Skopas. There was an immediate reaction. Several said they disliked the book and that the band had thought of suing Skopas. After some discussion in which we tried to find out something specific, the writer's first name came up and it turned out that the book under discussion was one by Leslie Skopas. An M.A. thesis on Indian political development, it had been written by the son of a storekeeper and resident of Bella Coola who had also written a general book on the Bella Coola Indians which was felt to express a condescending point of view toward the Indians and to be factually unreliable. It was this book, of course, which aroused the council. Later on, District Superintendent Ronald Witt explained that the elder Skopas also had taken a number of fine masks more or less in pawn from Indians who could not pay their bills and later, when they were not redeemed, had made a handsome profit on them.

On the whole we found that the native people have a strong attachment to their home areas and native villages. This is perhaps one of the reasons why, aside from economic difficulties, not too many have made the effort to acquire a college education, which would involve residence in Vancouver or Victoria and often eventual absorption into the white man's competitive world.

It seemed to us that there was always the sound of a small airplane taking off in the background wherever we went. And, indeed, without these 6-passenger Beavers, 14-passenger Ducks, Geese, and other assorted amphibians the isolated settlements in the various inlets, on islets and in deep river valleys on the North Coast would be almost unreachable. In these little planes, able to land on a strip or on the water, long-haired young men with packs on their backs in search of work at pulp mills, technicians and salesmen in business suits, Indians on their way to visit cities or returning to their little villages, plus the ever-present fisherman (who range from the long-haired youngsters with packs on their backs, to red-faced beer drinkers in parkas)—all these avail themselves of the reliable little planes as if they were taxis.

Port Hardy, on the north tip of Vancouver Island, offers a good-sized airport from which the small planes fan out into the hinterlands. From Port Hardy the jets fly back down the island to Vancouver. The town is a good example of the tentative, frontier character of small cities. Everywhere the rooted-up stumps of the trees that formerly covered the area are lying about. There is no grass, no public square, which an Easterner would expect to see. Instead, a few streets vaguely enclose empty lots filled with trash. The city seems to be organized around a dump. And yet there is a neatly designed modern hotel, a modern-looking bank and a well-planned arcade with sidewalks and shops. The rest is raw earth—and, no doubt, plans for the future.

The bush pilots, young men with the dash and flair of cowboys, go everywhere, undeterred by fog and rain, flight being the rule rather than exception in fall and winter. In planning a trip to the island of Bella Bella, there seemed no way to overcome the fact that there was, as yet, no place where we could find overnight lodging. Consequently, a chartered flight to nearby Ocean Falls was worked out from where a regular flight would return us to Port Hardy the next day. Ocean Falls is strictly a pulp mill settlement where Crown Zellerbach set up workers' houses, houses for executives, a school, and a hotel, and subsequently, deciding to pull out, turned the whole thing over at a loss to the Canadian government. Tall mountains seem to arch overhead; the settlement nestles at the head of the valley. That night it poured, and the following morning the valley was filled with pea soup fog. With no expectation of getting out we, nevertheless, went to the office of the Alert Bay Air Service. To our surprise the pilot soon called in by radiophone. "Oh yes," said the young woman in the office, "ceiling eight hundred feet, visibility five miles, wind velocity fifteen miles an hour." To the inquiry, "Do you have instruments?" she answered cheerfully, "Oh, no, I just look out of the window."

And through the mist we went, following the waterway with the snowcapped mountains bearing down on each side, only to find the airport at Port Hardy was closed, whereupon we landed in the bay and were bused in to the airport.

This was technological British Columbia of today, but the past is never far distant. While looking over Haida Village near Masset, we encountered a couple of young archeologists who had been digging all summer in an abandoned village nearby. The Gesslers had been working in the house of the brother of Charles Edenshaw, the famous carver. Working from the present backward, already having discovered a sequence of several hundred years, they hoped to go considerably further into the past. Among their interesting finds was a wooden cross embedded in a tree which they believed had been set up by the Spanish explorer Massena. They had already found artifacts of English, Spanish, and Russian manufacture. They were much interested in checking their finds against historical records.

Many cartons of small artifacts were stored in the abandoned schoolhouse in which they were camping precariously; their household included a young baby. They provided coffee, and, as we looked over their notebooks and photos, they told us that they were on leave from the University of British Columbia. They were commissioned to set up a museum in the former schoolhouse and were able to show us several fine old totem poles which had fallen and been rescued from the village. The poles consisted of handsome single figures, and, although weathered, the Gesslers hoped to restore them and make them the nucleus of the proposed collection. Among their finds were innumerable paintstones, testimony to the intense artistic activity of earlier generations of Haida.

It was in Bella Coola we encountered another link with the past in the person of Andy Schooner, who, we were told, liked to tell stories. Since he was generally to be found wandering about the streets, we waited for him beside the gate of his little red house. He soon appeared, an amiable little patriarch in a green jacket and a black cap. After we had chatted for awhile, he brought out a carton and showed us his family mask. It was the second one to have been made for his family and was at least a hundred years old. Grotesquely beautiful, with great staring eyes, it had a series of different mouthpieces ingeniously designed so they could be slipped into place to change the quality of the voice. It was a mask of Echo, Andy told us, and was used in potlatches. Treasured as a precious heirloom, it would be inherited by his son, a fisherman, who, he told us proudly, had made $50,000 that year.

We asked him if he had taken part in the old ceremonies and potlatches. This set him reminiscing:

First one I see when I was just a kid was in about 1905. I didn't see the whole performance but when this fellow was laying down on the floor in the old long house, his head was cut off.

We asked him how he reacted.

Oh, I was frightened, frightened all the time in those feasts called potlatches when they had what you call the Cannibal Dancer. He was sitting there all the time and when I'd move around like a kid he said, "OOOOAAAAH!" He was the law in any gathering, feast, or potlatch. He goes around to all the people to show how bad he is. And he bites them. He just takes the skin like that and let the blood run, that's all. And the people have to behave themselves all the time, all the time!

We chatted about the missionaries, which led us into talk of the Indian religion and eventually to a story which was a quaint mixture of the traditional, Andy's personal invention, and, if he is to be believed, an unrecorded footnote to history:

I got a different religion, the Indian religion. Every morning I go with my grandfather to see to the traps—he had five or six traps. And every morning that old fellow he splash water in his face and he look up to heaven and he says, "Protect us again for the day, during the day, protect us." And I ask him one day, "Who do you talk to?" He said, "My father living in the sun. If you don't do that, you have accidents." That's the first thing I heard from my grandfather. And then that night he told me the creation. I'll just give you the first part.

At this point we asked permission to turn off the television set, which had been running steadily and which we knew was playing havoc with the recording machine:

In the sun, where god lives, we call him Menachis, that's the name of our god, you see. And he's in a valley just like this here with trees and goats and all the other animals. Then Menachis created two persons, one was to go to the sunrise and the other to the sunset, east and west. And then God made the sunrise and the sunset. And he gave two articles to that fellow going to the sunset, a book and an ax. And he was holding that book and he looks it over, looks that book over. Finally he say "Useless" and he took the ax. And he discovers there's a sunset. The other fellow, he went to Europe or Asia. And that nation has that book because the other fellow was in Europe or Asia. I don't know whether it was China or what. Chinamen seem to be the first people over there in Asia. That other man he come down on a sunbeam, there was other people coming down on the sunbeams, too. And that fellow on the sunbeam, he tried to say good-bye to the others and they didn't understand him. God gave them a different language. And God said, "We're parting now, but we will meet again years, and years, and years afterward." He said good-bye and went down and that's how this guy, Alexander Mackensie, came to this coast, to Bella Coola. Now the people knew the whites were coming. They called them *mismismesolenich*—they didn't call them white men. The people didn't know the creation story yet, but they stopped the Bella Bella from murdering him, from killing him. This Bella Coola chief he puts feathers on his head, eagle down. And then this other Bella Bella fellow comes with bow and arrows and clubs and spears. When he saw that, the feathers on the chief's head, he just turned around and went away. That was what the Indians did in Bella Coola. And they took Mackensie down to see the ocean. And these other Bella Bella people came to kill him that night. But they put him in a canoe and took him up the other inlet and the Bella Bella people went up the river instead.

Mackensie was always afraid that he was about to be attacked and would have had no way of distinguishing the Bella Bella from the Bella Coola. It is just possible that Andy's account contains some traditional elements which have been handed down by word of mouth. He finally added a coda to the creation story:

At the beginning before they created the human beings, the Eagle was the one that flew all over and said you'll have this kind of tree, all this land and, you know, the salmon and the animals, the goats and the deer. And he's going to start a new world. And Raven says that he'll report him to God. And then Raven completed the world, this part here. He lost his son, the Eagle got his son and carried him up to the other world. So Raven made a whale, all out of pitch, like a ball, he put pitch inside the whale. He wanted to kill all the eagles, see. And the first one came down and tried to take the whale to the other world. And Raven drowned him. And the second one, and the third, and the fourth came down and Raven got them all. So he asked Menachis to make him another eagle, a small one that he could handle.

So once more we come back to Raven, who is never far away. At least in Andy's version, he triumphs in the end. And let us hope he watches over the Northwest Coast still and will lend his people some of his cleverness and toughness so that they, too, will attain what they seek in the end.

THE TWO METLAKATLAS

24

It is not often that one has the opportunity of encountering the last chapter of an historical episode and consequently we were eager to visit both Old and New Metlakatla of today. One bit of folklore we did encounter concerned the redoubtable Father Duncan. The famous clergyman, it seems, had red hair, and it happened once or twice, we were told with a wink, that in the old days red-haired children were to be seen running about the streets of Old Metlakatla.

At any rate, the old settlement was to be reached from Prince Rupert by the school ferry. As the ferry's first trip was at seven o'clock, and since we were obliged to wait until four to return we chartered the conveyance in the early afternoon, planning to go back on the return trip from busing the schoolchildren. The boat was a sort of roofed-over inboard with a dozen or so seats. It was a 40-minute trip through the handsome bay, along which the city extends, passing between evergreen-crowned capes and islands, the whole scene bright in a warm September sun. The village itself was strung out along the shore, about 15 or 20 buildings housing a population of 100. The gently sloping hillside rising from a narrow stony beach was slightly reminiscent of the coast of Maine. In the distance were small islands and jutting from the shore was a dock which led by steep stairs to the macadam walk which ran along the single street.

We had not been able to contact the band manager, a Mrs. Joyce Liesk, who was unfortunately in Vancouver, but as we strolled up the path we encountered a pleasant middle-aged woman in a purple-and-white blouse, purple slacks, and crimson slippers who turned out to be the wife of the chief councillor, George Leighton. She became our amiable guide to the little hamlet.

Back in the late nineteenth century at the time of Duncan's exodus, over 100 people had remained behind. Over the years the population declined until there were only two or three families left. Then some began to move back until the community has become a small village once more.

Except for a handful of children playing on the path and one or two women passing along it, the place seemed almost asleep.

Mrs. Leighton explained that the men were all away fishing in the neighborhood of the Queen Charlotte's Islands. They generally went off for two days a week, sometimes staying longer and flying home for the weekend. Most of them rented their boats and delivered their fish to Prince Rupert. The women were housewives except for a handful who worked in the cannery at Prince Rupert. As we strolled about we could see that the village was, as we eventually learned, the prototype of most Indian villages. In this case a single row of dwellings of three or four rooms ran along the shore, some unpainted, some painted white, one more modern of varnished wood, two merely dewheeled trailers. They were set among unkempt, nondescript bushes with no attempt at lawns or flower gardens. Mrs. Leighton agreed that, during the Duncan regime, there had been luxuriant vegetable gardens but somehow they had all disappeared. Everyone depended on Prince Rupert for frozen provisions. Having gotten a power plant three years before they had electric freezers. In the summer, however, they did all their home canning of salmon and abalone for the winter months. Their water system was bad and in need of improvement. A couple of government agriculturists, however, were supposed to be arriving to determine whether the soil was capable of supporting crops.

The councillors had two-year terms, and there were two others beside Leighton. Mrs. Liesk, who served as band manager, only came over from Prince Rupert periodically. She was paid by the band from funds it obtained from land and gravel leases. The community had no police officer and no health nurse.

Aside from the dwellings, there was a small wooden church which had replaced the ornate one of Father Duncan's time (destroyed by fire). To this an Anglican clergyman came on Wednesday because on Sundays he was too busy. According to Mrs. Leighton the village managed pretty well economically. There seemed to be no unemployment problem, at least in as good a fishing year as 1973.

The other public buildings consisted of a small coffee shop, which was apparently only open in summers when tourists sometimes arrived, and a little museum. The latter contained a few Indian artifacts such as halibut hooks, baskets, and some chipped spear points. There were also a number of photographs of the old Duncan church and the old leader himself. Groups of his converts, his brass band instruments, and other memorabilia stared at us from faded prints. He was now remembered by only one very deaf old man.

The members of the community on the whole spoke English; only a few knew Tsimshian, among them Mrs. Leighton. On the cultural side there was a flicker of interest in carving. Mrs. Leighton was taking lessons and showed us an unfinished plaque. Since they had television (we never entered an Indian home without a set), it seemed that this, and occasionally the movie in Prince Rupert, were the sum of their recreation. As there was only a kindergarten on the island, all the children went to Prince Rupert for their schooling.

"It's so peaceful here. I don't think I'd leave it for anything," said the councillor's wife. And indeed it was, with the quiet waterfront empty except for one fishing boat which had glided up and moored at the dock. Presently, however, the school ferry arrived and disgorged a dozen or so children of various ages who chattered and skylarked as they bounced up steps to the village.

We had seen Old Metlakatla, which had never regained its old importance after Duncan left. All that was left of his era were a couple of imported poplars by the path. However, Allan Hall, the district councillor, told us that roads were projected, one of which would run to Old Metlakatla, and if this occurs Old Metlakatla may cease to be the quiet backwater it is now.

New Metlakatla, on Annette Island, Alaska, could be reached by plane from Ketchikan—in our case, by a tiny four-passenger Cessna. It was our first experience with the small conveyances, and we never ceased to admire the skill of the pilot, who would glide up to the dock, leap out of the door (rope in hand) to the pontoon, and then hop lightly to the dock to take a quick turn of the rope around the stanchion securing the plane.

It was a gray day, as usual; we arrived rather early, and no one seemed to be about. The new community was a fair-sized village laid out in a conventional grid pattern. Since we had no specific contact, we headed for the administration building, which was new and well-designed in simple modern style. We were directed to the community development officer, Wally Liesk (a distant cousin of the other Liesk) and his assistant Solomon Atkinson. They were hospitable and well-informed. New Metlakatla, it seems, has the special status of being the only reservation in Alaska. (It should be noted that the Tlingit have always rejected the reservation system and simply stuck to it that they were citizens until they made their claim good.) Interestingly enough, this means that New Metlakatla does not share in land settlement which has been awarded the other natives of Alaska. Theirs was a special grant, and Liesk feels that they have enough land and no fear of overpopulation in the near future. The land is owned by the community, but individuals own and can sell their own houses—only, however, to natives, that is, Aleuts, Tsimshian, Haida, or Eskimo. Indeed, over the years such a number of these have joined the community that the Tsimshian are no longer dominant. According to the village regulation, outsiders can marry members and join, but women who marry outsiders lose their vote and their non-native husbands cannot vote. They wish, it seems, to keep the balance of power in the hands of the natives. The community has 12 councillors, a mayor, a secretary, and a treasurer; the councillors are in office for two terms. Women can run, and one has been a councillor. Each year the people vote for six councillors. This is the government for a population of about 1125, about 900 being natives. There is a weather station and a coast guard station staffed by Alaskans and, while the airport was operating, there were more whites. Much exposure to the whites has resulted in a good deal of intermarriage. Liesk's wife was from Michigan, Atkinson's from Washington. Both were ex-service men, Liesk having retired from the air force and Atkinson from the navy.

New Metlakatla is a rather prosperous community with little unemployment. The cannery and the sawmill continue from Duncan's era (though not the same buildings). A new cold storage plant built with a $600,000 federal grant was completed in 1971; it holds 500,000 pounds of seafood. All the buildings are owned by the community. The mill is leased to the Georgia Pacific Corporation. The community gets a nominal sum from this, but it profits more from the ensuing employment for its members. As Liesk remarked, in the old days with some lumber and $100 down it was easy to put up a mill and pay off the initial cost from the profits. In those days they built their own houses from the lumber it produced. Now the mill turns out only beams, most of which are shipped to Japan, some to Vancouver. About 7,000,000 beams a year are cut. Some is local timber, but the community has access to more elsewhere.

The cannery and storage plant has a local director but imports technicians to run it. Liesk said they were running into a tax problem. As a reservation they were not taxed, but the state had decided it wanted to tax their fish products. The issue is still being fought out legally. We brought up the matter of a percentage on the fish caught in the neighborhood, but neither

Liesk nor Atkinson had heard of it. They had fishing rights to 3000 feet of shore but fishing here had not been good. We were told they blamed it on the Japanese and the Russians. The fishermen sold to the cannery and when the cannery made money, so did the town. In the Duncan days they had fine gardens and grew potatoes but interestingly enough, just as in Old Metlakatla, the habit of gardening had died out and everyone depended on the frozen provisions—"If the electricity failed, we'd all die of starvation." A majority still canned and smoked salmon, however: as Liesk remarked, it was well worth while with salmon at $50 a case.

The town used to supply free electricity, but now, with their multimillion diesel and hydro-electric plant, they were obliged to charge. Since they own it, however, the rate is much less than elsewhere in Alaska. They are free of the profits of the big power company.

The loss of the airport was a sore point. It had been government-built in World War II and leased from Metlakatla. We were told that it had been more accessible than the present one, in Ketchikan, which was often fogbound, but politics had shifted it from their island. The Indians were hoping that they could find someone to take it over and run it once more. There were also plans for a ferry early in 1974.

Atkinson was kind enough to chauffeur us about the town, which has an old community house, a much larger new one, and a white church replacing the one of Father Duncan's time, which, like the first one in the British Columbian community, had also burned down. There is also a bank. The schools are impressive, especially the new and modern $2,000,000 high school which is experimenting with open classrooms. They are still run by the state but there are plans for taking them over. There is a well-stocked supermarket which, because the settlement is a reservation, cannot sell beer.

We took note of the small stone monument with a plaque dedicated to the pioneers of 1887 and were shown the spot where the new ferry terminal was to be built.

At the dock, near the sawmill, a Japanese freighter was waiting for cargo. The burning of sawdust in a curious turret-shaped furnace produces a good deal of smoke to the point of somewhat polluting the air along shore. The community wanted the sawmill to do something about it, but the company threw the problem back into the lap of the village with the rationale that New Metlakatla owned the mill.

As we chatted with Atkinson, it emerged that although he did not have an Indian name (he said no one did except the old people) nevertheless his parents had started to arrange a marriage for him. He had said no flatly and married a white girl. He was, it seems, running for the council and had decided that there was no reason why Metlakatla should go on importing technicians to run the canning factory. He therefore intended to propose a training program so that their own people could take over. Since the director of the canning factory, with whom we were anxious to talk because he could remember Father Duncan, was not available, we had lunch in the pleasant little coffee shop by the water and then returned to the cannery. All along the dock lay picturesque piles of net, but there were no fishing boats in port.

John W. Smith told us that, until about 1920, the Metlakatlans ran their two industries. After this they brought in outside technicians for the cannery and in the early twenties they leased it to Pacific American Fisheries. In the late twenties it was leased to William Priest, then a few years later the village took it back and put in its own director.

The cannery was having difficulty in obtaining a labor force because it paid about $3.50 an hour, while the sawmill paid nearer $5. Smith had tried the experiment of importing college boys in summer but felt they did not know how to work.

In the past steamers had stopped at New Metlakatla, bringing some tourists. The townspeople would line up on the dock selling flowers, baskets, and small carvings. Around 1952 Metlakatlans began to have cars. According to Smith, the incidence of heart trouble had climbed, for people had ceased to walk. The community has about 140 miles of road which lead to the airport and the coast guard station.

Although there was little Indian tradition left in Smith's family, which was Irish and Russian on his father's side, he did remember some of the Tsimshian customs handed down from his maternal grandfather. The old man told him that the old hunters, if they came to a settlement at night, would examine the totem poles until they found one indicating the owner was of their clan. Then they would be sure to be taken in and given lodging for the night.

When asked about Father Duncan, Mr. Smith told us he remembered him as a schoolchild. In the old days all the grades were in one big classroom with a huge fireplace in the center. Although the older boys kept wood on the fire, those far from it were pretty cold. When the wind changed, they sat weeping from the smoke that poured down the chimney. Duncan, although he no longer taught himself, had a Canadian teacher who was aided by some Indian girls whom Duncan had trained. By this time Duncan was head of his own independent church. According to Smith, Duncan liked "law and order" and objected strongly to newfangled religious sects, which nevertheless invaded the community. Smith remembered that at the end of the school year Duncan would set up a big table covered with toys for the little children of the first and second grades and he would let them come by and pick out a ball or a doll. In his playground he had a merry-go-round with an organ in the center. Smith remembered that it had to be pumped by hand to make it go round. There was also a sort of maypole with a swivel on top and seats hung from it which was turned by the older boys while the little children hung on for dear life.

With this (finally softened) picture of the old religious leader presiding over the children, we left New Metlakatla. The community is undoubtedly thriving and can be pointed to as a triumph of the old approach of de-Indianization. Yet it was the basic industries and the advantages of communal organization that have made it what it is. Although there are scarcely any vestiges of anything Tsimshian visible on superficial observation, when we spoke of the old culture we were told that the group would like to develop some carvers. There was even one, Jack Hudson, who had already made a name for himself working for the Smithsonian Institution and who, after some apprenticeship in silver in Vancouver, planned to return to New Metlakatla. In addition, since there were many artifacts in the possession of the older members, the council was working on the idea of a museum; if they could obtain a state grant, they hoped to have it ready for the Bicentennial. Thus, at this late date, the Indians were beginning to turn nostalgically to the heritage from which their grandfathers had been so stringently proscribed.

THE INDIANS UNITE AND FIGHT

25

Canadian Indians were granted the right to vote with the restriction that they must waive their tax exemption, in 1949, in both provincial and federal elections. Frank Calder, who had been secretary of the Native Brotherhood and was the adopted son of the first leader of the Nishga Land Committee, ran for a seat in the provincial legislature. He had received his education in the Anglican Theological College of Vancouver. It was a moment of great historical importance when a native candidate was chosen by the Cooperative Commonwealth Federation—and even more significant that he was elected to represent the Altin constituency, an area of 60,700 square miles in the northwest corner of British Columbia. Calder has been a significant leader, having been reelected almost continually until he was appointed minister without portfolio in 1972 to the New Democratic Party cabinet of British Columbia.

In 1951 the coastal Indians tried to establish a party of their own. Its founder, Guy Williams, announced that it would run either Indian or white candidates who were sympathetic to the Indians and their aims. The group held an organizational meeting but eventually, on the advice of Peter Kelly and Bill Scow, the project was dropped. At the coronation of Queen Elizabeth II, Bill Scow was chosen by the Native Brotherhood to attend the coronation. It was thought that this gesture would be good public relations for the Indians. He appeared at the ceremony in an embroidered blanket and headdress and presented a Chilkat blanket to the Queen.

The Progressive Conservative victory in 1957 resulted in an amendment to the Election Act allowing Indians to vote without any restrictions. The Nishga, who continued to press their lands claims (now that it was legally possible) had formed the Nishga Tribal Council with Frank Calder as chairman of its legislative committee. The Allied Tribes of the West Coast, which represented the Nootka, was organized in 1958 and affiliated with the Native Brotherhood. The North American Indian Brotherhood still existed and represented Frazer Valley and the southern interior. A Vancouver Island tribal federation was soon organized to speak for the Coast Salish. The Native Brotherhood continued to be the organ of the north and central coast. Although the Nishga Tribal Council, with Calder as its spokesman, demanded compensation for trap lines destroyed by the Columbia Cellulose Company on lands which were part of those claimed by the Tsimshian, the new drive for a general land settlement was slow to get started. Nevertheless, *The Native Voice* began to revive the issue by reviewing its history, and in 1959 at a large Native Brotherhood convention there was once more talk about ownership of the land, with Peter Kelly remarking that the province of British Columbia had taken possession of it simply because it was stronger than the Indians.

In 1960 Calder presented a brief to the federal Joint Committee on Indian Affairs asking for aid in obtaining a court judgment on Nishga land claims, which included aboriginal rights to about 1000 square miles in the region of the Nass River.

An important shot in the arm was the news that the United States court of claims had ruled that the 70,000 Haida and Tlingit Indians were entitled to compensation for 20,000,000 acres of land of which they had been deprived in Alaska.

When the provincial Department of Highways built 4 miles of road across the Kitwanga reserve near Hazelton in 1960, the Indians threatened to establish a tollgate. The minister of highways blamed it on agitators. The writer interviewed Joe Daniels, band manager of Kitwanga, a salty and outspoken character whose opinions are an example of local sentiment. Said Daniels:

The roughest deal we ever had was when they sneaked in with the Indian reserves. You see this area here. It's 4 square miles. In the old days you could roam down 3 miles to the Little Oliver River and 3 miles east on across the mountains to the Copper River. Those were our boundaries in the old days with other tribes. And they go way back here 40 miles and come out about 11½ miles northeast toward Kitwancoel. That's our ancient times boundary. Kitwancoel has its own, Hazelton, Kispiox; they all join. Like for instance you look at a European map. It was something like that, the way our ancient tribal boundaries were joined together. In the early days, anytime anyone was caught trespassing on another tribe's land, they'd put him up in front of a stiff court and if he had no reasonable explanation they used to do away with him as a thief. They were very strict about it. When the white man came he brought the Bible—you see, "Thou shalt not steal" and so on, and yet a lot of our people had that in their own laws and regulations historically. And the whites come along and said,

"Thou shalt not steal," and take all our lands away—well, what was the good of their commandments?

Efforts to unite the natives of British Columbia and the rest of Canada continued. In 1961 Frank Calder, then president of the Nishga Tribal Council, and Guy Williams, president of the Native Brotherhood, and George Manuel, president of the American Indian Brotherhood, joined in the formation of a National Indian Council which included representatives from provinces and was coordinated by an Indian lawyer from Saskatchewan, William Wuttunee. This body rejected the most recent report of the Joint Committee of the British Columbian Parliament on Indian Affairs, claiming that its findings were based on recommendations by officials in the Bureau of Indian Affairs and did not take into account Indian opinion. In 1963 George Manuel resigned from the North American Indian Brotherhood to become a member of the Native Brotherhood. Apparently dissatisfied with the progress of unification, he pointed out:

> Our most pressing needs are the Indian land question and the settlement of Indian claims. These questions are of equal concern to all Indians of our province, regardless of our cultural background, regardless of whether we live in the interior, along the Pacific Coast or in the timberlands of the north.

The National Indian Council fell apart, but the Nishga Tribal Council, backed by the Native Brotherhood, chose Tom Berger to fight the land title case. Berger had successfully defended the case of two Indians who had claimed the right, by a treaty which stemmed from the time of Douglas, to hunt deer out of season.

In 1966 a Confederation of the Native Indians of British Columbia was set up with the intention of pursuing the claim to the aboriginal title of Indian lands. It was supported by many leaders in the existing organizations. Still, not a great deal seems to have been accomplished, for, in February of 1967 when Frank Calder was elected to succeed Peter Kelly, who had died the year before, as chairman of the legislative committee of the Native Brotherhood, Calder presented a resolution calling for a meeting of the presidents of all significant provincial organizations to make new plans for Indian unity.

Meanwhile the Nishga—through their lawyer, Tom Berger—filed suit against the attorney general of British Columbia, still claiming their 1000 square miles of land. At this point the government attitude, expressed by Minister of Indian Affairs Arthur Latham, was that it would only negotiate with Indian delegates who represented 75 percent of the Indians concerned.

Another meeting, on February 1966, was called in Vancouver to set up another committee to negotiate concerning the land title. It was dominated by the big five organizations, to which Calder read a new constitution for Indian unity. The delegates were asked to accept this immediately. Some demurred, and arrangement was made for a referendum; but the leaders of the big five held another meeting a week later. Although there was still demand for membership participation, Calder went ahead in the names of the Native Brotherhood, the North American Indian Brotherhood, the West Coast Allied Tribes, the Southern Vancouver Island Tribal Federation, and the Nishga Tribal Council and sent a telegram announcing that Indian unity had been achieved over the land claims constitution. Immediately there were protests from groups and individuals, criticizing this lack of democracy and challenging Calder and Williams' leadership. There was particular dissatisfaction because the district councils, involving groups of bands, which by now were achieving importance, had been passed over. William Scow of Alert Bay, long active in Indian organizations, sent a telegram protesting the undemocratic nature of the proceedings, and Chief Philip Paull wrote in *The Native Voice* in April 1968: "There are 216 bands in the province; every chief and band councillor should be heard, and they should be allowed to elect their leaders, who will not manipulate them to serve their own ends."

In the past the Indian organizations had been led by a few individuals, whose names appeared again and again. These people were relatively well educated, but their constituents in the past seldom had advanced beyond the ninth grade. Since the rank-and-file had been somewhat apathetic, the leaders had acquired the habit of running things their own way. Now their constituency was becoming better educated and, as we shall see, changes in the attitude of the Department of Indian Affairs had made them more aware of democratic self-determination.

At the same time, Indians were more in evidence politically. Frank Calder was still in the provincial legislature. In August 1968 Leonard Marchant, an Okanagan Indian, was elected to the Canadian House of Commons for the Kamloops-Cariboo constituency by the Liberal Party. More recently Guy Williams was elected to the B.C. Senate.

Then, in 1972 Frank Calder was appointed minister without

portfolio in charge of Indians, and on July 23 he was dismissed on the basis that Premier David Barret "had lost confidence in him." *The Native Voice* expressed displeasure. It was suggested that the provincial government had finally, at a late date, come to the conclusion that his activity in pushing the Nishga land claim involved some conflict of interest with his functioning as a cabinet minister.

It should be noted that Indian women had formed their own organization by federating the 57 Homemaker's Clubs, also in 1968, and were beginning to take an interest in politics. In the same year, stimulated by developments both among the Blacks and the Indians of the United States, some of the younger people formed the Native Alliance for Red Power (NARP) in Vancouver. The first issue of the *NARP Newsletter* for June and July 1968 was full of ringing denunciations. It said:

> We have been called hippies, young punks, trouble makers, disrupters, and many many other names. We wish to say at this time that we are not interested in spending our time attacking other native organizations. However, we wish to present an alternative to their ideas, and that alternative is RED POWER.

In subsequently defining red power, the periodical declared that the white man had stolen the Indians' lands, made a mockery of their culture, and murdered many of their people. It called for unity, attacked the Indian Affairs Branch, and announced that Indians must fight for the future of the native nation. The second issue carried on its cover a picture of Geronimo scowling fiercely and clutching his rifle. An article quoted a statement of the Island Tribal Federation that only 36 percent of B.C. Indians were in the wage earning group of 20 to 60 years compared to 49 percent for non-Indians. It also stated that the average annual Canadian wage was $4000 while that of the Indians $1361, quoting the second Hawthorn report, and concluded: "We are a colonial people, living under the rule of a colonial administrator." The periodical also ran an article charging that the Bureau of Indian Affairs on the one hand published a circular stating that Indians' parents were negligent in caring for their children, while at the same time the organization failed to supply medicines to a hospital on the Prince Rupert Tache Indian reserve. The red power group also picketed the Association of Principals and Administrators of Indian Residences with the slogan "Residence schools are prisons."

The group was denounced by most established Indian leaders, and the *Ottawa Journal* (doubtless prejudiced) maintained that NARP never attracted more than 75 members. The writer occasionally asked informants if they knew anything of "red power." In most cases they were aware of the phrase but did not know if there was any organization. They spoke of individuals who were "red power types."

The Reverend Terry Whyte, a young Methodist clergyman now at Port Alberni who had been in community development and worked for the Department of Indian Affairs for six years, was conversant with the red power movement and could discuss it concretely. When the "red power type" was brought up, he said he knew a number of Indians who fit this "type." He went on, when asked if there was any organization and any literature:

I can give you one or two issues of a newsletter called *The Native Alliance for Red Power.* The NARP was a group of young people in their twenties, in Vancouver, but it's defunct; it's had its day. It was really vital at the time and it's led to good things since then. It was more anti than pro anything. And I worked with those same people. After the girl, Geri Larkin, turned up in Alert Bay as an employee of the band when I was working there for Indian Affairs, I said, "Are you the same Geri Larkin who sent me this paper some time ago?" "Yes," she said, "are you the same Terry Whyte I sent it to? I didn't know we sent it to non-Indians." I was doing community development and helping the band and I was paid by Indian Affairs, but I was helping the band even if it meant taking Indian Affairs to court—which it did. It settled out of court for $50,000 and then it sacked Community Development. Not just because of that. It was happening all over. I saw this NARP paper and I was working with a group of people who were very depressed. Their own self-image was very low; their own idea of accomplishing any of their goals was very, very low. And this thing seemed to me an organ which could help them fight. So then I sent in my name to this outfit. They said they wanted people to distribute their paper and I said I'd like to distribute it and I didn't say whether I was Indian or non-Indian and I certainly didn't say I was working for Indian Affairs. I distributed it, one copy, and then I hoped somebody else would write in and say they would distribute it, but nobody did. I got so much static from the old people that I had to stop.

On the whole, therefore, the older Indian community rejected activism, accustomed as it had been to a long tradition of negotiation and attempts at political pressure.

In 1968 a new national organization, the National Indian

Brotherhood, was formed to represent the native people. In June, 1969, 45 delegates from all over the province were invited by the federal government to consult on further revisions of the Indian Act. At first the Indians disagreed on priorities, but when the government officials maintained that treaty rights and land issues were irrelevant the Indians formed a united front and set up their own committee to negotiate on what they considered important. Nevertheless, Minister Chretien went ahead and issued a statement, containing pious sentiments against discrimination, saying that control of their own affairs should be transferred to the Indians and that the province should be given the federal funds of the Indian Branch, while that organization was phased out of existence. All this was to take place within five years.

There was a storm of protest from Indian organizations. The natives were disturbed at what they felt was premature abandonment of the Indian Act and the avoidance of the land questions. The president of the New National Indian Brotherhood rejected the report and pointed out that the Indians did not wish to lose their reserves. Since 94 percent of the Indians dropped out before grade 12 they were still a disadvantaged people. He announced his organization would draw up its own proposals. Chretien backed down publicly and said that the proposals were merely a basis for discussion.

As Terry Whyte put it

> And then they brought out the white paper, which was like waving a red flag. There was so much protest when Indians Affairs committed itself to going out entirely in five years. And the Indian people said, "No, wait, we're going to tell you when to go out of existence, you're not going to tell us. And as for the implementation of the program on your way out, you must put an absolute freeze on all that stuff, if there's any point to what you're saying. When you start telling us what you're going to do to implement this thing—nothing doing." Which is a good point and caught Chretien with his pants down—he was doing exactly the same thing that he talked of trying to avoid. He backed off completely. He said, "You've made your point. I withdraw the thing completely." But the Indian people—and I too—are pretty sure that he has not. He has been involved in that withdrawal ever since—with a lot of consultation, however.

This was the attitude of a liberal involved in Indian Affairs. The attitude of Harold Cardinal, radical spokesman for the Indian in his book, *The Unjust Society,* is that a mere handing over of Indian Affairs to other federal departments and to the provincial governments is entirely unacceptable, although he is ready to scrap the Indian Act as soon as new structures under joint control of the government and the Indian people are set up. He suggests a crown corporation under Indian authority which would be responsible for land trusteeship. He also insists that no change should be made until massive economic development is planned for at the reserve level.

Many things were happening in 1969. In January the first meeting of the Association of Non-Status Indians took place in the Vancouver Indian Center. There are 30,000 of these people, according to government count, in British Columbia who have lost their reserve status as Indians and hence all advantage to be obtained from the government which extends its privileges for one year after a status Indian leaves his reserve. The association initiated a self-help program and promoted a grant of $40,000 to help meet organizing costs. The provincial government gave $10,000. An executive director was hired and six field workers to organize locals. The organization has been perhaps more active than some of the older native groups ever since.

The *Vancouver Sun* of September 20, 1973, carried a story of a hearing by the B.C. cabinet and the New Democratic Party Caucus in which the Association's president, Fred House, pleaded the case of the 65,000 nonstatus Indians according to his organization's count. The chief said that, although they do not qualify for Indian Affairs aid, most of them "look Indian" and have difficulty finding a place in the mainstream of society.

Calculating that people of Indian ancestry make up 5 percent of the population of the province, figures show that in government employment less than 1 percent of the total number is of Indian stock. This was an indication of the difficulties Indians have in finding employment and of the general unemployment situation which was described as "a national shame." On the whole, the association said that grinding, soul-destroying poverty was the lot of the people it represented. There were also complaints about education on the basis that about 5 percent of Indian students graduate from high school as against the provincial average of 60 percent. Only about 120 Indians have graduated from all Canadian universities since 1867, and the B.C. figure is about 20.

The brief called for a program to give Indian children a head start, funds for Indian education field workers, and more and more consultation between the Department of Education and the Indian people.

Housing was a problem considered most pressing. The Association through its Native Housing, Ltd., had built 84 houses for its members in a year and a half and 71 others were under construction—but this was considered to be only a drop in the bucket:

Some of the shacks our people live in would not provide shelter for an animal, House said. "We are not requesting special treatment or special programs for our people; rather, we are requesting special government assistance to enable our people to achieve a measure of equality."

The brief was received sympathetically by the Cabinet, House reported. He stressed the fact that their organization was supported by the Union of B. C. Chiefs, which was also represented at the meeting.

As a result of the agitation over Minister Chretien's so-called "white paper," the Homemaker's Association and the North American Indian Brotherhood took the lead in calling a conference of Indian chiefs from the 188 bands in the province. A first Citizen's Fund with $25,000,000 in the kitty, set up in 1969 for the benefit of the Indians of British Columbia, contributed $50,000 to pay for the conference. About 150 chiefs attended. The Union of British Columbia Indian chiefs was set up with a council appointed from 14 districts. This was to meet every three months. The organization was run by a three-man executive committee with annual conventions. Its aims were to become the officially recognized organization of the Indian in relation to the provincial government. It was to encourage self-sufficiency in the bands, coordinate government services, improve communication with government, improve education and social conditions, and above all push for a settlement of the B.C. land questions.

Among other activities, the group prepared a "brown paper" to counter the government white paper. A report on the land questions was prepared and a publication, *Nesika,* a Chinook word meaning "us," started in 1972. The second conference, in 1970, stressed unity. The meeting opened with an Indian dance of welcome and an Indian prayer. Chief William Scow (who was presiding) likened the chairman's gavel to the traditional Indian speaker's talking stick. A politician who suggested that Indians might resort to violence if they were not given a better break was corrected by Scow. "Our people are sensible people. We trust the words of the White man when he says violence does not solve problems."

The effectiveness of the Union of B.C. Chiefs remains to be seen. The resignation of the executive committee amid various charges seems to indicate that some of the old problems of unity still exist. Some individuals feel a greater loyalty to the Native Brotherhood, which has always been Indian-supported and independent of government funding.

The attitude of James Sewid, the Kwakiutl chief, who has often been a vice president of the Native Brotherhood, represents a certain segment of opinion. When I asked him about the relationship between the two organizations, Sewid said,

The Union of B.C. Chiefs—they try to quash the Native Brotherhood. I remember when they began. I was on the centennial committee. So we had a meeting. And I was with my friend Bill Roberts and Ross Modeste and we was having coffee right before we went to bed. Ross Modeste was president of the Union of Chiefs and he says, "Jimmy, we would like to ask you a question. We've been talking to the executives of the Native Brotherhood, you see, because the government is going to give us so many thousands of dollars"—he mentioned the sum, it was two or three hundred thousand dollars—"and Guy Williams, the President of the Native Brotherhood, wants forty thousand dollars but we would like to have it all. There's one more vice president [of the N.B.] down south we haven't approached." "Well," I says, "you don't have to go any further. I can't understand our president," I said. "We are a self-supporting organization with no donations from any government. We're not going to start that. We're not going to take gifts from any person. And you can tell whoever you're going to talk to that you can take all the money because I will never go for that." And they thanked me. Both of them thanked me. And then I said, "I'd like to ask you a question. Can you name any person from your group that can handle the fishery problems of the Indians of the coast if you move in and the Brotherhood pulls out?" Neither of them answered me. Finally: "Nobody," they said. "That's why I asked," I says. "We're qualified because that's what we've been doing the last forty years." And I said, "If the money should stop, if the government says, 'No more money is going to you people,' what are you going to do?" And they says, "I guess we'd have to fold up."

On the other hand William Scow, who has also been active as a leader in many organizations, and helped form the Native Brotherhood, expresses a different point of view. A former president of the latter organization, he eventually retired from it. His criticism of it was that it had become the instrument of the vessel-owning fishermen—in other words, native capitalists—and hence it did not truly represent the rank-and-file of the fishermen. In his view, therefore (he is a member of the governing council of the B.C. chiefs), the new organization is more truly representative and he feels it has a greater democratic potential.

Howard Wale, the chief councillor of Hazelton Tsimshian, was a member of both organizations and felt that there was no conflict between them. The Union of B.C. Chiefs takes the attitude that the brotherhood should stick to fishing affairs and leave the rest to them. But the older organization had traditionally done much more and also notably concerned itself with the land questions.

The movement to change the condition of the nonstatus Indian has sparked a special activity in reaction to the provision of the Indian Act which states that an Indian woman who married a non-Indian loses her status and so do her children. As Daisy Neel, Jimmy Sewid's daughter, wrote:

Not long ago I visited my sister-in-law. She was very upset because she had to tell a nonstatus Indian girl that she could not take an Indian culture course that the Department of Indian Affairs was sponsoring for "status" Indians. The girl left in anger and probably humiliation. But who could blame her? She went to the course because she wanted to learn about her culture. She could see there were many white women in attendance that had Indian status and she felt she had more rights than they to learn about her ancestral heritage.

With the new political awareness among the Indian women of Canada, this provision of the law has been challenged, on the basis that it contradicted the Canadian Bill of Rights, by two Indian women, Yvonne Bedard and Jeannette Lavalle. Their status was upheld in a lower court and this resulted in a mixed reaction. According to Terry Whyte many Indians in British Columbia were pleased on the basis that the act was manifestly unjust. Other Indians objected. To quote *The Indian News* (an Indian Affairs publication):

Executive member of the Treaty Voice of Alberta, Vicki Crowchild, recently said that the Indian way of life would be destroyed if Indian women who married white men could keep their Indian status and live on the reserve. Mrs. Crowchild said that such a situation would result in the reserves being overrun by white men.

Daisy Neel, who had worked for Indian Affairs, pointed out that she knew of reserves which were being overrun by white women whom the male Indians married and hence the argument could only be sustained on male chauvinist grounds.

The decision was appealed by the Department of Indian Affairs and the supreme court ruled that, although the Indian Act was discriminatory, it was not made inoperative by the Bill of Rights. It was a 4–3 decision, the same as that as to whether Indians were subject to provincial game laws.

Daisy Neel, who had worked with Jeannette Lavalle, commented that the latter, after her court defeat, wondered what to do:

> I told her, you just remember that we were fighting by ourselves, we were fighting alone. Anyway, we're God's Indians, the ones in the bands are government Indians. . . . But now we're not fighting alone. The decision hit all Canadian women and now all sorts of organizations, including Women's Lib, are with us.

The Indian women have not given up. Neither have the Indians submitted to restrictions on their hunting rights. A flyer put out by the Cowichan River Band in 1973 protested restrictions on using weirs in the river. The right of the Indians to hunt and fish for food on their land and unoccupied Crown land was recognized by George III in 1763. In 1913 sport fishermen protested that the use of weirs restricted the spawning of salmon in the upper reaches of the river. A meeting was held in which it was concluded that the weirs did not restrict the fish but that logging had changed the channel and done away with natural foods. Because of sport fishermen pressure eventually weirs were prohibited and currently, the flyer maintained, nets and spear fishing were also restricted. The Indian demands were that the right to hunt and fish on their land should be unrestricted and that they should be allowed to manage their own natural resources. They wished to abolish permits and to establish a hatchery to propagate the salmon. The flyer called for the support of other Indians with similar problems to unite over the same demands.

Among the still unresolved issues between the Indians and the Canadian government, that of the land settlement still remains supreme. We quote William Scow to show what an emotional area this is:

This land question has always been a sore spot. When the pioneers came here they had nothing. All they had was the shirt on their backs. When they showed here and there in the province those Indians received them with open arms. They didn't make those people suffer. They took care of them even in the winter time when it was hard to get foodstuff and all that. In their own homes they looked after them—such as their own homes were in those days, you know. They became friends with them. Then, when the surveyors came, they hired some Indians to go and survey. And some of those surveyors even had friends among the Indians at that time. And they told some of those chiefs, "Look, you'd better put your stakes on what land you want." And those old chiefs said, "Why should I want stakes? This land is mine. I don't have to stake this land—it's mine, my domain." And some of those surveyors said, "Look, there's going to be lots of white men here some day." "We shouldn't worry about that," the chiefs said. "There's miles of land around here." The surveyors said, "The white men, the non-Indians, may be as numerous as the pine needles or the sand." Time went on—and, lo and behold, the white man began to squeeze the Indian in. He wasn't allowed to cut wood outside of his little piece of land. And he began to argue with the white man. "What do you mean by this?" And the white man said, "This is mine." "Well, how can you say its yours?" "I have papers to prove it. Papers to say the land is mine. Where's *your* papers?" "Don't have any. I don't have to have papers." "Well, that's where you're wrong. You've got to have papers to prove the land is yours." And that's how the Indians became aware of what was happening. So they took up the land question. And that's when they started the Allied Tribes.

In Scow's view this first organization had wide representation but foundered on the difference of interest between interior and coast groups. The Nishga, however, from the first went their own way.

Actually, the Nishga suit, the most important test case in the land affair, was denied by the Supreme Court in 1969, the court ruling that their rights had been extinguished when the Crown Colony of British Columbia was formed in 1866. The Nishga immediately took their case to the British Columbia Court of Appeals.

An example of the continual rankling of an unresolved land problem is the Masset Inlet dispute. Back in 1912, according to the August 1973 issue of *Nesika,* an agreement was made to set up navigation lights at the entrance to Masset Inlet on Queen Charlotte's Graham Island, the home of the Haida. The terms of the lease included $250 for the improvement of the cemetery and a drawbridge across the lagoon near the lights. The bridge was built in 1917—but it was not a drawbridge. Recently, the Ministry of Transportation wrote to the band asking permission to cross the bridge. Surprised, the Indians took the letter to their lawyer. They discovered that, when the lagoon was filled with water at the time of the agreement, it was under federal jurisdiction. With the "non-drawbridge" the lagoon ceased to be a useful harbor. Over the years it filled with sludge, the water drained out, and it became as it is now, a dry sandy basin. The piece of land now comes under the jurisdiction of the province and the law which says that any agency that wishes to pass over reserve land must have Indian permission to do so. The band realized that the Ministry of Transportation had already been breaking the law without asking for permission. Moreover, the band had no record of receiving the $250. The ministry said it had paid but offered no proof. Also, as the land eroded the lights have been moved back 4 times, eventually impinging on land not leased to the ministry. The band decided that the bridge had affected their way of life, in which fishing has languished. Their fleet has diminished from 200 to 13. The band demanded $170,000 damages and back payment for the lease, or they would tear down the light towers. The ministry offered $600. The offer was laughed at. The police were called in but the band council argued the legality sufficiently well so that the police did not interfere when the dismantling celebration took place. Over 300 people came to watch and participate. There was dancing and a special song was composed for the occasion. At the end nearly everyone joined to pull down one 80-foot tower. Chief Councillor Bruce Brown called a halt at that and waited for the ministry's next move. The hardware and light are in the band's warehouse waiting to be picked up. Nothing was done about prosecution, but if the ministry ever does attempt this Brown has said the Indians would go to court. The Ministry of Transportation put a floating light offshore.

The whole incident is an example of the emotional dynamite inherent in the land issue. Masset was a quiet little village—a few streets of frame houses—basking peacefully in the sun when I visited it a month after the event. It was hard to believe so much emotion lurked in the background. Clearly the poor economic condition of the area had much to do with setting it off.

There was a background to the amount claimed by the Masset

Haida. They had demanded $170,000 to buy 1000 acres joining their reserve which they felt they needed. Indian Affairs refused to pay this amount. According to Brown, the tribal group now numbered 1000 and were crowded into 700 acres, some of it swamp.

In the case of the long-fought Nishga claim, when the suit reached the Court of Appeals early in 1973, the judges arrived at a split decision.

Prime Minister Trudeau's speech on Aboriginal and Treaty Rights given in Vancouver in August of 1969 contained the passage

> By aboriginal rights this means saying, "We were here before you. You came and took the land from us and perhaps you cheated us by giving us some worthless things in return for vast expanses of land and we want to re-open this question. We want you to preserve our aboriginal rights and to restore them to us." And our answer—it may not be the right one and it may not be the one which is accepted but it will be up to all of you people to make your minds up and to choose for or against it and to discuss with the Indians—our answer is no.

In 1969 this was the same old position and did not accord with the recommendation of the Hawthorne report, commissioned by Trudeau's own government, as we shall see in the next chapter.

The split decision of 1973 was, however, hailed with triumph by the native people. There were intimations that if they would not press on legally the government would make a settlement; the sum of $3,000,000 was mentioned.

Difficulties, however, remain. Although Minister Chretien announced publicly that the federal government was now ready to compromise, the provincial governments, which hold the land under the British North American Act, also have to agree. David Barrett, prime minister of British Columbia, was not enthusiastic and said he did not have time to study the proposal. The New Democratic Party of British Columbia, which represented local opinion, was not happy with the decision—although the same party's national leaders had been calling on the federal government to recognize the Indian claim. Once more the conflict between the provincial and federal government, with the Indians as a football, has to be resolved.

In the last decade, it is clear that the native people of Canada have learned much about defending their own interests and have made strides in organizing themselves into effective groups to make their wishes known. On the other hand, there have been changes in government attitudes, thanks to various changes in the climate of opinion. And these changes could be a significant example to those in charge of Indian affairs in the United States.

A NEW DEAL FOR THE INDIANS

26

Events of the last five years indicate that the Indians are beginning to enjoy a new deal affecting their general condition. Terry Whyte maintained that much is due to the atmosphere introduced into the Liberal Party by Trudeau, who sent representatives to survey the condition of the Indians as soon as he was elected. On the other hand, when I twice asked the Tsimshian, Allan Hall, of the North Shore District Council, if he felt that Trudeau's policies were liberal in regard to the Indians, he didn't answer. When asked yet another time, he remarked that $320,000,000 was allocated to Indian Affairs for the year, and only $80,000,000 got to the Indian people. He also pointed out that, after Trudeau's first election, he remarked that he would never recognize aboriginal title, and this is born out by his Vancouver speech. According to Hall, it was on the occasion of Trudeau's second election, when the New Democratic Party, a party committed to recognizing aboriginal title, held the balance of power, that Trudeau began to alter his position.

Actually, there have been a number of forces which have worked together to bring about change.

In 1958 a book was published jointly by the University of California and the University of British Columbia Presses edited by Harry Hawthorne, C. S. Belshaw, and S. M. Jamieson entitled *The Indians of British Columbia.* It was a critical study of acculturation and a survey of the general situation of the natives. It along with Hawthorne's subsequent two-volume *A Survey of the Contemporary Indians of Canada: A Report on the Economic, Political and Educational Needs and Policies 1966–7,* and Harold Cardinal's book *The Unjust Society* (1969), were important agents in bringing about a new attitude in the Bureau of Indian Affairs and in changing its relationship with the Indians.

Hawthorne's first study was carried out from 1954 to 1956 by university students sent out to numerous groups where they remained for as much as a month. The students felt that the missionary and the Indian agent had not been highly successful in their drive to promote white men's goals. Lineage and household kinship groups were still the units of organization. Chiefs appointed by the white man's authority were universally a failure.

Although the clan houses were gone some patterns of living remained. The single row of houses on the beach had developed into a double row or sometimes into conventional blocks. The frame houses were simple and bare because of lack of money, but the desire for comforts and technological gadgets was growing. Food habits were changing, although the salmon was still the staple. Work was highly seasonal, with frequent changing of jobs. Some Indians were using English names, some lineage names. One woman ran up charge accounts in both names.

In summarizing attitudes toward the Indian, it was pointed out that up to 1850 the Indian was seen as a trapper—and a soul to be saved. From 1850 on he became an obstacle to the acquisition of desirable land. He was also seen as a nuisance because his mores differed from those of the whites; it was hoped he would vanish. After 1951 he not only ceased to vanish but began to demand a greater voice in his own affairs. The Indians were characterized as defensive and suspicious, although the Bella Coola and the Haida of Skidegate were able to maintain a feeling of superiority. There was still much ambivalence on both sides concerning intermarriage, but it was on the increase. There was little residence discrimination in cities like Vancouver, though it still lingered in small villages. Attitudes existed similar to those cultivated in the United States concerning Blacks. In the work area it was felt that there were problems concerning a different point of view held by the Indian toward tardiness and absenteeism, a habitual complaint of the industry-minded white toward the more relaxed view of time taken by most native peoples.

There was still a fundamental gap between the competitive, profit-oriented, money-and-amusement-centered Protestant values and the traditional native attitude toward acquiring prestige by using wealth ceremonially. On the whole, the Indian preferred self-employment; he disliked the authority of foremen, an element not in his culture. Hunting and fishing for survival were still important, and game regulations often came into conflict with the Indians needs.

There was a difficult problem, too, in competing with the Japanese and white fishermen who had the capital to buy their own boats; the Japanese, after being expelled from the coast in

World War II, had made a comeback with 25- to 30-foot gill-net fishing boats. In the south and elsewhere the Indians turned to logging as an alternative. Few Indians owned purse seiners and the amalgamation of canneries tended to reduce employment. It was felt that the owners and canners were content to keep the Native Brotherhood a separate organization because it could be used against the United Fisherman's and Allied Cannery workers. On the whole the Indians were said to be better at logging and handling log booms than the whites. The Indians sometimes started small business, such as shops or restaurants, but the rate of failure was high for lack of sufficient capital. The average income was calculated as about $3000 a year, which meant that half the native population lived in real poverty.

There was confusion in the housing area. Grants for this purpose depended upon the initiative of the Indian agents.

Crafts were not flourishing, except for a little carving and the knitting of sweaters. There was not even enough money forthcoming to keep Mungo Martin—the celebrated carver of Alert Bay, then seventy-five—working steadily for the University of British Columbia.

It was felt that the older people had lost much of their prestige while the young were not being taught the hereditary culture. Indian school organization was insufficiently staffed. No Indians languages were taught—though the isolated case of one teacher who learned the local tongue resulted in greatly improved relations with the community. There was a great lack of anthropological training among teachers. The rewards, however, were small, and thus it was difficult to get teachers for the Indian schools. There was a great need for adult education.

Drinking was also a problem: "The police officer and the magistrate expect the Indian to drink and be aggressive when he is drunk. The Indian who is drunk and aggressive expects, although he also resents, certain kinds of handling in return." The pattern was pretty much that of the Indian getting his pay and getting drunk on Saturday night, being locked up when he created a disturbance and then being let out the next morning.

At this period (1956) a child born to a white woman made pregnant by an Indian was not considered an Indian. A quarter-blood child born by an unmarried Indian mother was considered to be an Indian until the age of twenty-one. If an Indian child was adopted by a white family it remained Indian. In the reverse case the child remained white. There was still some fuzziness as to who was an Indian. As we have already pointed out this has been recently brought to a head.

The report felt it was not good for the Indians to be under the jurisdiction of the mounted police and advocated band constables. Under the Indian Act the band councils were elected. In some cases there was a desire to return to the traditional hereditary chief. There was considerable criticism of the Indian agents, who were often high-handed in making decisions. It was also felt that the district superintendents, although they were supposed to listen to Indian council decisions, had a tendency to want to run these groups.

The report went on to say that more heed should be paid to the Native Brotherhood and that the provincial government should assume more responsibility and try to make the Indians feel that it was sympathetic. At that time it had an Advisory Committee of unrepresentative Indians and uninformed whites. Although it suggested that the government should make more use of anthropology it never pointed out that, if anthropologists were more aggressive and activist, they could contribute to improving the condition of the natives.

All in all the report painted a picture of a people both economically and spiritually deprived. It had the value of putting on paper harsh facts of which, no doubt, many Canadians were aware but which had not been publicly faced. The book's recommendations were important.

The report started with the statement that it did not advocate "Further deliberate pressure on planning directed toward the changing of custom, attitude or belief. Such further changes should be a matter for the Indian's own decision." This was an important change from the attitude that the white men know best and the natives were unable to handle their own affairs. Summarized, the recommendations went as follows:

1. Indians should be citizens with rights and responsibilities.
2. These rights and privileges should be guaranteed by Canadian law.
3. Further changes should take place only at the request of the Indians.
4. Administration should neither hasten nor retard assimilation.
5. The administration should do more for mental health both for individuals and the general welfare of the community.
6. Administration should be flexible in changing its goals, aided by research.

7. Indians should more and more be encouraged to undertake self-administration and to take more and more responsibility in their own governing bodies.

The study was undoubtedly read by those concerned with Indians and must have had an impact. At the same time another force was effecting Indian affairs and that was the community development movement. A worldwide (and nonorganized) movement, it was relevant to many different types of disadvantaged peoples, had been used in U.N. projects, and on various continents with success. It seems to have been applied to Canadian Indians in Manitoba by the Department of Welfare and coordinated with the activities of the Indian Affairs Branch in 1961. The first year's report said: "It represents one of the most efficient and, at the same time, democratic methods of helping a nation or a community to coordinate its resources, to achieve social and economic improvements." The report went on to explain that the workers took residence in or near a community after having studied reports on the community in the office. They were advised not to organize anything for three months but to spend their time gaining the confidence of the people they were to work with to be able to form a partnership with them. They could then help them understand their problems, become technical advisors in self-help, and also teach them how to make use of government services and loans, how to get financing for such projects as housing, while supplying the labor themselves, and, in Manitoba, where fishing and trapping were proving inadequate, stimulating projects of clearing the land for agriculture. Much of this seems no more than common sense, but it had not often been tried.

According to Terry Whyte:

> The whole community development movement [in B.C.] started in 1965. A guy called Rudnick, he sold it to [the Bureau of Indian Affairs] to coordinate the thing. It was kind of anthropologically based. Indian Affairs was sold on the theory that if people worked on their own priorities as opposed to something laid on they would be better off. Now if people are to work on them they have to define them first. You need a body of trained personnel to live in communities and to help them define their goals and then help them to work on them. That was really a good insight. It's a worldwide movement, not just a local thing.

It was quite clear to the writer that the two persons interviewed who were trained in this movement, both Whyte and

Ronald Witt, superintendent for Indian Affairs for the Bella Coola–Bella Bella area, were liberal, enlightened, and vitally involved in what they were doing.

As Witt described the same events:

About six years ago some of the Indian Affairs officials discovered this community development work and what was happening. It started in India and in South America and in Mexico particularly. They felt that that was the answer here. The major problem the Indian people faced was paternalism on the part of the government, the church and Canadian society. So this paternalism had to be knocked out. It had to be coped with in two areas; the Indian's dependency on the white man had to be altered and Indian Affairs had to do its bit in getting off the Great White Father kick and starting to work as a teammate and especially as a trainer. So it hired a team of community development workers. I was one of them and our job was very clear cut. We were hired by the Department of Indian Affairs to fight the Department of Indian Affairs. It was a fun job. It was really great. Very fortunately I was able to convert the district supervisor where I was. Although on the surface I was fighting, he knew what we were doing and why we were doing it. And he believed in it. He saw that every time there was a little confrontation the Indian people were taking another step forward when he lost. It was a game and he enjoyed it. For me it was just a beautiful field to work in. In some cases the supervisor fought back, really fought back, and they just had a miserable time. The majority, of course, were the old-time supervisors and eventually they sold out the community development program. They said, "If the Indian People want to take over responsibility, take over management, give *them* the community development." So they got rid of us. We were absorbed into the Indian Affairs Department and so the war is over and the Indian people won it—and in the end community development did transform Indian Affairs.

Replying to the question as to whether it was in this period that the district councils of the Indian bands were set up, Witt continued:

Oh yes—I was instrumental in forming one. And that's when the provincial brotherhoods became really political bodies. They weren't involved in really significant challenging issues before that. . . . So it's really interesting, really interesting, and the result is we're trying to find out what the people really want, what changes in policy. And our government has been very, very flexible. They've made some changes in the last twelve months to accommodate me here, not me in person, but for the Indian people channeled through me, that would not have been possible two years ago and unheard of ten years ago.

The community development influence was strongly felt in the late sixties. It was in the same period that Hawthorne's second report was commissioned, this time by the government, evidently on the strength of his first one. Both are evidence that—as E. Elmer Patterson II has pointed out in his recent history, *The Canadian Indian*—the situation of the Indian in America has at last, at least in Canada, become related to the worldwide rejection of imperialism. On the one hand, governments have begun to feel that the exploitive colonial relationship is dated and unworthy of an alleged civilized society. On the other, the exploited peoples have taken heart from each other's successes. Awareness of the parallel was slow in coming, in the case of the American Indian, and still does not seem to have penetrated the necessary areas in the United States.

The second Hawthorne report is hard-hitting and uncompromising in its recommendations. It was commissioned by the Ministry of the Department of Citizenship and Immigration and carried out by the University of British Columbia in conjunction with other universities. More than 40 scholars collected data and many special and field reports were synthesized. The result was a two-volume work, the first volume dealing with economics and government policies, the present condition of the Indian; it was published in 1966. The second concentrated on Indian education and the new trend toward self-government.

The opening statements of the report are significant.

> The Indians do not now have what they need . . . and cannot at present get what they want. Their income levels and average expenditure are rising but on the average are now far less than equal to the national or regional average and the gap is ever widening.

Once and for all a government publication acknowledged the claims that Indians had been making all along and stated that they had a right to be treated as "citizens plus" and this right—

> . . . derives from promises made to them, from expectations they were encouraged to hold, and from the simple fact that they once occupied and used a country to which others came to gain economic wealth in which the Indians have shared little.

This was revolutionary thinking and the report went on to point out that public knowledge of the Canadian Indians did not even match public misconception. The general indifference and lack of information was so great that there had never been any general interest in the solution of the problems which this segment of the Canadian community faced. Nevertheless, it was the duty of the Canadian government to regard its natives as "charter members of the community."

There were a great many recommendations. The most important were:

1. Integration or assimilation should not be imposed upon them.
2. Economic help was needed in many areas.
3. Educational and vocational training should be major points of assistance.
4. An Indian Progress Agency should be established.
5. The Department of Indian Affairs should act as the conscience of the community to expose injustices.
6. Indians should be regarded as citizens plus.

Much larger appropriations were needed for training and help in job placement outside of reserves. It was also felt that capital should be extended to bands in commercial areas to help them start their own businesses. Where outside groups rented land from the reserve, the band members should have priority in training and opportunities for undertaking the new jobs opened up by tenant enterprises. The role of the Indian Affairs superintendent was to become advisory and the district councils encouraged to play a greater role. It was necessary to take more pains to train Indians to understand white government techniques. The report called for more cooperation between the provincial and federal government and the pooling of their resources. It also stated that the move toward more self-government should continue and that, more and more, the bands should take over the control of their revenues.

The report was an important blueprint for the future and was even cited by Harold Cardinal in *The Unjust Society*. Admittedly a polemic, written by an educated Cree of Alberta, this book is significant as one of the first in which an educated Indian articulately attacks government policy and speaks out against the injustices he feels have been perpetrated against his people. All in all, it is an attack on the whole concept of wardship and what it has done to the Indians. He starts from the premise that the Indian people were adult, capable of managing their own affairs, and had created a society that worked (at least before the white man came). After he surrounded and overwhelmed them with superior numbers and technological culture, he proceeded to treat the natives as naive children who did not know what was good for them. This concept, more or less sophisticatedly implemented, has obtained in government circles ever since. Cardinal is unsparing in his attack on missionary activities and missionary education. He points out that by supplanting the medicine man and the successful emotional and spiritual involvement with nature which was at the basis of the Indian way of life, the missionary substituted a series of "thou shalt not" ethics—an inhibiting and irrelevant system which has had much to do with the creation of apathy among the indigenous people today.

The Indian Act comes in for violent attack as a discriminatory and paternalistic set of laws which have had a similar castrating effect upon the Indian. In his view, an anonymous group of bureaucrats in Ottawa for over a century had been deciding what would happen to Indians—about whom they knew absolutely nothing and from whom they made no effort to learn anything. They decided where children should go to school (near home or far away), what houses should be built and where, whether they should have inside or outside toilets, and what sort of social development should take place and how it would be controlled. Cardinal's charges range from castigating a pig-headed bureaucracy to insisting that much has been done by skillful politicians to divide the natives and to prevent them from uniting to present their demands. Worst of all, he maintains, the bureaucrats have come to believe their own propaganda and have convinced themselves that they act from the best of intentions.

In his criticism of education he maintains that nothing really serious was done until the 1950s, because the various church groups, with their narrow aims of conversion, were satisfied if the Indians were taught enough reading and writing to pay lip service to their various doctrines. Like others, he also charges that the warring sects have played their role in dividing the energies of the native people.

Again and again he stresses the point that all sorts of projects and plans for improving the condition of the Indians are made without consulting the people themselves, and he insists that only when the Indians are supported in developing their own resources, aided by a development corporation with adequate funds administered by Indians, can they really make the kind of progress they need.

Thus, in many ways, Cardinal's book vividly and emotionally implements the more academic statements of the Hawthorne report. Government critics might reply that his case is overstated, but there is too much truth in it to brush aside. It can also be seen from the events of the past five or six years that some part of the measures he advocates are slowly and unevenly being put into practice. Since his book was published in 1969 he spends a good deal of time attacking the white paper, which he feels is ominous: although the Department of Indian Affairs is due to be phased out, a departmental letter explains that the employees will still be needed as experts in the other ministries which will take over parts of Indian Affairs, and also in the provincial ministries. In other words, more bureaucracy looms ahead.

The matter of self-government is central to the new deal for the Indians. Originally, with the intense interest in and respect for lineage, Indian leadership was based on prestige, as we have seen, both inherited and acquired through potlatches. There was the house chief, recognized as the head of a family group and also the village chief based on clan status in the tribal hierarchy. There were occasional weak federations and chiefs who extended their sway beyond one village. On the whole, authority, however, rested upon respect, community approval—but, of course, since the natives had no police force, not upon coercion. The punishment for the individual who transgressed traditional codes tended to be community disapproval.

With the formation of agencies, the government eventually decided that the bands—that is, the coherent area groups, generally consisting of one village or tribe which had become the units with which the agencies dealt—could have elective councils. This was a part of Indian Act revisions of 1950. It was, according to James Sewid, on a voluntary basis. He explains that he was in favor of the change in Alert Bay because a council, consisting of an elected chief councillor and three councilmen, seemed to him more democratic than a single village chief. Nevertheless, he waited until the old chief died before he pressed the agent to apply for an elected council. It was granted in 1950, Sewid being elected chief councillor. Today all the bands have elected councils. The institution of hereditary chief exists. Hawthorne's 1956 report states that some groups were reluctant to give up rule by the hereditary chief and today his role varies from taking no part in the governing body to being himself elected to the position of chief councillor. Thus the two systems overlap slightly, although the election system is already dominant in the area of politics.

Terry Whyte, however, cited the case of a Kwakiutl chief who passed his hereditary position down to his son with a traditional potlatch, the son also being the chief councillor. In Prince Rupert the hereditary chief knew nothing of modern government but was always consulted in ceremonial matters. Wilson, the elective chief councillor, always said, "I am not a chief but the government likes to call me that."

In Bella Coola and Bella Bella everyone knew who the chief was—but, again, he was not a political figure. Ronald Witt analyzed the situation in the Bella Coola band. The Bella Coola nation which, as a result of epidemics in the past, had shrunk from 27 villages to one settlement, amalgamating seven, had chiefs for all seven, but one was the ranking chief of the whole group. Though not on the council, he spoke officially for the group. He made the oration when the hospital was opened, and when visiting V.I.P.'s arrived he greeted them. As Witt put it, "I get the impression that if he really decided that the band council was doing something that was wrong, if he decided to stop them, he probably could."

In this area it can be seen how the hereditary culture has compromised in various ways with the exigencies of contemporary Canadian life. The institution of chief still carries with it profound resonances. As Jimmy Sewid never tires of stressing, it is the word respect which says much about Indian culture, respect for lineage ("My daughters are both married to men from 'noble' families," as Jimmy put it), respect for custom, respect for hereditary authority. Yet, in order to deal with problems involving the white man's world, the Indians realize that special competence is necessary. According to the second Hawthorne report, in 1968 among the bands a high proportion of the councillors was over fifty years of age. Today more young men, because they have more education, are infiltrating the councils. That of Bella Coola, which the writer met, contained two older men and the other eight or so were in their forties and thirties. The chief councillor was one of the youngest. Women were not allowed to vote or run for a council until 1950, but now there is a growing number of women councillors—in fact, the writer met the daughter of a Nootka chief who was chief councillor of the Gold River band.

The changeover to the elective system, while satisfactory to the white authorities, was certainly a wrench for the Indians, in whose culture the respect for lineage and hereditary prerogatives were so deeply ingrained.

Ken Harris, a Tsimshian and the hereditary chief of the village of Gitsegyukla, expressed a conservative point of view when interviewed in Prince Rupert. He is one of the organizers of the Indian Benevolent Association, a voluntary organization which owns a craft shop in Prince Rupert that sells Indian craft objects, the proceeds being used by the Benevolent Association Charities. He pointed out that, although he was a chief of his village, because his mother married a chief from Kitwanga Village he belonged to the Kitwanga band and had no influence in his own village. He blamed this situation on the reserve, the system which set up a structure worked out by the white authorities. He related this problem to the land question: "As a hereditary person I can deny all this and say, 'Look you're dealing with an alien structure and if you want to deal with hereditary rights of the Indians [in land] you have to deal with the hereditary system.' " He went on to elaborate his feelings in the matter:

> When we talk about hereditary rights, we mean that we have hereditary rights which have been established since time immemorial. And these rights have been badly infringed upon by the Indian Act, which is a new structure that dictates the lives of the Indians. And they say, "According to the Indian Act you've got to do this, you've got to make this change," and so the Indian structure suffers. This has to be thrashed out whether it is good for the contemporary Indians or not.

Thus, although, from the white point of view, elections are the accepted method of setting up democratic government, in the case of the Northwest Indians, particularly, it conflicts with profound and strongly held emotional attitudes.

It is a fact the band councils are the cornerstone of the new era of self-government. As the district superintendent of the Campbell River area, Mr. Frye, put it, "We give them as much responsibility as they are willing to take. In some cases, as in very small bands around Alert Bay, they were told they must take over certain services or they would not get them. Whyte explained that he persuaded Bill Scow, who had retired after being three-time president of the Native Brotherhood, to unite the groups and act as their chief councillor. At first Scow said he was too old and been out of it too long. (He was in his seventies.) Gradually he was persuaded, took over the job, and has proved to be one of the more forward-looking leaders of the new regime. In Whyte's view, many of the old leaders were accustomed to work personally with the agent through the back door. The new ones work democratically and learn how to use political pressure. Likewise, the new type of superintendent trains the band councils so that they can take over such services as their welfare program, their public works, water system, sanitation, fire prevention, and housing programs.

Much has depended on leadership. The Bella Bella band, a Heiltsuk Kwakiutl group, is notable for initiative. In this case the chief councillor, Cecil Reid, has been a teacher and has a master's degree in English. The community numbers 1150, plus 200 who are members of other bands, nonstatus, or whites, the last mostly technicians. Here the Indians have set up their own construction company, their own boatyard, and are planning to build a hotel. They have their own hospital, and although the department is still running the schools they plan to have their own school board and, when they can mount enough pressure, they will push for a high school. They plan for a telephone system since now they can only be reached by radiophone, Bella Bella being on an island north of Vancouver. At present it can, of course, be reached by water but the main transportation consists of six-passenger Beavers.

When we visited Bella Bella we were chauffeured about by the combination police constable and fire chief, Mike Wilson, who pointed with pride to the sewage system, the three schools they had built, and the neat houses they had erected especially for the teachers. They had built a general store to replace one that had burned down and this stocked everything from hardware to foodstuffs, being owned and operated by the band. A second store was also being built. As Witt pointed out, the Bella Bella had suffered from exploitation from the whites who live on the fringes of Indian settlements and this had been a stimulus to setting up their own enterprises. Wilson proudly ran out the shiny new fire engine, evidently his pride and joy, and showed us over the spotless new hospital, built with church funds; and from a strategic height we could look down on the extensive boatyard.

On the cultural side Reid states:

> We have not participated to any great extent in cultural reawakening. However, we are developing a written language form and hope to teach our language to our young people. Also, currently we have engaged a competent anthropology student to research museums for Heiltsuk artifacts and designs which will help to authenticate the art work in our proposed arts and crafts program in our new Secondary School to be built by next December.

Like all waterside Indian towns, the fishing fleet rode at anchor by the dock. In a letter dictated in answer to some of the writer's questions Cecil Reid stated:

> Recently there has been more money for education and four years ago an Economic Development Branch was finally funded for limited economic development of Indian Reserves. I say limited because the degree of poverty on Indian reserves requires long-term loans with low interest rates for any appreciable reversal of the poverty among Indian people.
>
> As far as Bella Bella is concerned we have been able to take advantage of the Department of Indian Affairs, new funding program for the establishment of local government facilities. We have been able to negotiate with the Department for essential machinery and funds for limited operation and maintenance of roads, sewer and water services.

Reid goes on to say they have been able to train carpenters to build new homes and repair old ones, but there is a great need to improve employment opportunities and, as yet, they have not been able to institute programs for social development. He substantiates Witt's sketch of the difficulty of arousing the general membership and complains that, as yet, the progressive and active condition of the band depends too much on a small group of leaders. As Witt pointed out there are a number of new jobs coming up in the marine shipyard and also in public works and in the fish-processing plant. As no trained people are available, the council is planning a training program. So they hired a university student to make an inventory of the job and he asked the unemployed people: "Where do you see yourself fitting in? If you have an ambition, tell us. If there are enough people with a particular ambition, we'll feed that to the band council and perhaps be able to create a business." It seems the apathy the young man ran into made him quit three times.

The resistance is no doubt partly a discouragement resulting from so much recent history of downgrading and discrimination and perhaps partly a slow adjustment to what is admittedly a white man's ideal of progress. It should always be remembered that the Indian cultural goal was to amass goods in order to give them away, not to work in order to make a profit and keep it.

Bella Bella is an example of the way in which an Indian band has proved its ability to manage its own affairs and to learn how to get what it needs. It seems clear that the new deal can work. The effects of two centuries of hidden colonialism, however, cannot be immediately overcome.

One of the worst problems which still persists is alcoholism. Terry Whyte spoke of the recent death of a young man from alcoholism. Jimmy Sewid complained that his crewmen were in the habit of dissipating their wages by drinking them away over the weekends. He advocated teaching Indians how to drink "socially" and said he would be glad to give such a course himself.

The prohibition against selling liquor to Indians had always rankled because it treated the natives as less than adults. It was removed in 1951, but the psychological reasons for drinking were not removed.

Judge Roderick Haig Brown, who has had 30 years of experience of dealing with Indians in court and also has a wide circle of Indian friends in his area, felt that the Indians were no more prone to alcoholism than any other group. He was inclined to think that the problem was more acute in isolated villages than in regions where the Indians were in contact with a large community. This related to the problem of apathy, for in such communities, where the old traditions had been lost, there was little opportunity for a variety of activities and other ways to spend money than on liquor.

Witt had some interesting things to say concerning the situation in Bella Coola which contrasted in many ways with Bella Bella. In this beautiful river valley, which once numbered 50,000 in its 27 villages, the population is now down to 600. Traders came through the area in the nineteenth century selling blankets infected with smallpox. They would then return, strip them from the corpses, and resell them. Witt feels that this group has never recovered its drive after this decimation. When I asked the band council what was its "number one problem," they replied it was economic. The band manager, Edward Moody, explained that although most of the fishermen owned their own boats (they were built locally) many were now rundown and this curtailed the activities of their owners. Another source of demoralization was the discriminatory attitude of the white residents, mostly Norwegians of U.S. stock. The Indian children had to be bused twenty miles to the one high school—which was dominated by the whites. Witt pointed out that there was a 35 percent dropout rate the preceeding year, on the basis of testimony of the children and the parents because of harassment by the whites. Demoralization is obviously related to the drinking problem.

In the past year there had been 14 deaths, nine directly attributed to alcohol, some through accidents; but some Indians drank so much that their internal muscles were paralyzed and they simply died. Said Witt:

> I think they're struggling in limbo, they're struggling for identity—for religious identity as much as anything else. . . . They don't want to be white people, they don't want to be materialistic capitalists. But they don't see the old way as a viable way to live. You can't live off the land, we don't give them land to do that any more. . . . When you really talk to them, and I've talked to them for three or four hours at a time, they say the people are drinking because they don't really have anything else to do. They have no ambition to live. There's nothing to look forward to. . . . I think it's because of this religious thing.

As has often been pointed out the missionaries destroyed the old culture but did not succeed in putting anything in its place. It will take considerable time to overcome this heritage of demoralization, which amounts to, in popular psychological language, the Indians' having "a low image of themselves." This is beginning to change, as we shall see later, in terms of the cultural revival. Hence, the new deal will eventually result from, not only a changed policy on the part of Indian Affairs, but also from a psychic change on the part of the people themselves, a rebirth of their own egos. And this, of course, is related to the resurgence of colonial people and minorities all over the world.

So far we have been discussing the administrative changes which have improved the Indian condition. On the economic side progress has been slower. The massive training program and the job placement program called for in the second Hawthorne report does not seem to have come through. The Tsimshian villages near Hazelton were felt to be a depressed area. Although there was fishing, in the winter help was needed to take up the slack. The band manager of the tiny village of Glen Vowell asked my wife to help him fill out an application for a government grant which would put some of the men to work improving the road and enlarging the cemetery. On the other hand, Joe Daniels, of the village of Kitwanga, maintained that a nearby pulp mill gave plenty of work to his people.

Much depends on local conditions and the resources of the reserve. The Campbell River reserve (Kwakiutl) is situated on the very edge of the town. Campbell River is proudly pointed to as one of the fastest-growing towns in British Columbia, and consequently it will need to expand in the direction of the reserve, which already has plans for a shopping center which can be built on land leased from the band. This would be a case, as suggested by the second Hawthorne report, where training and priorities should make jobs available to the band members.

Fishing remains the basic activity and the salmon, everywhere along the coast, is the basic food. In Alert Bay the writer saw Mrs. Agnes Kranmer, daughter of Franz Boas's chief informant, George Hunt, preparing great filleted strips of salmon which would be hung over a fire and smoked for winter use. Everywhere along the coast the fish is smoked and home-canned, as it has been from time immemorial by the coastal people, to serve as winter provisions. In Alert Bay the majority of the fishing fleet is owned and operated by Indians. One of the white residents maintained that the fishermen would do better if their local of the brotherhood amalgamated with the United fishermen for they would thus have control of the local. At any rate, the owner of an up-to-date vessel who is a skilled operator can, in a good year (such as 1973), make as much as $25,000 to $50,000. One owner, it is said, made $100,000. Crew members, who work on shares, may earn from $7,000 to $8,000. In September 1973 Minister Jean Chretien, in charge of Indian and "Northern" affairs, announced that the Indian Fishermen's Assistance Program, with a budget of $10,196,000, had been renewed for another five years. Financed by the Department of Indian Affairs and administered by the Department of Environment, the program provides loans and grants to Indian fishermen for the construction, purchase, conversion and modification of fishing vessels, equipment, and shore facilities. The Assistance Board was now emphasizing on-the-job and institutional training facilities. The staff was to be expanded with a head councillor and three field councillors who would provide information concerning the program and advice and assistance in the area of business organization and marketing. In addition, the minimum down payment was being reduced and the eligible age for borrowers dropped from twenty-one to nineteen. There was a representation of three Indians on the six-member board. *The Indian News* maintained that the program, started in 1968, had brought the Indian fishermen closer to the economic level of the non-Indian members of the B.C. fleet. What seems particularly significant is the inclusion of three Indians on the six-member board.

Of course, there are still many marginal boat owners without the capital to obtain loans and crewmen, and these do not have the minimum down payment to become vessel owners.

The condition of the individual band varies greatly. Terry Whyte explained that the Nootka of Port Alberni were fortunate in possessing funds from lumber. The band had $40,000 to loan to its members, who were able to buy boats and repay the loans from their earnings. When the Department of Indian Affairs built floats, the Nootka bid on the job and got it. They also bought their own bulldozers to clear the land for new housing.

Allan Hall, a member of the North Shore District Council in the Prince Rupert Area, felt that the amalgamation of the big canneries by mergers had thrown many Indians out of work in the fishing industry. This, plus the government licensing program, which meant that many marginal boats were scrapped, stimulated the council, which had prophesied unemployment, to set up its own project of building a fish processing plant. He said:

> We'll be putting a lot of people back to work, about 180. Outside of this we're going to have a fishing fleet of boats that will be employing and training the young people. . . . The processing plant will go into herring, shellfish, shrimp, and sea urchins, the last for the Oriental market.

Hall also mentioned another Indian project being put into execution by the Tsimshian of Nass River. They were constructing a half-million-dollar sports complex out of their own timber. This would be for the use of fishermen and would be a source of revenue for the band.

The Salish of the Duncan River area, however, were one of the few groups who had not had a good year's fishing. Norman Joe, their band manager, complained that this resulted from improper logging in the area. This brings up the whole question of ecology and the protection of the salmon, so essential to the economy of both Indian and white in British Columbia. Judge Haig Brown, an expert on the ecology of the salmon, pointed out that improper logging had the effect of silting and caused the small streams to dry up in summer—and these were the streams particularly frequented by the Cohoe salmon when spawning.

He speculated on the instinctive balancing of the ecology practiced by the Indians in the past. On the whole, he felt that ceremonies had helped. When the first salmon was caught, for instance, it was laid on shore and several days elapsed while religious rites were carried on. During this time there was no fishing—which meant that there was an opportunity for the rest of the fish to escape upstream to spawn. The Kootenay used one official spearman and if, by chance, he did something which caused to him be seriously ritually polluted, he had to cease fishing for several days while he purified himself. Thus it seems that ritual, even if not consciously, resulted in ecologically sound behavior. As Judge Haig Brown pointed out, in the past there were probably acute ups and downs in the salmon runs with much unsuccessful spawning. Now much is known about management, and the number of salmon can be controlled so as to have the right number of females in the spawning area, one per yard. Any more than that must be reduced to avoid waste. The spawning areas will need to be rehabilitated; silt, caused by improper logging, removed; dams removed which impede progress of the fish upstream; and above all improvement in the spawning situation is needed. Some of the northern channels, it seems, are not using the potential rearing area of the lakes. And in some places the genetic stock of the fish that were acclimated to certain rivers have been lost and must be replaced. Although the government has projects for hatcheries costing $14,000,000, Judge Haig Brown felt that such a project would not count for a fraction of the good that repairing the damaged spawning areas and replacing the stock could accomplish. He concluded, "In this case I think we can vastly improve on conditions as they originally were in nature and be able to come out with more salmon than we ever had."

When one thinks of the damage that has been done to the lakes and rivers of America already, it becomes clear that British Columbia can thank its less dense population for a reprieve and, perhaps, the time to adopt sophisticated programs which will save its natural resources for all its citizens—including, particularly, the Indians.

It was among the Cowichan Salish that we learned of the only agricultural undertaking that seemed to be going on among the Indians who—traditionally, of course—never cultivated the soil. The Cowichan band is a large one, about 3500, located in and around the town of Duncan only about an hour's drive from Vancouver. Norman Joe explained that the band possesses about 1000 acres of arable land. Agriculture had started early. "In the early seventies," he said, "the Indians had the first combine in the valley." Then during the 1940s, with the changeover to logging, in which salaries are high, the fields were allowed to return to brush. Now a cooperative has been founded and some 15 acres have been planted in blackberries, 40 in strawberries, 12 in raspberries, and a few more in garden vegetables. Since berries always loomed large in the coastal Indian diet, it seemed another example of the strength of tradition.

Like the band around Campbell River, this one also leased some of its holdings to the city and considerable areas to shops and even a motel. This particular band, however, grants certificates of possession to individual owners of land who are then able to lease it, subject to the approval of band, which takes a cut of 10 percent.

If the economic new deal seems spotty and slow to be realized, housing is the area where there is real hardship. There definitely has been a population explosion among the Indian people. In Bella Coola, where the government was financing eight houses there was a need for 70, people who were waiting for housing were obliged to crowd in with relatives. In nearly every village visited there was a shortage of living space, and while some of the new housing was neat and attractive, by and large only minimal facilities were available. The Indian Assistance Board spent $2,069,664 in 1967–1968; yet, with the rising birth rate, to remove the accumulated backlog it was estimated that 353 new houses were needed for the following year. Norman Joe said that the large Cowichan reserve got financing for three houses last year but had a waiting list for dozens. The best that can be said, it seems, is that something is being done but far from enough.

Once again we turn to Bella Bella for more hopeful and constructive activity. It will be remembered that here the group has its own construction crew. Mike Wilson brought us proudly to a new section at the edge of the town. Roads had just been put in, and he told us that 18 houses would be erected next year. When asked about the financing, he answered that it would be done with government aid. "And how do you get that?" he was asked. "Pressure," he said firmly.

WARDS OF THE NATION

27

Despite the changes in attitude of the Indian Affairs Branch and the general improvement, in some areas of the Indian situation, so long as the government does not phase out its control the Indians remain wards of the state and federal government is responsible for their health, welfare, and education. Under the revised Indian Act of 1952–1953, it also still assumes many powers which can be considered arbitrary and paternalistic. We have already brought up the question of Indian status, in relation to women who lose their privileges in the reserve by marrying whites. Interestingly enough, the same women can, in marrying again, regain their status by marrying Indians. Again, the illegitimate child of a woman who is a band member becomes an Indian. The exception is that, if the child's addition to the membership list is protested by the band on the basis that the father is white, within 12 months the child can be disbarred from Indian status.

The powers of the Minister of Indian Affairs and Northern Development are sweeping, as they affect the lives of all the Indians on reserves. For instance: "No Indian is lawfully in possession of land in an Indian reserve unless *with the approval of the minister* possession has been allotted to him by the council of the band."

Although in most situations, according to the act, the approval of the band or band council is required, the approval of the minister hangs like a veto over the whole act. He may refuse approval of the allotment of land by the band and declare it to be available for reallotment by the council. No transfer or agreement of transfer of land is effective in a reserve until approved by the minister. If a band does not keep up its roads, bridges, and fences as directed by the superintendent, the minister may cause the work to be carried out at the expense of the band. The minister may declare the will of an Indian void if it is deemed to have been executed under duress, the deceased being incompetent, land being disposed of contrary to the interest of the band, or if the provisions are too vague or difficult to carry out or against the public interest. Likewise, all jurisdiction and authority in relation to property of mentally incompetent Indians is vested exclusively in the minister. In other words, many situations which would in the case of ordinary citizens be handled by relations or the courts come under the paternal jurisdiction of the minister. Not the least of these is the case of desertion by either married person in which any income accruing to either the husband or wife may be used by the minister to support the deserted individual; similarly, the income of either or both can be used by the minister to support an illegitimate child.

One of the valuable provisions of the Act is section 91:

No person, without the written consent of the Minister, may acquire title to any of the following property situated on a reserve, namely:

(a) An Indian grave house;
(b) a carved grave pole;
(c) a carved house post; or
(d) a rock embellished with paintings or carvings.

The section goes on to say that no person may remove, disfigure, or destroy any of the above without written consent of the minister on pain of a $200 fine or three months' imprisonment. The minister of finance, according to the act, may advance loans for social and cooperative projects on the reserves not to exceed the outstanding sum of $650,000.

Some of the most important regulations are those which "the governor in council may make." These include conservation and protection of game and fish, and as we have seen, bring up rights, dating back some time, claimed by the Indians. Another rather curious regulation may provide for the operation, supervision, and control of pool rooms, dance halls, and other places of amusement on reserves. More important, the regulations may provide for loans for housing, plus inspection to prevent overcrowding and to provide for sanitation. On the medical side, the governor may provide medical treatment, health services, compulsory hospitalization, and treatment for infectious diseases. In addition the minister may require an Indian child who has attained the age of six to attend school and provide for transportation to school and make regulations in respect to standards involved in equipment, teaching, and discipline. The minister may also enter into agreement for support of religious schools. The minister is empowered to apply truancy regulations, including fines and force if necessary. The child is expected to remain in school until the age of sixteen and, if he or she refuses to attend or is expelled, is then deemed to be a juvenile delinquent.

Statistics dealing with the conditions of the Indians, dating from 1966–1967, indicate that in certain areas the government has not fulfilled its wardship satisfactorily. According to the Fields and Stanbury report of 1970, in the case of social welfare, dependency among Indians living on reserves is eight times that of the general population of British Columbia. The report states that the Indian affairs branch employs only one professional full-time field worker. In other words it provides only money and does nothing about rehabilitation or finding employment for those who are employable. The provincial social service department does provide such services, in the case of status Indians, for one year after they leave the reserve, for which it is reimbursed by the federal government. But an examination of the case load in British Columbia in 1967 showed that the provincial social welfare service had about 100 cases which it was handling *on* the reserves. The province was at that time attempting to get federal reimbursement.

The health situation parallels welfare. The relative number of hospitalization cases is twice as great among Indians as among the general population and the average length of stay is 10 percent longer. Medical treatment is the responsibility of the federal government. It maintains some Indian hospitals, which it is trying to phase out. As it seems to work out, about half the amount paid to general hospitals in British Columbia is borne by the federal government. Medicare, adopted in 1968, is a still greater health responsibility borne by the federal government, but it is a fact that a large number of Indians will need help to cover their share.

The Fields and Stanbury report states:

> The Province of B.C. in some Divisions of the Department of Health Services and Hospital Insurance regards the Indians as "wards of the Federal government" and therefore the complete financial responsibility of the Federal government. For some Divisions in the Department the Indians are not seen as citizens of the Province entitled to "free" medical service as such.

Once more we are confronted with the contradictions between the two governments. Apparently the Indian health service wants to integrate public health services and withdraw the Indian health personnel in accordance with its gradual phase-out policy. As it works out now, the province has to step in where the federal government doesn't operate and then negotiates for reimbursement. The report concludes that "the present set of arrangements between the Indian Health Service and the Provincial government are at worst inconsistent and at best unclear."

That all this does not work out well for the Indian is attested by a letter published in the *Queen Charlotte Islands Observer,* a small mimeographed sheet printed in Masset.

Masset, which we have mentioned in connection with the land conflict, is a small village with a neat little new hotel and a settlement of naval and air force personnel in new modern government houses. It is one of the chief towns of the Queen Charlotte Islands, which have always been the home of the Haida. The village of Haida is about 9 miles away from the town of Masset and is not economically well off. A local cannery has cut its personnel from 90 to 20 and, as far as logging goes, Frank Collison, the band manager of the Haida village, felt that this industry was becoming more mechanized in his area with the result that a good deal of special training was needed to get jobs:

Masset. September 18, 1973

The Honorable Graham Lea
Parliament Building
Victoria, B.C.

Dear Mr. Lea:

I am writing this letter on behalf of the Queen Charlotte District Teachers' Association and in support of the Masset-Haida Health and Human Resources Council to bring about improvements in the medical and social resources available to the people of the islands.

The efforts of the teachers have been to a large degree negated by inadequate diagnostic services and to a lesser degree by the inadequate medical treatment and social services available to the students of the schools.

To be specific, the students do not listen when they have infected ears, they do not watch when they cannot see, they do not learn when they are hungry and they do not attend school at all when, due to lack of support from parents or other adults, they reach a level of frustration which is beyond their limits.

The Masset-Haida Health and Human Resources Council, in discussion with the Honorable Dennis Bocke, the Minister of Health, and the Honorable Norman Levi, the Minister of Human Resources, has stressed the need for the following:

1. Adequate hospital and laboratory facilities in Masset.
2. A full time doctor to be available to all the people in the Masset-Haida Area.
3. A public health nurse to be based in Masset.
4. An extra Social Worker to serve the Masset area.
5. A Diagnostic and Treatment Centre for Hearing Disabilities in the western end of the Skeena Health Unit to service the island.

The teachers here understand the needs expressed by the Council and ask that you in your capacity as our Member of the Legislative Assembly help convince the respective Government Departments of the needs of the people of the Charlottes.

Yours sincerely,
Brian K. Loadman
Political action chairman

This document is an example of unfulfilled needs resulting from the present state of things and is particularly interesting because the existence of a Masset-Haida Health and Human Resources Council shows that the whites and Indians, supported by the teachers, have, in this case, joined together to make their needs known.

The second volume of the Hawthorne report of 1967 is largely devoted to education. Obviously the economic condition of the next generation of Indians will be related to the amount of training. If, as the report suggests, they need to be provided with much more off-the-reserve work, then they must be able to compete in the white man's world. On the other hand, if they are reluctant to become potential competitive capitalists, must they fit into the mold of the general Canadian educational pattern? Up the the recent past, the main drive on the part of Indian leaders was for integrated schools, because it was felt that the exclusively Indian reserve schools did not achieve the standards of the provincial schools. Likewise, segregation implied a certain ghettoization and lack of equal status with white Canadian children.

Harold Cardinal has strong words for his own early education in a residential school:

In plain words the system was lousy. The curriculum stank and the teachers were misfits and second-raters. Even in my own elementary school days, in grade eight I found myself taking over the class because my teacher, a misfit, has-been or never-was, was sent out by his superiors from Quebec to teach savages in a wilderness school because he had failed utterly in civilization, couldn't speak English well enough to make himself understood. Naturally he knew no Cree. When we protested such inequities we were silenced as "ungrateful little savages who don't appreciate what is being done for you."

Joe Daniels of Kitwanga, near Hazelton, who complained that the whites in the valley refused to integrate their school with that on the reservation, also charged that the teachers were inadequate and couldn't speak good English.

Cardinal's more general criticism of the Indians' educational past is that the church-dominated schools alienated the child from his family and his way of life without really preparing him for white society. The unfamiliar disciplines, and the failure to relate what was taught to anything in the immediate environment turned the child against education and prevented him from appreciating whatever was good in the white man's teaching. Once more he objects strenuously to what he considers the aim of schools which try to process the Indian into a white man without consulting his own inclinations and also the failure to include Indians on school boards. He complains that integration is a one-way street, the Indian child does all the integrating, and the schools have done little to prepare themselves to handle Indian children or to look after their interests. He also complains that Indians do not know where to start to make their criticisms or desires known in the chain of supervisors which makes up the school bureaucracy.

The schools now are partly integrated except for areas where the reserves are not near any provincial school and hence make use of residential or Indian day schools. In 1967 there was an enrollment of 1686 in such residential schools as against 5666 in provincial schools. There were 723 Indians in parochial schools and 3427 in federal Indian day schools. There seems to be a shortage of high schools, for, in a number of cases, Indian children had to be bused long distances to attend these.

On a statistical basis the dropout rate for Indian children at various levels is still unsatisfactory compared with the general figures for the province. According to the 1961 census 76.2% of Indian children, aged 5–14 years, were attending school compared to 85.2% of all B.C. children in the same age group. By 1966–1967 about 61% of the Indian population, aged 5–24 years, were attending school as compared to 58.8 in 1961—all of which indicates that some progress is being made in retaining Indians in school. Further, in 1956–1957 only 7% of all Indian children in school were enrolled in grade 7 or higher while by 1966–1967 the proportion was 26.5%.

As can be seen, about half the children living on reserves are attending integrated provincial schools, but it is prophesied that in the near future all students proceeding beyond grade 7 will attend provincial schools.

Granted that not enough Indian children remain in school as long as they should, the question arises: How well are provincial schools adapted to Indian children?

First, there is the problem of language. As Judge Haig Brown of Campbell River pointed out in a remote village where his son had been a schoolteacher none of the children spoke a word of English before they came to school. There are a sufficient number of such villages to be significant. Other Indian children may know English but suffer from a disability because their vocabulary is smaller than that of white children from more advantaged homes and they use the language with less fluency. The Indian affairs branch takes no position on native languages and normally does not use them in connection with education. (In Mexico, in the south, the government finally availed itself of the native language, at least in early grades, and found it much easier to lead the young people into higher education in Spanish.) At any rate, Hawthorne concludes that this disregard of aboriginal speech is really the result of the ideology of assimilation—if you wait long enough there will be no Indians to worry about. The Indians themselves, however, are taking a new interest in the speech of their various groups, as will be discussed in a later chapter.

Another point made by the report is that, in the first place, material displaying attitudes offensive to the native population should be removed. (Norman Joe, band manager of the Cowichan, mentioned that his son said to him, "Daddy, why is it when the whites win it's a victory and when the Indians do, it's a massacre?") The cliché in popular literature of Indians always biting the dust is, however, changing and this will probably soon cease to be an issue. As Mr. Witt remarked, Indians nowadays are getting a good press and a new sympathy for them has arisen. On the positive side, it was suggested that material dealing with Indian culture should be developed because it would both help the morale of the Indian children and also be of value in moulding the attitudes of young non-Indians. It is evident that something is not being done in this area for the first book of the Nootka writer George Clutesi, *Son of Raven, Son of Deer,* is now used as an elementary English test in British Columbia schools. The writer also chanced to see a workbook in which use was made of Jonathan Green's narrative and the study so oriented that it pointed out the biased, narrow-minded attitude of the missionary.

The Hawthorne report also stressed the fact that teachers needed to know more about native culture and should take more interest in the general social situation of their students—which meant not calling in the parents exclusively when the child was in difficulties.

On denominational education the conclusion was unequivocal that government subsidy should be discontinued: "Multiplicity of denominational schools is a factor in the disastrous division within the reserves and is finally proving to do more harm than good." Likewise, I.Q. tests which were not oriented toward the background of Indian children were denounced as not valid. They sometimes had the effect of placing the Indian children in the lowest category, branding them "uneducable."

It was true also that there were certain elements in the background of native children which did not promote achievement in the white man's school. In the first place there was the matter of the "deprived" home, as in all low-income groups, where there were few toys, little privacy, and often not very stimulating communication with adults. In the past there would have been a handing down of traditional myth, customs, and, in general, the poetry of the culture. With all this wiped out by the missionaries and with the addition of punishment in school for speaking an aboriginal language (every informant we spoke to brought this up), enriching relationships between the generations were destroyed. The Indian family is permissive toward children and does not always support the white standards of punctuality, attendance and discipline. The Canadian school—with its specialized subjects, its strict sense of time, its goals of competitive achievement—can still seem alien to a nonindustrial people. The parents, although they often generalized that education is a good thing and helps you to get ahead, had not really accepted this fact emotionally, had perhaps not seen enough specific examples to prove it, and were often not wholeheartedly supportive. When a child was needed at home, school lost out.

Among the Cowichan there was awareness of some of these problems, and the band manager, Norman Joe, explained that they had initiated a project for the youngest children similar to the Head Start program in the United States. He felt they had had good results.

The aspirations of the Indian children, the report concluded, have up until now been too limited. They do not see enough Indians achieving professional status, well-paying jobs, and positions of community importance. Hence they identify with work opportunities on a low level. Finally, they are "hurt" by failure and tend to drop out. Here the whole basis of the traditional culture with its shame–prestige orientation should be remembered. Historically it is ingrained in Northwest Indian emotional life that shame is not to be endured. It is no wonder, therefore, with so many adverse circumstances making academic achievement difficult, that the dropout rate is high.

All these circumstances militate against many Indians' going on to a higher education, but, above all, there is the problem of cost. The Indian Act says nothing about college education. In 1966–1967 only 36 Indians attended B.C. universities. It does not seem to be clear whether Indian Affairs assumes the complete responsibility of subsidizing all qualified Indians who desire a college education. At the present time some assistance is given. The Fields and Stanbury report concludes, "We strongly urge the Branch to unequivocably support all eligible Indians to obtain a university education. The non-pecuniary rewards in the form of examples of the progress of Indian people (not mere tokenism) will bring hope and determination to thousands of others."

In a discussion of this problem with Judge Haig Brown of Campbell River, he said that, in his opinion, in his area more Indians should be going on to a higher education. He himself had worked on the idea that there should be Indian groups within the University of Victoria to encourage college attendance. It was his belief that a group could be developed which could go out and recruit. He felt that parents needed to be indoctrinated with the idea while their children were still young. Then, if the youngster had the capacity to go on, nothing should stop him or her. Concerning early preparation, he said:

> This should be done rather than going to a child when it is 15 or 16 and saying you're pretty bright and you ought to go on to the university. It *can* be done this way. My wife, who was librarian at the senior high school here, used to talk them into going on to the university. But then it's really too late and not in the parents' minds. You, when you have children, assume that if they can they will be going to the university. There is no such assumption among the Indians and that's the situation you have to deal with.

He went on to say:

I was hoping that in the University of Victoria there would be a group of Indian people on the campus who would watch for those who came in and who would individually give them support and push them on to get support elsewhere.

There is no doubt that education is a key activity in changing the condition of the Indians. More than once, when a band manager or chief councillor was asked what he thought of the future of assimilation he replied that it would take place when the Indians had produced enough professionals to take their place among other Canadian groups.

IN SEWARD'S ICEBOX

28

The voyage up the broad Clarence Strait, the marine highway which cuts through the center of southern Alaska, in the large steamer which functions as a ferry is a pleasant experience and is doubtless even more agreeable in summer when the ferry plies every day. The coastlines are the same as those of British Columbia, rugged and handsome as the light plays over the mountains, furred with evergreen. The weather is admittedly rain and fog most of the time and Ketchikan, strung for 30 miles along the shore, boasts that it has 220 inches of rain a year. It lived up to its boast.

If much of British Columbia seems frontier, Ketchikan seems more so. The town possesses a large fishing fleet, canneries, sawmills, a library with a small museum attached and a whole string of craft shops, for the steamers bring in tourists in summer. The shops stock Tlingit and Eskimo art of varying quality. Near the municipal building stands a handsome totem pole erected by Chief Johnson in 1901, described as the last of the original totem poles. It depicts the legend of Fog Woman, Raven's wife, creating the salmon and is painted in muted blues and greens.

We stayed in the poorer of the two hotels, the sort of hostelry which has no elevator and places the sink in the bedroom. It had the loudest plumbing (which seemed to function all night) we ever encountered.

Mrs. Bertha Johnson, our contact in the Bureau of Indian Affairs, had told us that there was a serious drinking problem among the Indians. We saw some indication of this when we dropped into a bar which was undeniably full of Indians of both sexes. On the shelf behind the counter we spotted a fine carving of a bear clan speaker's figure. We made some tentative overtures, but it was firmly not for sale. A drunken Indian, who seemed disoriented and anxious to buttonhole other patrons of the bar, kept repeating "I lost one of my sons in Vietnam." For some reason he irritated the bartender, who eased him out. Later as we were having dinner in one of the two or three restaurants, this one run by a Rumanian, the same Indian appeared in the same state and was again eased out.

Later that night, on our way back to our hotel we saw two pretty teenage Indian girls lurking rather too suggestively on the streetcorner.

We had arranged an interview with the mayor of the nearby village of Saxman, named for the missionary who had decided to transfer the Tlingit to that spot from their traditional home at Cape Fox. The village is located along the shore a few minutes from Ketchikan. The houses were mostly neat and well-painted with, however, no lawns or gardens, not differing greatly from those on the outskirts of Ketchikan. A shingle factory with its mess and disorder and black furnace of burning sawdust stood next to the house of Joe Williams, the mayor, and it was there that he was employed. It was notable that the settlement possessed a Pentecostal Evangelical Church, and Pentecostal Church of God, and a Salvation Army Church, the same multiplicity of sects of which all the coastal Indians have been victims. The only sort of focus for the village was the Saxman Totem Park which includes a number of poles—a few originals brought from Cape Fox, the majority replicas carved by modern artists and was set up mostly in 1934.

One of the oddities of the park is a replica of the Lincoln pole which was carved by an imported Tsimshian artist from Port Simpson to commemorate an event in Tlingit Indian history. In 1868 the Kagwantan clan of the Eagle moiety were at war with the Tongass Ravens burning their towns, murdering women and children, and enslaving others. While the Tongass were besieged on Village Island, in Clarence Strait, they learned that the revenue cutter *Lincoln* had arrived with a company of soldiers to set up a customs house and a fort. The Tongass quickly availed themselves of the protection of the station and, under the shelter of the guns, finally made peace with the Kagwantan, a peace which lasted. In the late 1870s or early 1880s the original pole—with the figure of Lincoln on top and Proud Raven, emblem of the Tongass Ravens, on the bottom—was set up. A photograph shows the original statue (said to be the oldest of Lincoln and now in the Juneau Museum), though much eroded, to be a rather naturalistic portrait. The replica is not as fine a piece of carving. It seemed a pity that, when we visited the park, the poles were being repainted in far too bright acrylic colors.

Some 13 miles north of Ketchikan there is a long house, in an old Tlingit campsite at Mud Bight. In 1938 a totem pole restoration program was started with the intention of setting up a village with several houses with Tlingit and Haida carvings from all such groups in Kasaan, Hydaburg, Klamwak, Saxman, and Ketchikan. Copies of carvings from deserted towns as well as new specially designed poles were planned. World War II put an end to this ambitious project but the Saxman workshop with the aid of CCC workers did construct the present building with its portal pole and another free-standing totem pole. The whole was designed by Charles Brown, head carver of the Saxman workshop.

The painting on the housefront is a stylized raven with double eyes. On poles on each side of the house a man in a spruce root hat with a cane in his hand ready for a potlatch is sitting. Within the house are posts depicting stories of the Cape Fox and Tongass tribes.

It is significant that these restoration activities took place as early as 1939 and indicate a recognition of Tlingit art and a stimulation of native carving, a precursor project which helped pave the way to the cultural reawakening of today.

In 1968 as a result of a suit by the Tlingit–Haida Central Council the U.S. Court of Claims awarded the Tlingit and Haida Indians $7,546,053.80 for lands lost or damaged plus 2,500,000 acres of land. The Tlingit and Haida Central Council is administering these funds. Meanwhile, the Bureau of Indian Affairs has been conducting an enrollment of Tlingit and Haida Indians residing in the United States and Canada. There are 10,000 to 12,000 Tlingit in Alaska and about 200 Haida, who migrated from Canada to the vicinity of Hydaburg in the eighteenth century.

In 1966 when the matter of oil and gas leasing came up in Alaska, the native organizations protested and a general land freeze was instituted. A federal field committee was set up to look into the native claim situation for all of Alaska. This committee in 1969 concluded "that Alaska Natives have a substantial claim upon *all* the lands of Alaska by virtue of their aboriginal occupancy. . . ." As a result various bills were drawn up in 1970 and 1971—bills of a truly revolutionary character which are having an effect upon the situation in British Columbia.

As the Cummings-Mickenberg study *Native Rights in Canada* points out: "The past has witnessed native disillusionment with the large and costly Bureau of Indian Affairs and the poverty and alienation of the reserve system." The Tlingit of Alaska have fortunately escaped this system by insisting, since the United States took over Alaska, on their citizenship and organizing to legalize it. They are therefore in a much better position today than the southern tribes of the United States, who are only belatedly unifying for the purpose of dealing with the government. The combined natives of Alaska are now using about 60,000,000 acres, or approximately 17 percent of the land, to which they have a valid claim. The Act of June 6, 1900, states that, "Congress and the administrative authorities have consistently recognized and respected the possessory rights of the natives of Alaska in the land actually occupied and used by them." Once again the low density of the white population has spared them much of the mistreatment that reserve Indians of the United States have suffered.

An example of the newly enlightened point of view is the statement of Senator Fred Harris, author of S-835, the bill which was drafted with the aid of the Alaskan Federation of Natives, an organization founded in 1964. Harris stated: "We know that the native people need vast areas of land if they are to continue their traditional way of life." In other words, because of the large areas of land in minimal use, as far as the whites go, in Alaska, for the first time it was proposed to allow the natives to live as they had been doing. And with the new appreciation of the ecology crisis, it is beginning to be realized that land used by native peoples will result in protection of the environment rather than raping it. As the Alaskan Federation of Natives put it, they demanded: "A bold and imaginative approach which fully resolves all claims, ties the settlement to the lands in question and permits the natives to improve themselves and their land and determine their destiny."

Old attitudes died hard, however, and the final settlement was not achieved without a struggle. Although Harris fought for an adequate settlement, the Senate at first passed an unacceptable bill cutting down the acreage and cash settlement to a fraction of that allowed in his bill. The native organization did not give up but pushed their case hard. Harris and Senator Edward Kennedy introduced a bill which was adequate and Representative Lloyd Meeds a companion piece of legislation in the House in 1971. The AFN managed to impress President Nixon sufficiently so that he came out in support of the figure of 40,000,000 acres. Committees from the two houses worked out joint legislation and the Alaska Native Claims Settlement became a law on December 18, 1871. It was a historic piece of legislation which is bound to have an effect upon government attitudes toward native peoples in other parts of the world.

In addition to the acreage, the Natives receive $462,500,000 over an 11-year period from funds in the treasury and an additional $500,000,000 from mineral revenues. This settlement, which abolishes reservations and "trust" arrangements, extinguishes all aboriginal claims. The act sets up 12 regional corporations for the administration of these assets, and these are to be managed by boards of directors all of whom, except for the initial boards, shall be stockholders over 18 years of age. Since only natives are stockholders this allows for native control. Funds are to be channeled through the regional corporation (on a population basis) to village corporations which actually invest the assets or exploit them. These village corporations must submit their plans for the approval of the regional boards. The number of board members and manner of elections of the directing groups of both types of corporation are to be determined when the articles or incorporation are drawn up. Thus there are checks and balances which are intended to safeguard the interests of the village residents.

A native village is defined as a settlement containing a minimum of 25 natives in the 1970 census or by other evidence satisfactory to the secretary of the interior. The definition of a native is perhaps not wholly adequate but it is certainly better than that of the much-attacked Canadian Indian Act. The Alaskan Settlement Act specifies one-quarter blood and goes on to say that in the absence of proof, anyone who claims to be a native and is so regarded by the village or native group of which he claims to be a member and whose father and mother are regarded as natives by such village or any other village or native group listed in the legislation will be accepted as a native. This also applies to individuals whose adopted parents are not natives.

The act states that the secretary of the interior shall prepare, within two years from the date of the enactment of the law, a roll of natives living in the various villages and those not living permanently in any one village are to be assigned to one of the 12 corporate regions.

The Tlingit–Haida group are listed as one of the regional corporations and, as are all the villages, each community is to receive 23,040 acres. The balance of the land awarded under the settlement is not shared by the Tlingit–Haida because of their earlier settlement.

The residents of New Metlakatla, in virtue of their special position and historic agreement, do not come under the Settlement Act. The general nature of the settlement had evidently already influenced the 1971 Dorion Report, which advocates a development corporation for the province of Quebec for the social, economic, and cultural advancement of the native communities. It will be remembered that one of the proposals put forward in Harold Cardinal's book was for a development corporation and it appears that his basic demand that Indians be in control of their own destinies is gradually being met.

A footnote to the matter of the land settlement was the attitude of a Ketchikan businessman that it meant the Indians were prying more money out of the government: "I never saw so many Tlingit and Haida turn up as when the land settlement went through." There is evidently a feeling among right-wing whites akin to that evidenced toward relief clients in other parts of the United States.

Mrs. Bertha Johnson, who worked for the Bureau of Indian Affairs, told us that the bureau exercised no control over the Saxman Tlingit. Its chief function was that of handling matters of welfare. There was a cannery and cold storage plant for crab and shrimp nearby which had shut down—but the B.I.A. was taking it over and presumably would run it for the benefit of the Indians, which, she felt, would take up the slack at Hydaburg, which was the home of the local Haida group. She herself was of Tsimshian stock, having been born in New Metlakatla, but she had lived most of her life in Seattle and Ketchikan. We discussed question of discrimination. She had never encountered discrimination, she said; but she did tell us that by law the pulp mill had to employ a certain quota of minority groups—here, of course, Indians—and this meant that whites who were at least as well qualified felt they lost out to the natives, with the result that there was a certain backlash.

Joe Williams, the mayor, who governed Saxman with an elected council, was both knowledgeable and amiable. He told us that the move from Cape Fox had taken place about 70 years ago. There had been an Indian Bureau school but now the school was integrated with those of Ketchikan. He was particularly pleased with the fact that under the Farmers' Home program the settlement had built 18 new homes and with financing obtained through the Indian Bureau the Tlingit and the Haida of Hydaburg were in the process of obtaining 20 more. A pulp mill, a spruce mill, and two cold storage plants in Ketchikan plus the Alaskan Cedar Shingle plant next door afford an adequate amount of work for the men of Saxman. Some also found employment building the new homes, a couple were in the public health department working in the sewage treatment plant (Williams boasted that it was better than one in Ketchikan). A few women worked in the canneries. A couple of young people worked for the state, one near the top in the Indian Affairs Administration.

Williams had 2 families, the older boys now grown up, all high school graduates, and several young children by his second wife, a white woman. Fishing was still important as a partial source of livelihood: "It's in the blood, fishing. My son took my boat out recently but he didn't want me aboard. He said it was too late in the season. I was out last summer and I enjoyed it." Salmon, as elsewhere on the Northwest Coast, was home-canned and -smoked for the winter. In addition, some meat was frozen when deer hunting took place. Williams insisted that in this area no one need starve.

We discussed the Alaskan Native Brotherhood which flourishes currently. Williams had been grand president for two years. He was enthusiastic about the gains which this organization had made for the Indians. Like every older native we spoke to, he remembered how he had been punished for speaking his language when a boy at school. He credited the brotherhood with having pushed through citizenship for the natives, achieved integrated schools, old-age pensions, and public health services. He also maintained that it had done much to eliminate discrimination. When he was a boy Indian children did not play with whites; if they did there were fights. As a young man, because he was an Indian he was not allowed to enter a pool hall and even certain restaurants. In the movie house the Indians were segregated in a sort of glass cage. All this was far in the past, for now he felt his children and grandchildren were fully accepted in the white community.

We asked about hereditary chiefs and were told that they still existed, although there did not seem to be any one who was outstanding in the area. This being the northern and matriarchal region, the office passed down not from father to son but to the lineage of the mother's brother. In each clan there was still technically a chief. As he explained, a friend of his was the last of his clan and that automatically made him a chief. The moiety regulations in marriage are still preserved. His first wife, when they thought of marrying, immediately asked him about his clan. He was a Beaver of the Raven moiety, she a Killer Whale under Eagle, and thus the rule of exogamy was not broken. In the case of his second wife's being non-Indian, she was properly adopted into a clan of the opposite moiety and given a Tlingit name.

Williams's own name was The-Spirit-Comes-from-Up-Above. Everyone in the Saxman community had Tlingit names; two of

Williams's grandchildren were named, respectively, Whale-Jumping-out-of-the-Water and Great-Bear-Lying-Dead.

Williams was vitally involved in the cultural revival. "It almost got away from us," he said, "but we are trying to put it together again." A few ceremonial objects had been saved but many were destroyed during the period of missionary dominance. Today the Tlingits have repaired what they could of the older pieces and have made replicas of those that were too far gone. Joe proudly put on his halibut hat with five potlatch rings and assumed his button blanket regalia. He also possessed an abalone mask headdress and he brought out a series of button blankets which his wife had made for his children and grandchildren.

He had been fortunate in that his uncle (mother's brother) had lived with the family and had passed down knowledge of the dances and song as well as myths. Thus Williams knew how the songs were sung and the relation of the myths to the various clans. All of this he was determined to pass on to the younger generations. He told us that about 60 to 80 of the Saxman Tlingit participate in the dances, sometimes performing for tourists who come to Ketchikan in summer. His sister was also able to help transmit the dances. When we asked about the younger people he told us that one son who was in his second year at college in Anchorage would come home to dance the bow and arrow dance.

Ketchikan is not alone in these activities; Haines has a large group, also Juneau, Kluckwan, Sitka, and several other villages. The November of the previous year there had been a statewide convention at which the Indians had spent a day and a night dancing.

He also pointed out that the Haida group at Hydaburg had their own group, whose dances he had often seen and enjoyed. He said he had been in Kluckwan not long ago and heard little children there talking to each other in Tlingit, which made him feel very good. Indeed, as he proudly told us, his granddaughter knew many songs and stories at the age of thirteen, and his ten-year-old grandson knew many songs and could do the chief's dance. Still another element in the revival was the fact that a Miss Fanny Brown was teaching Indian culture in the school, and the Tlingit language was in the curriculum.

Joe Williams was our first introduction to the coastal revival of culture. We spoke further concerning it with a Tlingit carver and dancer whom we encountered in the Ketchikan museum, Nathan Jackson, whose Indian name was Raven

Chick. One of his plaques hung on the wall of the museum, and we were to see some of his screen prints later at 'Ksan. We discussed the future of Northwest art. He felt that the tradition must become freer and less imitative of the past. He also had done restoration work for the University of Alaska and felt that the Northwest tradition should be used more widely in architectural design. He told us that potlatching was going on in four or five places in Alaska (there had been one at a wedding recently in Ketchikan). In his view it had never wholly died out and hence some material was being handed down without a break with tradition. He, himself, was on his way to a potlatch in Haines, taking with him a garbage can which was to be his contribution. His white girlfriend, who was learning how to make Chilkat blankets, was accompanying him. He was not sure if she would be allowed to participate in the potlatch.

Jackson has shown work in a New York gallery. He told us he felt there were about a dozen serious Tlingit artists in Alaska. It was evident that in the last few years much has happened to strengthen ethnic consciousness in Alaska. The custodian of the museum said the movement was quite recent. Among the various arts which are now respected is basket making, but few younger people have learned the true cedar bark, finely woven technique. Actually, a hat and basket in the museum collection were made by an old Haida woman of eighty-four who lived in Masset.

If the cultural revival is in full swing in Alaska, when we turn to the coast of British Columbia we find that the peoples of the other six nations are equally active, even though they have been officially inhibited for so many years.

TO BE AN INDIAN

29

"I think the whole priority for the Northwest Coast is to get the younger people interested in the old culture," Mrs. Johnson, chief councillor for the Nootka Gold River band, told the writer. And indeed the cultural revival which is now going on from Alaska to Vancouver is perhaps the most exciting thing which is taking place among the Northwest people. The fact that a reawakening of interest in the cultural heritage has occurred to a greater of lesser degree in every one of the seven nations is of the utmost importance both for the morale of the people and because efforts are now being made to create a continuity with a magnificent tradition and to carry it further. Kenneth Muldoe, band manager of Kispiox, said of it, "It has been the greatest thing in my lifetime."

Changes had to take place in both the government attitudes and the general social sophistication before the dead hand of the missionaries could be shaken off. It will be remembered that in 1951–1952 a new and liberalized Indian Act at last removed the shameful prohibition which had made potlatching illegal for decades. For decades the Indians had protested and devised ways to circumvent it. Daisy Neel told the writer that her grandfather cleverly gave a potlatch at Christmas time and wrapped the potlatch gifts as Christmas presents. Some Indians went to jail and that memory has rankled. Several times Indian leaders told me that they remembered how their forefathers had been forced by missionaries to cut down and burn their totem poles. With the 1951 laws the Indian once more breathed freely; they were no longer forced to be white men by legal penalties. It was not long after that the first stirring began. The whites had even done something in the way of restoring totem poles a few decades earlier, specifically the Canadian National Railway and the federal government in the Skeena area, in the twenties, and some were set up in Stanley Park at Vancouver, in the same era, which decayed and were replaced by the present group. The Provincial Museum took an interest in totem pole preservation in the forties and hired

Totem Poles Restored

the carver Mungo Martin to restore and create new carvings. Eventually Thunderbird Park was created on the museum grounds. The University of British Columbia, also in the forties, began restoring and establishing totem pole exhibits. This meant that other carvers, Bill Reid, Doug Cranmer, and Henry Hunt were given work and able to carry on when Martin died in 1962.

All this had value in preserving and reestablishing carving tradition. The Gitksan of the upper Skeena had continued carving poles into the fifties, and the Kwakiutl of Alert Bay and father south were carving poles with only a hiatus of a few years before the renewed work in the contemporary period. Thus it can be said that Northwest carving has never wholly died out. In some cases the purity of the classical style had declined, but the spark has been kept alive and in some areas carving families have now reestablished their art in a tradition which goes back for three generations.

The art, however, was always an integral part of the whole richly imagistic culture. Despite the attacks of the whites, some parts of the old structure remain. Awareness of the clans and rank in clans still exists. Claude Davidson, the argillite carver of Masset, maintained that the moieties were here remembered, he being an Eagle. He told us with approval that his son was going with a Raven girl. We have already seen that the same retention of moieties and clans was attested to by Joe Williams, the Tlingit. Terry Whyte informed us that in the Skeena area everyone knew the clans, even children, and the ranking was known from top to bottom. In the Nootka area, he felt the tradition was remembered in less detail, though the top three positions in a clan were known. In the Cowichan area Norman Rose also stated that the clans were known and respected. In general, there was an agreement that the young people did not always adhere to the exogamic rules and obviously much of the elaborate mental bookkeeping as to what privileges each individual was entitled to can no longer be kept up because the knowledge is now fragmentary; but it is clear that many lineages are fully aware of their prestige, crests, and remember some of their family mythologies. Nevertheless, there is a hiatus because of the white man's schooling which has deprived many of the youngsters of their heritage and, in order to regain it, they must turn to the few old people with important connections and good memories. In some cases the situation is felt to be acute. Mrs. Johnson said, "In our band we have only five or six of the old people left, and once they are gone there will be a complete loss."

One of the significant and interesting areas is that of names. As we have seen in earlier chapters, names were acquired at various times in a man's life in connection with crests and privileges. With adjustment to the white man's world came the problem of easily pronouncible names. It was solved by acquiring English names in various ways. Sometimes a simple first name eventually was turned into a surname, as Jimmy Dick, the master carver of Alert Bay, or Norman Joe of the Cowichan band. Often the name was handed out by a missionary at baptism and in this case the missionary's own name was often used, as in the case of Frank Collison of Haida, who was aware that he was named for the first missionary to the Masset area. Sometimes when the Indians worked in canneries, we were told the boss charged $10 for a name and handed out anything that occurred to him; sometimes, not being aware of relationships, he gave different surnames to two brothers. In a few cases where the Indian name was not difficult for the English-speaking world to pronounce, that was used—as in the case of George Clutesi, James Sewid (pronounced *seaweed*), or Kenneth Muldoe. The latter name is an example of what happens to tradition. It belongs to the frog clan of the Hazelton area and should traditionally pass down the maternal line, but now that it has become a surname, it passes down the male line and is born by people of other clans. Duff cites the case of Maquilla of Salmon River who became Johnny Moon, a translation of the Indian name, and another individual whose boyhood name was Frog-Sitting-in-a-Spring-of-Water-in-Bright-Sunlight who became Michael Inspring Bright.

We often asked those whom we interviewed for English translations of their Indian names. In some cases they had none, testimony to a complete loss of tradition, but in many cases the names were interesting and often poetic.

Muldoe, for instance, was Big-Angry-Man. Andy Schooner, as might be expected, was able to oblige with three of his names, Crazy-to-Make-a-Potlatch, Raven, and The-Sun-on-My-Back. Benson was called Gives-Presents-All-Over. Norman Joe told us he had just been given a name in a ceremony the winter before—and a fine one it was. The-Sound-of-Rocks-underneath-the-Water. Bill Scow's name was, appropriately, Born-to-Be-a-Leader.

The actual revival, stemming from Indian areas, takes similar forms. In 1960 the Provincial Museum had a replica of a Kwakiutl house in its Thunderbird Park. The report of that year records that the Nootka writer and artist George Clutesi put on an impressive program of Nootka dances in this structure. This was evidently a pioneer effort. Most active and important was Jimmy Sewid, who tells the story of what he initiated in his region. In 1963 he convinced his band council that Alert Bay should have an arts and crafts center. With a building committee of Henry Speck, Simon Beans, Arthur Dick, and others he planned a replica of a long house, first constructing a small-scale model. The carvings made use of crests from several of the nearby tribes, the front house posts with the supernatural *quolus* bird and the Grizzly Bear—the back ones, the *tsunuqua* or wild creature of the woods and the thunderbird, while the crossbeams were ornamented with the *sisiutl.* The building was 70 by 50 and required logs three feet in diameter. Sewid was able to draw a little money from the winter works program and eventually from the Board of Trade of Alert Bay:

> In the back of my mind one of the main reasons for building that community house was to have a place where we could try to preserve the art of my people. I knew it was going to be lost if we didn't try to pick it up and it wasn't just because the people were losing interest. The main reason that our customs, dances and art were dying out was that they had been forbidden by the law against our will. In fact, many of our people had been put in prison for refusing to give up our way of life.

Sewid eventually formed the Kwakwala Arts and Crafts Organization to support the activities of the center which was completed in June 1965. The opening was held in the Centennial year of 1966, the potlatch and the Hamatsa ceremony being given by Chief Knox of Fort Rupert, who was related to the Sewids and whose son was eligible to become a Hamatsa. Over 500 people attended, Bill Scow acting as announcer and interpreting the meaning of the dances because some of the spectators were whites. The young Hamatsa and many of his relatives danced. Finally Sewid himself and his friend Charlie Peter from Cape Mudge danced the feather dance. As Sewid explains:

> James Knox was very happy to have me dance for him because it was always the feeling of the chiefs to get all their relatives wherever they were from. It didn't matter how many dances you put on but it was

important to use all your relatives that you could. That showed that you were a prominent man, you were a big man, and you were related to all the different tribes.

Jimmy's wife Flora and his daughter also danced, all being related to Chief Knox. After the dancing ended at midnight, cake and sandwiches were served and gifts given. Sewid handed out $10 to the leading chiefs, $5 to the older people and $2 to the young men.

Eventually, with the aid of the Alert Bay Board of Trade, Sewid worked out an arrangement with the steamship line which stops at Alert Bay on its way north during the summer. The Kwakiutl put on dance programs in the clan house which were sold to the passengers as a part of their fare. The program—adorned with a killer whale, the symbol of Alert Bay—lists the dances and welcomes tourists to the area. In the first year over 3000 people saw the community house programs. The participants were paid out of admissions and the balance went into the Kwakwala Arts Fund. The occasion of the performance was also used to sell craft objects produced by the local people.

Recently, in the field next to the long house, the village has erected what they designate as the tallest totem pole in the world, a monument which towers above the house and combines the crests of a whole group of neighboring Kwakiutl tribes. The summer programs have already become an institution.

Interestingly enough, Bill Scow's contribution to the cultural awakening was his father's house. Since it had fallen into disrepair, he decided to sell the house poles to the Pacific Science Center Foundation, the permanent installation of exhibits which followed the Seattle Exposition of 1962. We made a special effort while in Seattle to visit it. Reconstructed indoors, the impressive facade and portal pole has been restored and the interior arranged as a museum of Northwest artifacts. When it was opened Scow told us he had gone with a dance group from one of the islands near Alert Bay to put on a program. He had been impressed by the clever way in which a fire in the center of the building is simulated by means of electric light and strips of cellophane agiated by a fan, commenting that in Sewid's clan house the tourists sitting around the fire during dance programs got smoke in their eyes.

In Bella Coola during the last five or six years, a replica of a clan house has been built using the motifs of old portal poles of the past. It serves as a carving center and meeting hall and one room is devoted to a fine collection of masks, old and new. Carving continues to go on and dances and potlatches are held; but in this area they are not, as they are in Alert Bay, oriented toward the tourist. Ronald Witt told the writer that the ceremonies carried out are very much for the benefit of the community, although a few outsiders are allowed to become spectators. Masks, too, are mostly being made for specific purposes and not as craft for sale. Here, therefore, the cultural revival appears to be very self-contained and deeply rooted.

In contrast, the town of Campbell River has organized a salmon festival in which the white community and the neighboring Indian bands combine to participate in the events. The 1973 program booklet includes pictures of Kwakiutl carvers and their work and basket makers and articles by Daisy Neel on family history, native customs, and the nonstatus Indian problem. In 1972 the Heritage Park Pavilion, a skeleton clan house with carved posts and poles was built in a park on the shore of the bay, and in this area the events now take place. The four days of the festival, which includes some aspects of a county fair and some of a circus, involve Indian arts and crafts, an Indian salmon barbecue, Indian war canoe races, a dance program by Indian children, and another program by the Alert Bay group.

A well-publicized program paralleling to some extent that of Alert Bay goes on at 'Ksan, a cultural center with six replica clan houses which has been built near Hazelton. The buildings are lined up along the Skeena River (when we were there flanked with the gold of fall cottonwoods), and, looming up in front of them, the great bulk of Rocher de Boule with its eternal snows. The actual Indian village consists of houses scattered along the outskirts and within the town of Hazelton, while the cultural center is set in a green meadow, actually a park, of over 50 acres set aside by the Hazelton band council. Howard Wale, the present chief councillor, told us they had to wait until the old hereditary chief died because he was not in favor of the project.

Actually the first stirrings took place in the fifties when a group of Indians and whites under the leadership of the Hazelton Library Association began to revive the arts and crafts of the Gitksan Tsimshian of the region. Locally $10,000 was raised to build the first building of the group, The Skeena treasure house in 1958 which functioned as a museum. It was also the library association, in which Polly Sargent was active, which took the lead in sparking a restoration program of totem poles in the four neighboring villages: Glen Vowell, Kispiox, Kitwancool, and Kitwanga. Today all have small parks which contain some of the finest old poles and excellent reproductions in the Gitksan style.

The treasure house led to the raising of $100,000 locally and with matching government grants the building of a feast house, a larger museum, a display area and craft shop, and eventually a building which houses a workshop and a school of carving. The federal and provincial governments now cooperate in a training school for the artists.

The buildings of 'Ksan village display handsomely decorated facades in traditional style; portal poles with the crests of the clans in the area are constructed with the heavy beams and carved house poles of the Northwest clan houses. The feast house contains figures in Gitksan dress and artifacts to illustrate the activities of the past.

Thanks to the government and missionary attacks, the arts had almost come to a stop with the death of the old master carvers and the lack of young artists to continue the style. The revival came just in time when there were still enough of the older folk to transmit traditions and also was aided by artists and whites from other regions. Bill Holm, the author of the classic work on West Coast art, was a consultant and also aided in the reconstruction of the dances and ceremonies, which has been continuing along with the revival of the sculpture and graphic art. The Kwakiutl carvers Doug Kranmer and Henry Hunt contributed knowledge of carving, as did the Haida, Robert Davidson, and the Tlingit, Nathan Jackson (whom we have mentioned). Doris Gruber aided in recapturing blanket weaving techniques, and Duane Pasco is credited with successfully managing the project, which was officially opened in 1972.

There were, of course, some family regalia still in existence which aided in recapturing the patterns of the past and in 1971 an historical project was set going. With the use of cassettes Indian interviewers have worked industriously at recording history, legends, and songs in the original language. These have then been translated into English with the aid of older people who still understand the archaic classical terms. Protocol of potlatches, lists of foods and medicines, and additional data concerning artifacts and regalia have been recorded. The famous button blankets of dark blue with red borders and crests outlined in pearl buttons have been produced. The beautifully carved masks for frontlets of the headdresses, new masks, rattles, wooden potlatch hats, Chilkat blankets, cedar bark hats and headbands and other articles of apparel are being made, so expertly that they constitute a continuation of tradition. The most ambitious project has been the production of a 1500-square-foot painted screen for a new bank building in Vancouver.

In short the production of traditional art forms has become a flourishing industry, and indeed a few master carvers can make as much as $20,000 a year. Alongside the craft house are stacked great cedar poles which will be made into totem poles, for now the West Coast is becoming conscious of its important aboriginal tradition. Newly created poles and replicas of old ones are sought for as decorations in front of hotels or set up near municipal buildings in cities. The names of the master carvers are well known and most of the new art objects are signed.

As has been said before, all of this work can be regarded as a continuation of tradition, many of the pieces as good or better than those of the ancient traditional masters. On the whole the classic style has not been degraded by commercialism. So far, it must be admitted, not much that is new and original has yet emerged from it. Many screen prints are being made in which there is considerable freedom of composition, but the elements used are all those already formalized by the overall cultures. The Northwest Coast still awaits the young new genius who will create something completely new from the old roots—but the chances are that, within a few years, this, too, will happen.

Something should be said of the very special Haida craft of argillite, or black carbonaceous shale, carving. This material occurs only in the Queen Charlotte Islands and the right to use it had been granted the Haida as a monopoly by the government. Actually the craft started around 1820 and was always used to produce trade items for the whites, and many of the early pipes and small pieces of sculpture depict the nineteenth-century traders in their high boots and stovepipe hats.

All sorts of small objects, including amulets, pendants, dishes, boxes, brooches, and the like, are now being produced, most of them decorated with incised totemic patterns. We watched Claude Davidson (son of Robert Davidson) at his workbench in his house when we visited Masset. His son was sawing up pieces of argillite into convenient sizes, for the material can, when it is fresh, be worked like wood. We purchased a pendant engraved with the eagle crest of the carver. When the work is finished it is sanded and finally polished with a touch of shoe blacking.

With the revival of carving, argillite is one of the materials being worked with a fresh impetus and the modern products are often thought to be equal to the best created in the past.

Needless to say, the dance ceremonials of 'Ksan have become an institution viewed by thousands of tourists during the summer months, and the same spectators are also taken through the structures in the 'Ksan cultural center. On November 3 and 4, 1972, the 'Ksan dancers performed in the National Arts Center Theatre in Ottawa, while an art exhibition was concomitantly displayed in the lobby.

What has happened with the work in Alert Bay and 'Ksan is something parallel to the development of the Mexican Folklore Ballet, in that the native art forms are being recaptured and recognized as an important part of the heritage of Canada.

Terry Whyte told us something of activities in the Port Alberni area, where there was a good-sized dance group. This is the home of the writer–artist George Clutesi (who was unfortunately away making a film when we passed through). At Port Alberni four bands organized an Eagle cultural council. An old chief stood up in a meeting, however, and said that Eagles banded together as brothers, so, as a result, the name was changed to and became the Titska Brotherhood Council. It is noticeable that the Northwest Indians have been partial to the word brotherhood in a number of their organizations.

A number of meetings were held at the Indian center of the town which Whyte attended and found most exciting. Groups from all around chartered six-passenger Beaver planes and flew in to participate; some were even bedded down in the church because of a shortage of accommodations. For once the elders were the center of attention and loved it. As Whyte described what went on:

> This time it was the oldsters, instead of sitting back in a meeting and wondering what a lease or a mortgage was, were trying to remember, helping each other to reconstruct the past. The old timers were heroes. You could see a birth taking place as they revived what they had known. Then they revived the gambling game with sticks. The two teams face each other as a drum is beaten. They try to guess which hand has the sticks and make points. The team that wins the most points then gets the sticks. It goes on with singing and story telling. It was mostly young men playing it for the first time. They got so interested that it overshadowed everything else and they played all night.

It might be pointed out that the gambling sticks are often beautifully painted or carved and that all the early traders made mention of this activity, which they maintained was a positive passion with the Indians.

We discussed the point of whether the cultural revival was in danger of becoming commercialized. Whyte felt that such things as the salmon festival meant that the town took an interest in the native arts and ceremonies, which was good for the Indian ego and really did not hurt the movement. As he pointed out there are two attitudes. Sewid doesn't mind performing for tourists, and his work involves a certain amount of modification of tradition. A few purists, however, say, "They don't know what they're doing—dances are sacred and their versions are blasphemous."

This attitude, however, is bound to die out. Both Ken Harris and Judge Haig Brown brought it up in connection with carving. In some cases there was a reluctance to use any image which did not belong traditionally to the carver. This naturally breaks down and we were told that many of the mortuary poles in the Nimpkish cemetery in Alert Bay were not strictly traditional. In a discussion with Deirdre Norman, archivist of the Anthropological Museum of the University of British Columbia, she accepted an evolutionist point of view: the culture was changing, but by modifying and adapting it would survive and new forms would emerge.

The influence of Christianity, however, is still an inhibiting force. Scarcely any Indians are willing to return wholeheartedly to their own religion; instead, they insist there is no conflict between the two, rationalizing their own culture as "not a religion." Some are even inhibited about the word potlatch, now that is has been revived, and insist on substituting the word "feast." Others insist on the legal aspects of potlatching. In their rationalization, it was a ceremony to impress the nature of a transaction or a social event on the minds of a number of witnesses since the culture had no writing. Norman Joe told us he had recently been married, in church, the following day with an Indian ceremony. We asked Ed Moody of Bella Coola what the attitude of local clergymen was toward the cultural revival. He said in his area they merely paid no attention. The Anglican was too busy teaching music and organizing a band. (Always those bands!)

Daisy Neel, who continues her father's interests and has taped material preserved by her maternal grandmother, said, "My grandmother taught me a lot of the Indian religion and I tell you honestly I don't think I could have coped with all I have gone through in this life if it wasn't for that." She went on to say of the reawakening that people accused her of wanting to return to the past: "What I am talking about is the spiritual philosophy of the Indian people. That's what I want. Only a fool would return to the canoe when you can get somewhere in a matter of hours by plane. That's being unrealistic." Daisy felt strongly that for decades Indians had been taught to be ashamed—they did not know what for. When they knew nothing of their own culture they had no weapons to fight whites who tried to downgrade them; they simply withdrew and hatred built up. This, she felt, led to their being attracted to red power, to which she was unsympathetic.

Thus, although the British Columbia Indians do not actively reassert their religion as some of the younger U.S. Indians do, it is significant that in August 1973 *The Native People,* which calls itself "Canada's First Native Weekly Newspaper," quoted Chief John Snow as saying, at an Ecumenical Conference at Stoney Reserve in Alberta, that the Indian people "have given Christianity every opportunity to flourish and, although it is sound theoretically, it just doesn't seem to work."

The conference, which included Indian delegates from both the States and Canada, was dedicated to reviving what was good in the old religion. The drift of the conference was to point out that, now that non-Indians were beginning to examine the native point of view, "They are starting to come around to a way of thinking about ecology and nature that we have been practicing for a long time," as Snow said. The conference was addressed in a militant vein by a twenty-two-year-old Ojibway who had been wounded in the siege of Wounded Knee, but his approach was rejected by a Saskatchewan Indian, Ernest Tootoosis, who summed up: "Living in harmony with people and things the Creator has seen fit to put on this earth is the only way of life."

To sum up, Louis Demerais, acting director of the Union of B.C. Indian Chiefs, wrote concerning the cultural revival:

> . . . There is no question that this is happening on a large scale in B.C., and, while somewhat fragmented (many of our 192 bands are attempting to do things in this area on their own), at the present time it would not surprise me in the least to see a complete revival of Indian religion as our people once knew it and practised it.

The new attitude is of incalculable value for the morale of the Indian people. There is no doubt that the revival goes much deeper and that much more in the way of ceremonial has now begun to take place in the last two decades that can be seen by the outsider, for in many areas there are dances and activities to which whites are not admitted.

We were fortunate enough to see a small festival involving potlatching in Port Alberni. We went at the suggestion of Terry Whyte, who told us to ask at the door and, if there was no objection, we would be allowed to watch. A family by the name of Sutherland had had a fire in which their boy had been badly burned. A white neighbor had saved the child's life and gotten him to a hospital. The festival was being given in thanksgiving for the child's recovery. It was also a kind of social payoff.

The affair took place in a little whitewashed former church which had been rebaptized Friendship Center. Over the door was painted a traditional Nootka design. People were coming and going, the whole atmosphere highly relaxed and informal. We inquired at the door and were told to go in. The auditorium was filled with benches and chairs, at one end was a small stage on which a group including the family, the M.C., and some dancers were sitting. The stage was flanked by two carved poles in Nootka style. On screens, at the sides of the stage, eagles were painted.

The room was crowded with a great variety of people. There were oval-shaped old Indian women in house dresses, old men in shirtsleeves or sweaters. There were chic young girls in miniskirts, many of them pretty, some of whom lingered in clusters in corners with their boys, most of whom sported long hair. It is interesting to note that while the older generation of Indians tends to be short and chunky the youngsters have slimmed themselves down and seem, on the whole, to be taller than their elders. Mothers held babies in their laps, little children milled around drinking Pepsis and clutching comic books. The same cheerful informality, much moving around and chattering between events, prevailed inside as outside.

When we arrived an old man stepped forward on the stage and made a speech in Nootka. After this, which was received with applause, some dancing went on on the crowded stage. The orchestra consisted of skin drums and sticks struck together. The dancers, half a dozen girls and half a dozen boys, were led by an old lady. The girls wore black shawls with a Nootka design done in sequins and (alas) beaded headbands with a feather in the rear. The boys merely wore T-shirts and slacks. They danced in a line around a small portion of the stage in a simple up and down step, moving their hands back and forth. The dance elicited many cries and yips from the audience. The M.C., the uncle of the boy, then made a speech in English, which ended: "You all know we have come here to give thanks because the boy is well. I hope you are feeling it the way I am feeling it. That's all I have to say."

The grandparents and the boy himself came forward and sang together, in Nootka. They then also spoke in the same language.

There was another dance in which the girls circled a man wearing the traditional Nootka wolf mask and a black cloak with a Nootka sequin design on the back. He moved agilely, raising and lowering his body, but he did not seem actually to mimic the animal. This, dance, too, provoked cheering, cries, and applause. Although the dancers did not wear the traditional headgear, some of the women on the platform and the M.C. did have on the cedar bark circlet.

Then the actual potlatching began. The M.C. would call out a name and the person designated would come up to the stage and receive money. We could see that one middle-aged woman received $5. The white man who had saved the teenager's life was present and, we were told, received a handsome monetary gift.

We were subsequently told that in an open potlatch, such as this, one would not see the really fine regalia, still owned by many families, which was used only in important closed ceremonies.

What was heartening about the affair was that it seemed happy and spontaneous. For us it was especially interesting, because it was not a performance put on for outsiders (none of which we had a chance to see) but rather a group feeling their way back to their roots and, although the visual magnificence of the past was no longer there, they were at home with themselves.

As we left we saw notice in the lobby calling for volunteers to form a basketball team. Outside tables were stacked which suggested that later in the afternoon the group would have refreshments.

One element of the culture which the native people are now realizing as basic is language. It has taken a long time for them to become aware of how rapidly it is being lost and what it means to them. Of course, once more it is the missionaries and the white man's schools that have taken it away from them. As Harold Cardinal, in his angry book, never tires of pointing out the government's policy of assuming eventual assimilation was arrived at without reference to Indian opinion. Every Indian over the age of thirty with whom we spoke mentioned the fact that he or she was punished for speaking the native language in school. Obviously the downgrading effect, the destruction of respect for native tongues in several generations of Indians, has been incalculable. In general it can be said that most young children do not know their own language. Among young people in their twenties and thirties the knowledge is spotty; many said they could understand it but could not speak it. The older people still know their own tongue, but many younger ones said that the old timers spoke "classically" with a big vocabulary while they, themselves, were reduced to almost a pidgin.

At any rate, with the reawakening of pride in what it is to be an Indian, desperate efforts are now being made to regain the native tongues. Most important is the creation of written languages, which up to now no one has bothered to do. We have already seen that in Bella Bella experts have been brought in to aid creating teaching aids for Heiltsuk. Daisy Neel has worked on a Kwakiutl grammar. In Bella Coola we obtained a mimeographed vocabulary with pronunciations which showed that this group is not lagging behind. 'Ksan also was working on a language problem. In other areas, such as those of the Nootka and the Cowichan Salish, efforts were being made to obtain government adult education programs for teaching the local language. As we have seen in most regions there have been moves for Indian control of the schools, in Bella Bella, Kispiox near Hazelton, and among the Cowichan, for example. As this movement continues there is no doubt but that the Indians will succeed in breaking through the century-old official resistance to native languages and getting them into the curriculum.

If the Indian languages are, in some measure, preserved, it will mean that the old songs and stories can still be handed down. Above all, with the development of more native literary men, more of the tradition will be preserved in English and the cultural heritage will undoubtedly receive a new imaginative impetus.

The Northwest Indian people are a great people. We have tried to sketch their colorful past, something of their indigenous way of life, and their valiant struggle to preserve their identity. To the writer they mirror countless peoples of the colonial world who have been carelessly brushed aside by the arrogance of Western technological civilization and, like so many of these peoples, they had built a balanced society and succeeded in creating something magnificent from their relation to the planet, an achievement which we are only just learning to respect, particularly in the light of the threat that technology will impose a universal featureless culture upon the whole world.

For over a hundred years the Indians have been frustrated by the pressures of an alien majority, but they are showing enormous reserves of vitality and their new self-confidence will win them the economic and social status which they deserve. They will also go on to new expressions of their cultural energy. They are still dancing and, as long as they dance their own dances, they will remain Indians.

BIBLIOGRAPHY

PART I
THE HISTORY

CHAPTER 1
THE RUSSIANS, SPANISH, AND ENGLISH DISCOVER AMERICA

Bancroft, H. H.
History of the Pacific States of North America: Vol. 22, "The Northwest Coast," Vol. i, San Francisco, 1884.

Chevigny, Hector
Russian America: The Great Alaskan Adventure, 1741–1867, New York, 1965.

Colder, Frank A.
Russian Expansion in the Pacific, Cleveland, 1914.

Cook, Captain James
The Voyages of Discovery of the Resolution and the Discovery, 1791–1794, Part I, Boston, 1967.

Coster, James C.
"The Last Days of Juan Perez," *Journal of the West,* Vol. 2, No. 1.

Fernandez, Justino, ed.
Tomás de Suría y son viaje con Malaspina en 1791, Mexico, 1939.

Nova y Colon, Pedro de
Viaje alrededor del mundo de las corvetas, descubierta y atrevida, 1791–1794, de Capitán Don Alejandro Malaspina, Madrid, 1885.

Wagner, Henry A., ed.
Journal of Tomás de Suría, San Francisco, 1930.

Ybarra y Berge, Xavier de
De California a Alaska: historia de un descubrimiento, Madrid, 1945.

CHAPTER 2
THE FRENCH ADVENTURE

Emmon, G. T.
"Native Account of a Meeting between La Perouse and the Tlingit," *American Anthropologist,* No. 13 (n.s.), 1911, pp. 294–298.

La Perouse, de Jean Francois de Galaup
Le Voyage de La Perouse sur les côtes de Alaska et de la Californie, Cahier X, Institut Français de Washington, Historical Documents, Baltimore, 1937.

CHAPTER 3
THE IMPERIALIST CONFLICT

Chapman, C.
A History of Spain, New York, 1945.

Dixon, Captain George A.
A Voyage around the World Performed in 1785–1790 and 1790–1793 (narratives of Robert Haswell and John Box Hoskins and John Boit's log), The Massachusetts Historical Society Collections, Vol. 79, Boston, 1941.

Meares, John
Voyages Made in the Years 1788 and 1789 from China to the Northwest Coast of America with an Introductory Narrative of a Voyage Performed in 1766 from Bengal in the Ship "Nootka," London, 1791.

CHAPTER 4
VANCOUVER TAKES OVER

Howard, Frederick E., ed.
Voyages of the Columbia to the Northwest Coast, 1787–1790 and 1790–1793, Boston, 1941.

Vancouver, George
A Voyage of Discovery to the North Pacific Ocean and Round the World (facsimile edition), Amsterdam, 1967.

Ybarra y Berge, Xavier de
De California a Alaska: historia de un descubrimiento, Madrid, 1945.

CHAPTER 5
MACKENSIE MEETS THE BELLA COOLA

Mackensie, Alexander
Voyages from Montreal on the River St. Laurence through the Continent of North America to the Frozen and Pacific Oceans, 1783–1789, London, 1927.

CHAPTER 6
THE YANKEE PRISONER

Howay, Frederick E.
"Indian Attacks upon the Maritime Traders of the Northwest Coast, 1785–1805," *Canadian Historical Review,* Vol. 6, 1925.

Jewitt, John R.
Narrative of the Adventures and Sufferings of John R. Jewitt, Only Survivor of the Ship "Boston" during a Captivity of Nearly Three Years among the Savages of Nootka Sound, Fairfield, 1967.

CHAPTER 7
A COLONY IS BORN

Bryce, Reverend George
The Makers of Canada Series, Vol. IX, London, 1926.

Campbell, Marjorie Wallace
The Northwest Fur Company, N. Y., 1957.

Finlayson, Roderick
The History of Vancouver Island and the Northwest Coast, Joseph P. Connely, ed., St. Louis University Social Studies, Series B, St. Louis, 1945.

Green, Jonathan
Journal of a Tour on the West Coast of America in the Year 1829, New York, 1915.

Haig Brown, Roderick
Fur and Gold, Toronto, 1962.

Lennert, Edwin M.
Alcohol and the Northwest Coast Indians, University of California Publications in Culture and Society, Vol. 2, No. 6, Berkeley and Los Angeles, 1954.

Rich, E. E.
1. *The Hudson's Bay Company, 1670–1870,* New York, 1961.
2. Editor of *Publications of the Champlain Society,* Vol. 4: Hudson's Bay Company, Series I, 1825–1838, and Series II, 1839–1844, Toronto, 1938.

CHAPTER 8
RUSSIAN BEARS AND TLINGIT RAVENS

Chevigny, Hector
Russian America: The Great Alaskan Adventure, 1741–1867, New York, 1965.

Krause, Aurel
The Tlingit Indians, tr., Erna Gunther, Seattle, 1956.

CHAPTER 9
THE ATTACK ON THE INDIAN WAY OF LIFE

Actander, John W.
The Apostle of Alaska: The Story of William Duncan of Metlakatla, New York, 1909.

Beynon, William
"The Tsimshian of Metlakatla, Alaska," *American Anthropologist,* Vol. 43 (n.s.), 1941.

Large, R. G.
The Skeena, River of Destiny, Vancouver, 1957.

Mayne, Commander R. C.
40 Years in Columbia and Vancouver Island, London, 1862.

CHAPTER 10
PIONEER PREACHERS AMONG THE HAIDA, TSIMSHIAN, AND SALISH

Collison, William H.
In the Wake of the War Canoes, London, 1915.

Crosby, Thomas
Up and Down the North Pacific by Canoe and Mission Ship, Toronto, 1914.

Lennert, Edwin M.
"The Life and Death of an Indian State," *Human Organization,* Vol. 13, No. 3, 1955, New York.

CHAPTER 11
THE WAR AGAINST THE POTLATCH

Benedict, Ruth
Patterns of Culture, New York, 1948.

Codere, Helen
Fighting with Property, Monographs of the American Ethnological Society, New York, 1950.

La Violette, Forrest E.
The Struggle for Survival: Indian Cultures and the Protestant Ethic in British Columbia, Toronto, 1961.

CHAPTER 12
INDIAN AGENT TO THE KWAKIUTL

Ford, Clellan S.
Smoke from Their Fires: The Life of a Kwakiutl Chief, Hamden, 1971.

Halliday, William
Potlatch and Totem, London, 1935.

Sewid, James (ed., James P. Spradley)
Guests Never Leave Hungry, New Haven, 1969.

CHAPTER 13
IN UNION THERE IS STRENGTH

Chevigny, Hector
Russian America: The Great Alaskan Adventure, 1741–1867, New York, 1965.

Drucker, Philip
The Native Brotherhoods: Modern Intertribal Organizations on the Northwest Coast, Smithsonian Institution, U.S. Bureau of American Ethnology, Bulletin, No. 168, Washington, D.C., 1958.

Hulley, Clarence C.
Alaska 1741–1953, Portland, 1953.

Jones, F. Livingston
A Study of the Tlingit of Alaska, New York, 1914.

Kopas, Leslie
Political Action of the Indians of British Columbia, Master's Thesis in the Department of Anthropology and Sociology, the University of British Columbia, 1972.

Mayne, Commander R. C.
40 Years in Columbia and Vancouver Island, London, 1862.

Sewid, James (ed., James P. Spradley)
Guests Never Leave Hungry, New Haven, 1969.

PART II
THE CULTURE

CHAPTER 14
THE SHARED CULTURE

Drucker, Philip
1. *Indians of the Northwest Coast,* American Museum of Natural History, N.Y., 1963.
2. *Cultures of the North Pacific,* San Francisco, 1965.
3. (with Robert Heizer) *To Make My Name Good,* Los Angeles, 1967.
4. "Sources of Northwest Coast Cultures," in *New Interpretations of Aboriginal Cultural History,* 75th anniversary volume, Anthropological Society of Washington, D.C., 1955.

Duff, Wilson
The Indian History of British Columbia, Vol. 1, The Impact of the White Man, Memoir No. 5, Provincial Museum of British Columbia, Victoria, 1944.

Waterman, T. T.
"Some Conundrums in Northwest Coast Art," *The American Anthropologist,* (n.s.), Vol. XXV No. 4, Dec. 1923.

CHAPTER 15
TOOLS AND THEIR USES

Drucker, Philip
Indians of the Northwest Coast, American Museum of Natural History, New York, 1963.

Gunther, Erna
Indian Life on the Northwest Coast of North America as Seen by the Explorers and Fur Traders during the Last Decades of the 18th Century, Seattle, 1973.

Jewitt, John R.
Narrative, Fairfield, 1967.

Mackensie, Alexander
Voyages from Montreal, London, 1927.

Murdoch, George P.
Rank and Potlatch among the Haida, Yale University Publications in Anthropology, No. 13, New Haven, 1936.

Vancouver, George
A Voyage of Discovery, Amsterdam, 1967.

CHAPTER 16
FROM BIRTH TO DEATH

Boas, Franz
Kwakiutl Ethnography, ed. Helen Codere, Chicago, 1966.

Ford, Clellan, S.
Smoke from their Fires, Hamden, 1971.

Garfield, Viola
Tsimshian Clan and Society, University of Washington Publications in Anthropology, Vol. 7, No. 3, Seattle, 1939.

Jewitt, John R.
Narrative, Fairfield, 1967.

Krause, Aurel
The Tlingit Indians, tr., Erna Gunther, Seattle, 1956.

McIlwraith, Thomas
The Bella Coola, Vol. I, Toronto, 1948.

Swanton, John R.
Social Conditions, Beliefs and Linguistic Relationships of the Tlingit Indians, United States American Ethnology Bureau, Annual Report, Vol. 20, Washington, D.C., 1904–1905.

CHAPTER 17
OF MAGIC AND GHOSTS

Barbeau, Marius
Tsimshian Myths, Bulletin National Museum of Canada, No. 174, Ottawa, 1961.

Boas, Franz
1. *Indianische Sagen der Nord Pacifischen Küste Amerikas,* Berlin, 1895.
2. *Kwakiutl Culture as Reflected in Mythology,* Memoirs American Folklore Society, Vol. 38, New York, 1935.
3. *Religion of the Kwakiutl Indians,* Columbia University Contributions to Anthropology, Vol. 10, Part 2, New York, 1930.

Dawson, George
The Haida, Geological Survey of Canada, Report of Progress for 1878–1879, Montreal, 1880.

Drucker, Philip
The Northern and Central Nootkan Tribes, Smithsonian Institution, American Ethnology Bureau Bulletin, No. 144, Washington, D.C., 1951.

McIlwraith, Thomas
The Bella Coola, Vol. I, Toronto, 1948.

Müller, Werner
Weltbild und Kult der Kwakiutl Indianer, Wiesbaden, 1955.

Niblick, Albert P.
The Coast Indians of Southern Alaska and Northern British Columbia, Report of the National Museum, Washington, D.C., 1890.

Pierce, William
From Potlatch to Pulpit, Vancouver, 1933.

Swanton, John R.
1. *Contributions to the Ethnology of the Haida,* Memoirs of the American Museum of Natural History, Vol. VIII, New York, 1909.
2. *Haida Texts and Myths,* Smithsonian Institution, American Ethnology Bureau, 31st Annual Report, Washington, D.C., 1916.
3. *Social Conditions, Beliefs and Linguistic Relationships of the Tlingit*

Indians, United States American Ethnology Bureau, Annual Report, Vol. 20, Washington D.C., 1904–1905.

CHAPTER 18
THE EPIC OF RAVEN

Boas, Franz
1. *Kwakiutl Tales,* Columbia University Contributions to Anthropology, Vol. 26, New York, 1935.
2. *Tsimshian Mythology,* United States American Ethnology Bureau, 31st Annual Report, Washington, D.C., 1916.

Garfield, Viola, and Linn A. Forrest
The Wolf and the Raven, Seattle, 1973.

Newcome, C. C.
The Haida Indians, Congrès internationale des Américainistes, Quebec, 1902.

Swanton, John R.
Contributions to the Ethnology of the Haida, Memoirs of the American Museum of Natural History, Vol. 8, New York, 1909.

CHAPTER 19
CARVERS OF MAGIC

Boas, Franz
Primitive Art, New York, 1951.

Davis, Robert Tyler
Native Arts of the Pacific Northwest, Stanford, 1949.

Duff, Wilson
1. "Contributions of Marius Barbeau to Northwest Coast Ethnology," *Anthropologica,* Vol. 6, No. 1 (n.s.), Ottawa, 1964.
2. "Histories, Territories and Laws of the Kitwancool," Provincial Museum of British Columbia, Anthropology in British Columbia Memoir No. 4, Victoria, 1959.
3. "Stone Clubs from the Skeena River Area," Report of the Provincial Museum of British Columbia for 1962, Victoria, 1963.

Garfield, Viola
1. *The Tsimshian, Their Arts and Music* (Paul Wingert, Tsimshian sculpture; Marius Barbeau, Music), Publications of the American Ethnological Society, No. 18, New York, 1950.
2. *The Wolf and the Raven,* Seattle, 1973.

Gunther, Erna
Art in the Life of the Northwest Coast Indians, Portland, 1966.

Hawthorne, Audrey
The Art of the Kwakiutl and Other Tribes of the Northwest Coast, Seattle, 1967.

Holm, Bill
1. *The Crooked Beak of Heaven,* Seattle, 1972.
2. *Northwest Coast Indian Art,* Seattle, 1965.

Inverarity, R. B.
The Art of the Northwest Coast Indians, Stanford, 1950.

Keithahn, Edward L.
Monuments in Cedar, Seattle, 1963.

Lévi-Strauss, Claude
1. "The Art of the Northwest Coast at the American Museum of Natural History," *Gazette des Beaux Arts,* Vol. 24, September 1943, Paris.
2. "Le dédoublement de la représentation dans les arts d'Asie et de l'Amérique" *Renaissance,* Vol. 2 and 3, New York, 1944–1945.

Meade, Edward
Indian Rock Carvings of the Pacific Northwest, Sydney, 1971.

Paalen, Wolfgang
Dyn, No. 4–5, December 1943, Mexico.

Reid, Bill, and A. Demenil
Voices Out of Silence, Toronto, 1972.

Wingert, Paul
American Indian Sculpture, American Ethnological Society, New York, 1949.

CHAPTER 20
NORTHWEST THEATER OF VIOLENCE

Artaud, Antonin (ed., Jack Hirshman)
Anthology, San Francisco, 1965.

Boas, Franz
1. *Kwakiutl Ethnography,* ed., Helen Codere, Chicago, 1966.
2. *The Social Organization and the Secret Societies of the Kwakiutl Indians,* United States National Museum Annual Report for 1895, Washington, D.C., 1897.

Clutesi, George
Potlatch, Victoria, 1969.

Curtis, Edward S.
The North American Indians, Vol. 10 (Kwakiutl), Vol. 11 (Haida and Nootka), Cambridge, 1907–1930.

Drucker, Philip
1. *Kwakiutl Dancing Societies,* University of California Press, Anthropological Records, Vol. 2, No. 6, 1940, Berkeley.
2. *The Northern and Central Nootkan Tribes,* Smithsonian Institution, Bureau of American Ethnology, Bulletin No. 144, Washington, D.C., 1951.

Ford, Clellan S.
Smoke from Their Fires, Hamden, 1971.

Hawthorne, Audrey
The Art of the Kwakiutl and Other Tribes of the Northwest Coast, Seattle, 1967.

Jewitt, John R.
Narrative, Fairfield, 1967.

McIlwraith, Thomas
The Bella Coola, Vol. II, Toronto, 1948.

CHAPTER 21
INDIANS AS POETS

Boas, Franz
1. *Primitive Art,* New York, 1951.
2. *The Social Organization and the Secret Societies of the Kwakiutl Indians,* United States National Museum Annual Report for 1897, Washington, D.C.

Drucker, Philip
The Northern and Central Nootkan Tribes, Smithsonian Institution, Bureau of American Ethnology, Bulletin No. 144, Washington, D.C., 1951.

Duff, Wilson
"Contributions of Marius Barbeau to Northwest Coast Ethnology," *Antropologica,* Vol. 6, No. 1 (n.s.), Ottawa, 1964.

McIlwraith, Thomas
The Bella Coola, Vol. II, Toronto, 1948.

Roberts, Helen
Musical Areas in North America, Yale Anthropological Publications, No. 12, New Haven, 1936.

Swanton, John R.
"Haida Songs," *Tsimshian Texts,* New Series, Franz Boas, Ethnological Society Publications, Vol. 5, Leiden, 1912.

CHAPTER 22
THE UNSEEN POWERS

Boas, Franz
Kwakiutl Ethnography, ed., Helen Codere, Chicago, 1966.

Castaneda, Carlos
The Teachings of Don Juan, New York, 1972.

Curtis, Edward S.
The North American Indians, Vol. IX, Cambridge, 1913.

Krause, Aurel
The Tlingit Indians, tr., Erna Gunther, Seattle, 1956.

Waterman, T. T.
"The Paraphernalia of the Duamish Spirit Canoe Ceremony," *Indian Notes* (Museum of the American Indian, the Heye Foundation), Vol. VII, Nos. 2 and 4, 1930, New York.

Wingert, Paul
American Indian Sculpture, American Ethnological Society, New York, 1949.

PART III
THE NORTHWEST COAST TODAY

CHAPTER 23
RAVEN'S COUNTRY

Tapes. All quotes not otherwise identified are taken from tapes recorded in September, October, and November 1973 during a trip to the Northwest Coast of British Columbia and Alaska.

CHAPTER 24
THE TWO METLAKATLAS

Tapes.

CHAPTER 25
THE INDIANS UNITE AND FIGHT

Tapes.

Cardinal, Harold
The Unjust Society, Edmonton, 1969.

Cummings, Peter A., and Neil H. Mickenberg
Native Rights in Canada, Toronto, 1972.
Heritage, Festival Souvenir Booklet, 6th Annual Campbell River Salmon Festival, Campbell River, June–July 1973.
The Indian News, September 1973.

Kopas, Leslie
Political Action of the Indians of British Columbia, Master's Thesis in the Department of Anthropology and Sociology, the University of British Columbia, April 1972.
Native Alliance for Red Power, newsletter, June–July and September–October, 1968.
The Native Voice, August, 1973.
Nesika, August 1973.
The Vancouver Sun, September 20, 1973.

CHAPTER 26
A NEW DEAL FOR THE INDIANS

Tapes.

Annual Report Community Development Service, Manitoba, 1961.

Cardinal, Harold
The Unjust Society, Edmonton, 1969.

Hawthorne, Harry, C. S. Belshaw and S. N. Jamieson, eds.
The Indians of British Columbia, Vancouver, 1958.

Hawthorne, Harry, ed.
A Survey of the Contemporary Indians of Canada, 2 vols., Ottawa, 1966–1967.
The Indian News, September 1973.

Reid, Cecil
Letter dictated by Reid, Chief Councillor, Bella Bella Band, November 19, 1973.

CHAPTER 27
WARDS OF THE NATION

Tapes.

An Act Respecting the Indians, Ottawa, 1970.

Cardinal Harold
The Unjust Society, Edmonton, 1969.

Fields, D. B., and W. R. Stanbury
The Economic Impact of the Public Sector upon the Indians of British Columbia, Vancouver, 1973.
Queen Charlotte Island Observer, September 1973.

CHAPTER 28
IN SEWARD'S ICEBOX

Tapes.
Alaska's People, Booklet, Department of the Interior Bureau of Indian Affairs, Juneau, 1972.

Anderson, John II, Acting Director, Bureau of Indian Affairs, Juneau, letter, December 7, 1973.

Cummings, Peter A., and Neil H. Mickenberg
Native Rights in Canada, Toronto, 1972.

Garfield, Viola, and Linn A. Forrest
The Wolf and the Raven, Seattle, 1973.

Jones, Richard S.
Alaska Native Claims Settlement of 1971 (Public Law 92-20), History and Analysis, Library of Congress Research Service, Washington, D.C., 1972.

CHAPTER 29
TO BE AN INDIAN

Tapes.

Demarais, Louis H., Acting Director, Union of B.C. Chiefs, letter, July 11, 1973.

Duff, Wilson
The Indian History of British Columbia, Vol. I, Provincial Museum of British Columbia, Memoir No. 5, Victoria, 1964.
Heritage, souvenir booklet, 6th Annual Campbell River Festival, Campbell River, June–July 1972.
'Ksan, Booklet, National Museums of Canada, Ottawa, 1972.
The Native People, August 1973.

Sewid, James
Guests Never Leave Hungry, Yale, New Haven, 1969.

Index

ABOUT THE AUTHOR

H. R. Hays has written poetry, plays, novels, and nonfiction works. He has taught literature and headed the drama department at Southampton College and headed the drama department of Fairleigh Dickinson University. Among his most notable books are *In the Beginnings, The Dangerous Sex,* and the now classic work *From Ape to Angel.*